JACQUI HURST/A

RIVER COTTAGE

1 Much of East Devon is an Area of Outstanding Natural Beauty. These Devon ruby red cattle are enjoying the pasture near Shute. **2** Fishing boats still set out from Beer for the catch of the day. **3** Lacemaking was Honiton's main industry for centuries, and provided the lace for Queen Victoria's wedding dress and veil. **4** Participants in a cookery class run by River Cottage learn how to prepare sustainably caught fish. **5** On Seaton's popular tramway, heritage trams amble their way to Colyton.

EXETER CITY COUNCIL

HISTORY

From great manor houses to little places of worship, and working mills to heritage centres, East Devon is steeped in history.

1 Shute Barton, a medieval manor now owned by the National Trust. **2** Axminster Heritage Centre's traditional loom offers visitors a hands-on experience of carpet weaving. **3** Clyston Mill, part of the Killerton Estate, is owned by the National Trust. It still produces flour during weekly demonstrations.

4 Sir Walter Raleigh greets passers by from a garden in East Budleigh. 5 The church at Ottery St Mary looks like a cathedral because it was modelled on one – Exeter's, in the 14th century. 6 'The Red Indian' carved bench end at East Budleigh church. Experts have long speculated on what is depicted here – perhaps an early representation of a native American or a Green Man with a leafy headdress? We'll never know. 7 The Baptist Meeting House at Loughwood, near Dalwood. 8 Who knows what is going on here?! Tiny Luppitt has one of the most interesting churches in the region. This font may be a thousand years old and depicts what seem to be pagan scenes.

THE JURASSIC COAST

A UNESCO World Heritage Site, the Jurassic Coast stretches from Dorset's Studland to Devon's Exmouth, a distance of 95 miles. Visitors can identify the three eras that comprise the Age of the Dinosaurs by the colour of the cliffs: Triassic, Jurassic and Cretaceous.

1 The red (Triassic) stacks of Ladram Bay, at the western end of the Jurassic Coast, show that this area was once desert. This is the oldest part of the coast — around 185 million years.

2 The chalk (Cretaceous) sea stacks of Old Harry Rocks mark the eastern, and geologically the youngest, point of the Jurassic Coast. **3** Exmouth's geoneedle, at Orcombe Point, marks the Jurassic Coast's western end. **4** Durdle Door, eroded from the limestone rock by the sea, is one of the Jurassic Coast's most iconic sights. **5 & 6** Grey Jurassic rocks yield up their fossils, most notably ammonites. It can take hours of painstaking work to reveal the treasures of a find like this one, near Lyme Regis. **7** On the shore between Seaton and Lyme Regis are The Slabs, huge fossil ammonites set in smooth lias rock.

ACTIVE EAST DEVON

With two long-distance footpaths and several dedicated cycleways, East Devon and West Dorset are perfect for leisurely exercise but also attract watersports enthusiasts.

1 The South West Coast Path provides the best way to appreciate the Jurassic Coast's 'walk through time'. 2 The Jurassic Coast plays host to a variety of watersports, from kitesurfing (shown here in Exmouth) to canoeing, kayaking and stand-up paddleboarding. 3 Several riding stables offer leisurely hacks over the heathland and bridleways of East Devon. Here are riders from Devenish Pitt Farm in the Coly Valley. 4 Cycling the Exe Estuary Trail.

AUTHOR

Hilary Bradt's career as an occupational therapist ended when potential employers noticed that the time taken off for travel exceeded the periods of employment. With her then-husband George she self-published the first Bradt guide in 1974 during an extended journey through Latin America. Since then she has seen Bradt Travel Guides grow to be an internationally recognised and award-winning publisher. In 2008 she was awarded an MBE and other awards have followed. Now semi-

retired, she writes regularly for the national press and travel magazines, and has recently started exhibiting as a sculptor. She lives in Seaton. (⊘ hilarybradt.com)

CO-AUTHOR

Janice Booth's working life has included professional stage management, archaeology, compiling puzzle magazines and travelling widely. She initiated and co-wrote the early editions of Bradt's *Rwanda* guide, has edited other Bradt guides to various far-flung places, helps to judge Bradt's annual travel-writing competition and, with Hilary Bradt, has co-written and/or contributed to the other two Slow Devon guides. Janice settled in East Devon in 2001 with a sense

of 'coming home', having lived briefly in Colyton as a toddler and tasted her first clotted cream in Sidmouth aged eight. She lives peacefully within earshot of the sea.

Second edition published April 2020
First published February 2016
Bradt Travel Guides Ltd
31a High Street, Chesham, Buckinghamshire HP5 1BW, England
www.bradtguides.com
Print edition published in the USA by The Globe Pequot Press Inc, PO Box 480, Guilford,
Connecticut 06437-0480

Text copyright © 2020 Hilary Bradt & Janice Booth
Maps copyright © 2020 Bradt Travel Guides Ltd; includes map data © OpenStreetMap
contributors
Photographs copyright © 2020 Individual photographers (see below)
Project Managers: Emma Gibbs and Anna Moores
Cover research: Pepi Bluck, Perfect Picture

ISBN: 978 1 78477 476 9
British Library Cataloguing in Publication Data
A catalogue record for this book is available from the British Library

Photographs © individual photographers credited beside images & also those from picture
libraries credited as follows: Alamy.com (A), Dreamstime.com (D), iStockphoto.com (i),
Shutterstock.com (S), Superstock.com (SS)

Front cover Sidmouth (Marc Hill/A)
Back cover Weir at Ottery St Mary (Nigel Jarvis/S)
Title page Otter Estuary (SS)

Maps David McCutcheon FBCart.S

Typeset by Pepi Bluck, Perfect Picture and Ian Spick, Bradt Travel Guides

Production managed by Jellyfish Print Solutions; printed in the UK

Digital conversion by www.dataworks.co.in

ACKNOWLEDGEMENTS

We are generalists, not experts. Many people lent their extensive knowledge to the first edition and some of their information remains in the book, so second-time-around thanks to Steven Edmonds (Wetlands), Karin Frewin (Seaton) and Karen Whittaker (East Devon AONB).

For this edition, I (Hilary) would like to thank Jon Gardner, who somehow fitted us in to his busy schedule to provide plenty of new information on Trinity Hill Local Nature Reserve; Kim Strawbridge kindly updated the Pebblebed Heath box; and Peter Burgess likewise updated the beaver box. Brian Lane Smith corrected my information on the Upottery Heritage Museum and Caroline Cornwall gave me help and information on Wildwood Escot. Finally I know a lot more about wine after spending the afternoon with the knowledgeable Mike of Dalwood Vineyard.

Janice would like to thank Marc Millon for his additional information on food and the Topsham scene.

And of course many, many thanks go to Bradt's long-suffering editorial team, for their unfailing cheerfulness, patience, encouragement and painstaking work.

AUTHORS' STORY

Janice was the first to move to East Devon, having checked out local places that held family memories before finally choosing Seaton. Hilary followed seven years later, having gradually got to know and love this part of the world. Together we have walked most of the South West Coast Path (Hilary somewhat more energetically than Janice), deep into Dorset and south to Torquay and beyond, and have delighted in the emergence of Seaton as an important cultural and wildlife centre.

I think the moment when I (Hilary) knew I'd made the right decision to move down here from Buckinghamshire was when I found a baby grass snake near the bird hide and a slow-worm on the esplanade. The wetlands now are as familiar to me as the ever-changing sea. We swim from the pebbly beach in the summer and in winter battle our way against the wind and spray to watch breakers smashing against the rocks.

I (Janice) have always loved living near the sea, listening to the beat of the waves from my garden late at night. Among my hoarded memorabilia I have an old Post Office Savings book, which records a deposit my mother made for me in Colyton in August 1940, so settling in Seaton (only five miles from Colyton) more than 60 years later felt like 'coming home'.

We researched this book together and apart so the 'I' could be either of us. You'll have fun guessing!

CONTRIBUTORS

The following experts generously wrote boxes on their specialist subjects. They all gave their time and knowledge, but we'd especially like to thank Mike Green who gave far more of his time, and far more quickly, than we could have hoped.

Mike Green, who wrote text on the Jurassic Coast (pages 26 and 154) as well as advising on the Beer section, is a Jurassic Coast Ambassador (see ⊘ jurassiccoast.org).

Dr Sam Bridgewater (*The Pebblebed Heaths*, page 118) is the Nature Conservation Manager at Clinton Devon Estates. His contribution was updated by Kim Strawbridge.

Donald Campbell (*Botanical Secrets of the Undercliff*, page 194) is one of the most respected naturalists in the area.

Mark Elliott (*Beavers in the River Otter*, page 130) is the Devon Beaver Project Lead at Devon Wildlife Trust. His contribution was checked by Peter Burgess.

Philip Knowling (*Sidmouth Orné*, page 164) has been sharing his knowledge of Devon's follies (architectural rather than human) through all three volumes of this guide.

CONTENTS

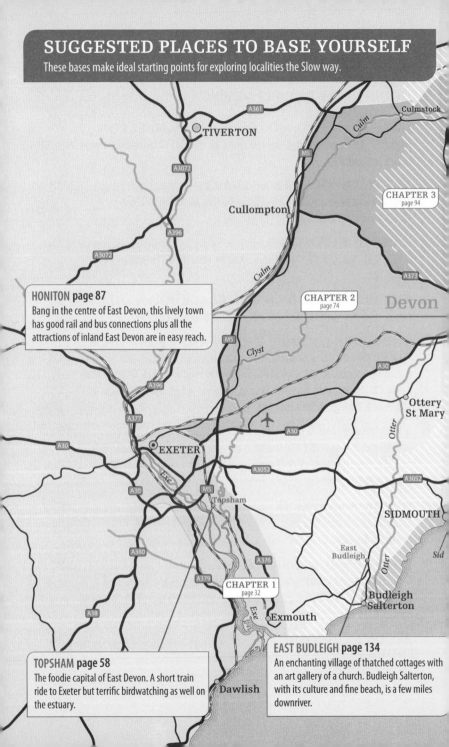

SUGGESTED PLACES TO BASE YOURSELF

These bases make ideal starting points for exploring localities the Slow way.

TIVERTON

Culmstock

CHAPTER 3
page 94

Cullompton

CHAPTER 2
page 74

Devon

HONITON page 87
Bang in the centre of East Devon, this lively town has good rail and bus connections plus all the attractions of inland East Devon are in easy reach.

Clyst

EXETER

Ottery
St Mary

Topsham

SIDMOUTH

East
Budleigh

Sid

CHAPTER 1
page 32

Budleigh
Salterton

Exmouth

TOPSHAM page 58
The foodie capital of East Devon. A short train ride to Exeter but terrific birdwatching as well on the estuary.

Dawlish

EAST BUDLEIGH page 134
An enchanting village of thatched cottages with an art gallery of a church. Budleigh Salterton, with its culture and fine beach, is a few miles downriver.

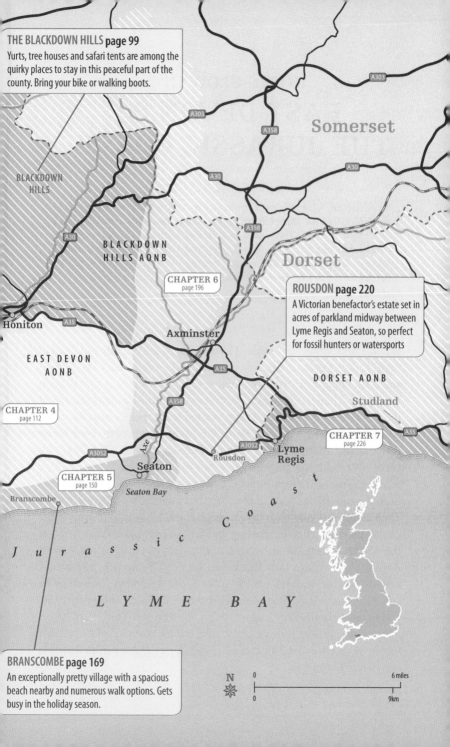

THE BLACKDOWN HILLS page 99
Yurts, tree houses and safari tents are among the quirky places to stay in this peaceful part of the county. Bring your bike or walking boots.

Somerset

BLACKDOWN HILLS

BLACKDOWN HILLS AONB

CHAPTER 6
page 196

Dorset

ROUSDON page 220
A Victorian benefactor's estate set in acres of parkland midway between Lyme Regis and Seaton, so perfect for fossil hunters or watersports

Honiton

EAST DEVON AONB

Axminster

DORSET AONB

Studland

CHAPTER 4
page 112

CHAPTER 7
page 226

A303

A358

A30

A358

A30

A35

A358

A35

A3052

A35

Axe

Seaton

Rousdon

Lyme Regis

CHAPTER 5
page 150

Branscombe

Seaton Bay

J u r a s s i c   C o a s t

L Y M E   B A Y

BRANSCOMBE page 169
An exceptionally pretty village with a spacious beach nearby and numerous walk options. Gets busy in the holiday season.

N

0   6 miles
0   9km

EAST DEVON &
THE JURASSIC COAST

Any visitor who explores thoroughly the coastline from Lyme to Exmouth and the rich hinterland between this coastline and the main line of the Southern Railway will rightly come to the conclusion not only that East Devon has the Joseph's coat among English counties, but Benjamin's bounty in addition. In few places is it possible to find such infinite wealth in so small a compass.

S P B Mais, *Weekends in England*, 1933

When I first moved to Seaton, 11 years ago, it felt slightly ashamed of itself. It didn't draw the trendy crowds like its neighbours Lyme Regis and Beer, but just existed contentedly and unobtrusively as a small town by the sea. Then the Jurassic Coast received World Heritage status and the whole region woke up. Things started to happen; a new feeling of pride was apparent. Hikers along the undulating South West Coast Path realised that they were walking through time in a big way, with every mile covering an average of two million years. When funding was obtained for Seaton Jurassic, the town was reborn, and there has been a ripple effect all along the coast; but inland it's a different matter. The East Devon Way meanders through the landscape to provide some gentle, pub-interrupted rambling, but few holidaymakers stay north of the A3052, despite the attractions of this Area of Outstanding Natural Beauty; small villages busy themselves with local, volunteer-run events, and cyclists or walkers on the quiet lanes are rarely disturbed by something as vexing as a car. And yet there's so much history here too, and so much for the Slow visitor to enjoy. We stray into Dorset in *Chapter 7* just to describe its Jurassic Coast area, but for coverage of Dorset as a whole we recommend Bradt's *Slow Travel Dorset* by Alexandra Richards who wrote *Chapter 7*.

A TASTE OF EAST DEVON

Devon has long been known as a county of good food. Much of its meat is home-reared in small-scale and 'happy' conditions; and the seafood is exceptional, with Exmouth mussels sold throughout the UK (see box, page 69) and the 'brown crab' said to be at its biggest and juiciest along Devon's coast. For a while East Devon lagged behind South Devon but now there's a rapidly growing enthusiasm and expertise in food; really, how could it be otherwise when Hugh Fearnley-Whittingstall and his River Cottage have made it their home (page 223)? Also top chef Michael Caines, who has had such a positive impact on Devon's food scene, has

THE SLOW MINDSET

Hilary Bradt, Founder, Bradt Travel Guides

> We shall not cease from exploration
> And the end of all our exploring
> Will be to arrive where we started
> And know the place for the first time.
>
> T S Eliot, 'Little Gidding', *Four Quartets*

This series evolved, slowly, from a Bradt editorial meeting when we started to explore ideas for guides to our favourite country – Great Britain. We wanted to get away from the usual 'top sights' formula and encourage our authors to bring out the nuances and local differences that make up a sense of place – such things as food, building styles, nature, geology or local people and what makes them tick. Our aim was to create a series that celebrates the present, focusing on sustainable tourism, rather than taking a nostalgic wallow in the past.

So without our realising it at the time, we had defined 'Slow Travel', or at least our concept of it. For the beauty of the Slow movement is that there is no fixed definition; we adapt the philosophy to fit our individual needs and aspirations. Thus Carl Honoré, author of *In Praise of Slow*, writes: 'The Slow Movement is a cultural revolution against the notion that faster is always better. It's not about doing everything at a snail's pace, it's about seeking to do everything at the right speed. Savouring the hours and minutes rather than just counting them. Doing everything as well as possible, instead of as fast as possible. It's about quality over quantity in everything from work to food to parenting.' And travel.

So take time to explore. Don't rush it, get to know an area – and the people who live there – and you'll be as delighted as the authors by what you find.

his new luxury hotel and restaurant in Lympstone on the Exe Estuary (page 63), while Mitch Tonks has a branch of Rockfish in Exmouth and is planning another for Sidmouth. We share our favourite places to eat. Most seaside towns and villages have their own fish outlet, selling whatever the day's catch has provided: straight from the sea and glisteningly fresh. And don't forget the pasties! You'll find them everywhere, from a number of local producers, particularly the award-winning Chunk (♂ chunkofdevon.co.uk, based in Ottery St Mary) whose products and tasty fillings come in many shapes and sizes. The region is justly proud, too, of its fine restaurants and farm shops, and hosts several food fairs including the huge one in Exeter each April (see box, page 49).

CLOTTED CREAM

This is undoubtedly the best-known 'taste of Devon'. A Devon cream tea is as integral a part of a visit to this region as rain (indeed, the one often leads to the other). Clotted cream is quite unlike any other sort of cream, being as thick as butter and almost as yellow; it contains more fat (around 63%, while double cream is 48%), and traditionally was made by gradually heating fresh milk using steam or hot water, and allowing it to cool very slowly. The thick cream that rises to the top was then skimmed off. The original term was clouted cream, clout being the word for patch, referring to the thick crust that forms when the cream is heated.

True clotted cream is made only in Devon and Cornwall, and we Devonians are not only convinced that ours is better but that we got there first. After all, it was one of the wives of the Dartmoor giant, Blunderbus, who won her husband's affection by bringing the knowledge of clotted-cream-making to his kitchen. The story is slightly spoiled by the fact that Jennie was exiled to a cave in Cornwall at the time for being a lousy cook, and it was a Phoenician sea captain who taught her the process as a reward for saving his ship from wreckers.

Clotted cream is served with fresh scones, which should be warm from the oven rather than the microwave; purists prefer plain scones but others, myself included, love the fruit ones. In Devon we spread the cream on the scone first, instead of butter, and add strawberry or raspberry jam on top; in Cornwall it's the opposite: jam first, then clotted cream. Either way it's utterly delicious – and very filling. The Victorian Prime Minister William Gladstone was right when he called clotted cream 'the food of the gods'.

WORTH THE DIVERSION: OUR FAVOURITE RESTAURANTS

All of these restaurants, listed alphabetically, serve very good food, but each has something extra, something special, that makes them stand out. We can't eat everywhere and there are bound to be plenty of other wonderful places that we don't know about. We'd like readers to make their own recommendations, which we can add to our website. Send your recommendation to ✉ info@bradtguides.com with 'East Devon update' as the subject.

The Five Bells Clyst Hydon. The most attractive, rural place on our list, which also serves way above average meals. A thatched whitewashed former longhouse in a tiny village with food to savour. See page 83.

Half Moon Inn Clyst St Mary. Earns its place for offering smaller portions and for the indulgent puddings. Too many restaurants serve the same old sticky toffee pudding, but here there's treacle tart and jam sponge, and all those lovely things we oldies remember from our childhood. See page 116.

East Hill Pride Farm Shop Newton Poppleford. The best for a Sunday roast. Why? Because the owners are licensed slaughterers so you know this meat has had the best possible life – and end of life. The vegetables mostly come from the farm and are cooked to perfection, and the outdoor seating has views over the Sid Valley. In early summer there are home-grown strawberries for dessert. See page 147.

Jack in the Green Rockbeare. Conveniently close to the M5 and A30, a village pub in appearance but also recognised as (probably) the best restaurant in East Devon. Scrumptious food and attentive service. See page 86.

Neil's Restaurant Sidmouth. A little oasis of quality dining away from the sea-front crowds. Exceptionally good, fresh fish – the menu changes to accommodate the latest catch. Friendly, efficient service. See page 168.

The Rusty Pig Ottery St Mary. They call it a feasting house and conversation is encouraged by seating people (if they wish) at a large table and serving them dishes from whatever ingredients are seasonal and available. There is no menu. See page 127.

The Salty Monk Sidford. The classiest place to eat along the A3052. Excellent food in appealing surroundings. Options include a seven-course menu with wine flight. See page 148.

Steamers Beer. Andy the head chef has been here for 15 years and really knows his stuff. The fish is often 'the catch of the day' from the waters around Beer itself. It's family owned with a friendly atmosphere and pleasant staff. A happy place. See page 178.

Trill Farm Musbury. This organic farm does superb lunches three times a week using produce from their own garden. What makes it special is the ethos of the place and the fact that guests (like at the Rusty Pig) sit at big tables to encourage conversation, and help themselves from a large selection of delicious, mainly vegetarian dishes. See page 216.

Tuckers Arms Dalwood (see box, page 108). What's special here is the community feel and warm welcome. Portions are huge and delicious, and they serve the village's own wine. See page 110.

BEER, CIDER & WINE

Of course East Devon isn't only about clotted cream. The county is no laggard in its production of alcoholic drinks as an accompaniment to all that good food. Leading the field is the Otter Brewery (🖉 otterbrewery. com), arguably the best-known brewery in the South West. This is still a family business, set up nearly 30 years ago by David and Mary Ann McCaig, and leading the way in sustainability as well as popularity. Five regular brews are produced year round, with a seasonal one to add warmth to the darker months. Every pub in this book will serve Otter ales; it is the local brewery. They claim that a pint of Otter is drunk every nine seconds in the UK!

There is also a bourgeoning wine-making scene, with small vineyards popping up all over the place producing some award-winning wines (see box, opposite). Devon cider (or cyder) is well known, including 'scrumpy' (derived from the dialect word 'scrump' meaning a small withered apple), which nowadays is the term used to describe ciders made in small quantities and using traditional methods. Several farms in this area do still press the apples through straw and use old-style crushers and presses. Prepared traditionally, four hundredweight of apples will make 40 gallons of scrumpy, and a good scrumpy normally has an alcohol content of at least 7% despite tasting deceptively light and refreshing. So beware: it's not just apple juice!

Cider has been drunk in Britain for more than 1,000 years, and in olden times farming landowners often paid their workers in scrumpy and other foodstuffs. Today the British consume nearly half of all cider made worldwide; the West Country is our biggest producer, followed by Kent.

For an immersion in the history of cider-making, visit the Whiteways Cyder room at the Whimple Heritage Centre (page 80).

SOME CIDER PRODUCERS IN EAST DEVON

Froginwell Vineyard and Cider Barn Woodbury Salterton EX5 1EP 🖉 01395 239900 🖉 froginwellvineyard.co.uk

Green Valley Cyder Darts Farm, Topsham EX3 0QH 🖉 01392 878200 🖉 greenvalleycyder. co.uk. 'During the apple pressing season you can hear our traditional cider-making machinery clunking away in the Cyder Barn, spreading the wonderful smell of fragrant Devon apples throughout the farm shop.' Customers can watch the process and, of course, taste the result.

EAST DEVON'S VINEYARDS

The Romans had their priorities: if they were to hang around in damp, chilly Devon they needed wine to ease the pain. So they grew vines on the south-sloping hills. Now, a couple of thousand years later, vineyards are our fastest-growing agricultural sector with three million vines planted in the UK in the last two years alone. East Devon has at least half a dozen vineyards, three of which can be visited for a tour: Dalwood (page 109), Lily Farm Vineyard (Budleigh Salterton; page 158) and Pebblebed Vineyards (Topsham; page 59). Others, such as Castlewood (Musbury), Sidbury and Lyme Bay Winery (see below) sell their wine from a shop or online. Most of these vineyards rely on volunteers to harvest the grapes, with a bottle of wine and a celebratory meal being reward enough. However small the enterprise, these wines win awards. Indeed, the sector is thriving!

Vines take four years to mature, so growers must curb their impatience. They also need to select the variety carefully. Pinot noir is the oldest cultivated vine in the world, but is delicate; seyval blanc and chardonnay are among other favourites that are tougher. Then there's solaris which has strong leaves that are perfect for *dolmades* (stuffed vine leaves). On a wine tour you will learn that every variety of vine in the world comes from the same root stock with a clone grafted on. The parasite *phylloxera* threatened to wipe out Europe's wine industry in the 1880s when vines imported from America (or reimported since the New World's vines originated from France) were infected by this tiny creature. There was no way of stopping 'the great wine blight' until growers realised that the American rootstock was immune and that grafting was the answer.

You'll notice that most of these small vineyards specialise in sparkling wine. The Devon climate is perfect for this: a good sparkling wine needs to not have too much sugar, which is created by too much sun. It takes two years to make, but the wait is worthwhile.

Cheers!

Killerton Estate Broadclyst EX5 3LE ☎ 01392 881345 ♕ nationaltrust.org.uk. Fifty acres of traditionally managed orchards and a 200-year-old heritage of cider-making. At the Killerton Cider and Apple Festival in October, the ancient press is in action.

Lyme Bay Winery EX13 7PW ☎ 01297 551355 ♕ lymebaywinery.co.uk. Between Shute & Musbury (page 203). Their Jack Ratt range of cider and scrumpy, made in traditional style from locally grown traditional cider apples and named after the notorious West Country smuggler Jack Rattenbury, has won numerous awards.

Ventons Devon Cyder Clyst St Lawrence EX15 2NL ☎ 07811 963853 ♕ ventons.co.uk. 'All we use are traditional Devon cider apples with no additions, natural yeast from the apples, a crusher, a twin-screw oak press barley straw and oak barrels.' That was four years ago. Now they've added a hydraulic crusher and large storage tanks. Around 6,000 gallons of cider are produced here each year, and many awards won. An online shop will soon be opened.

Wiscombe Cider Wiscombe Park, Southleigh EX24 6JG ✆ 07976 585465. Two ciders (Wiscombe Medium & Suicider), most likely to be found at real ale festivals, produced by Tim Chichester in traditional style using two horses to turn the granite mill.

THE APPEAL OF COUNTRY CHURCHES

A poem by E E Cummings starts: 'I am a little church no great cathedral' and we make no secret of the fact that it is East Devon's little churches that tug at our heart-strings, while the grandeur of the likes of its great cathedral is appreciated on a more intellectual level.

I love what rural churches can show us of village life through the span of a thousand years. Simon Jenkins, in his wonderful book *England's Thousand Best Churches*, sums up the appeal: 'Into these churches English men and women have for centuries poured their faith, joy, sorrow, labour and love.' In their artefacts and monuments these little churches tell the story of the village, revealing the lives of the poor farm workers as well as their rich employers up at the big house. They are recorded in the oldest Norman font to the newest WI kneelers. Nowhere else will you find this unbroken thread of history.

No old church is devoid of interest. Start with the lych gate where you enter the churchyard. Lych was the old English word for dead body, so a lych gate was a corpse gate. A few retain the slab on which the coffin rested during the burial service and the one at the former St Pancras' Church in Rousdon even rotates, making it easier to enter while the coffin was laid on the slab. In medieval times only the rich were buried in coffins; the poor used the parish reusable one, the corpse being wrapped in woollen material for burial. And it had to be wool or they paid a fine – a canny way to protect the wool trade.

"In medieval times only the rich were buried in coffins; the poor used the parish reusable one."

Look up at the eaves. Are there gargoyles with ferocious faces spewing water from the run-off from the roof? They may be there to protect the church from the demons and devils that try to get inside.

Old churches are full of words. You walk on ancient memorial slabs – ledger stones – from the 17th and 18th century, beautifully lettered with intriguing abbreviations and Roman dates so brush up on your Latin numerals. More recent memorials, on the walls in brass or marble, commemorate the rich, influential or brave. And painted on the wall of most churches is a list of rectors or vicars. They often start in the 1200s, with the French names of the Norman clergymen, and continue in an unbroken line to the women vicars of today.

Most intriguing of all are the carvings, because we can only guess at what they mean. The tops of columns, capitals, are often carved with detailed and enigmatic faces of man or beast – an elephant, for example, in Ottery St Mary – but where the carver gave most expression to his imagination is in the wooden bench ends of the pews. Benches or pews in churches only came into being in the 14th century – before that the congregation stood – and were universal in the 15th, which is the date of the earliest of Devon's examples. The subjects of the carvings are quite extraordinary. Where you would expect religious motifs you find, instead, creatures of the wildest imagination. And even in the 14th century these weren't a new fad. The French Abbot St Bernard of Clairveaux, who died in 1153, wrote:

> What mean those ridiculous monstrosities in the courts of cloisters; those filthy apes, those fierce lions, those monstrous centaurs, those half-men, those spotted tigers, those fighting soldiers and horn-blowing hunters; many bodies under one head, or many heads on one body; here a serpent's tail attached to a quadruped, there a quadruped's head on a fish; here a beast presenting the foreparts of a horse, and dragging after it the rear of a goat; there a horned animal with the hind parts of a horse?

He accurately describes the decorative church art that persisted for another five centuries until a more demure mindset took over. You will

FOUND SOME NEW SLOW PLACES?

East Devon and Dorset's Jurassic Coast are stuffed with people who have specialist knowledge of their part of the West Country and, although we've done our best to check facts, there are bound to be errors as well as the inevitable omissions of really special places. You'll find out before us when a fine new family-run hotel opens or a favourite restaurant changes hands and goes downhill.

So why not write and tell us about your experiences, so we know for the next edition? Contact us on ☎ 01753 893444 or ✉ info@bradtguides.com. We will put all updates on to our dedicated webpage (⌂ bradtupdates.com/eastdevon) as well as adding our own new finds. In addition you can add a review of the book to ⌂ bradtguides.com or Amazon.

find many different explanations for the carvings in church booklets; personally I enjoy the mystery. One of the best examples of secular bench-end carvings in all of Devon is in the church of East Budleigh.

Dividing the nave, where the congregation sits, and the chancel leading to the altar, there is generally a beautifully carved wooden screen, often called a rood screen since the rood, a beam on top, carried the figures of the Crucifixion; these were all removed during the Reformation or by the Puritans in the Cromwell period. In the panels between the supports you can still find charming painted portraits of saints, rich with symbolism. These, too, were often damaged – literally defaced – by the reformers. While on the subject of old wood, look out for the ancient alms boxes and chests used to store church documents. The oldest of these may be cut from a single log; many are bound with iron bands and have more than one lock to secure them.

Carvings, both in wood and stone, are found on and over the font. This basin holds holy water for baptism, and is often the oldest thing in a church. Rough-hewn Norman stone fonts are quite common, as are more intricately carved ones from the same period, sometimes depicting strange creatures or faces which may represent demons being expelled through baptism. Luppitt is the best example here. In the 13th century the Archbishop of Canterbury ordered that fonts should be covered to prevent the theft of holy water; the consequent carved wooden covers then became increasingly elaborate until they could only be raised by pulleys.

The aristocracy have their own lavish memorials. Some marble or alabaster tombs occupy quite a large proportion of the church, with elaborate canopies, heroic inscriptions and depictions of the nobleman either in life or death. Dead knights in armour have their feet resting on lions, to symbolise courage, whilst their wives often have a dog for fidelity. Studying these effigies and the memorial brasses set into the floor is an excellent way to learn the history of costume and armour. Ottery St Mary has some exceptionally interesting monuments.

Finally the most eye-catching and least enigmatic features of a church: the stained-glass windows. Being vulnerable to storm and sabotage, many of the medieval ones have perished and most are now Victorian. But early ones do survive and charmingly represent contemporary interpretations of the Bible stories.

Churches in Devon are rarely locked during the day. Give them the time and attention they deserve.

FURTHER READING
FOR CHURCH ENTHUSIASTS

A Cloud of Witnesses: Medieval Panel Paintings of Saints in Devon Churches Wilks, Diane, Azure Publications 2011, updated 2013. Many of Devon's churches contain historically important paintings of saints; some of the finest are illustrated here, with intriguing background details of the saints themselves.

Devon's Ancient Bench Ends Gray, Todd, The Mint Press 2012. A detailed examination of the history and significance of these often enigmatic carvings, illustrated in colour.

Devon's Fifty Best Churches Gray, Todd, The Mint Press 2011. A beautiful book, with some fine photos of the churches and their carvings, accompanied by location maps and informative text.

England's Thousand Best Churches Jenkins, Simon, Penguin 1999. The essential companion for any churchophile: knowledgeable and atmospheric descriptions of the churches (33 of which are in Devon) and their locations, in Jenkins's seductive prose.

The Pilgrim's Guide to Devon Churches Cloister Books, 2008. A practical, helpful little handbook, small and sturdy enough to carry in a backpack, systematically listing all of Devon's Anglican churches, with a small photo and brief description of each. Location maps are included.

NGS GARDENS & OPEN STUDIOS

East Devon has only four public gardens: Killerton, Bicton, Burrow Farm and Cadhay, but each year householders from all over England and Wales open their gardens for the National Gardens Scheme's Gardens Open for Charity Programme (⌀ ngs.org.uk). Since this guide aims to get under the skin of East Devon and West Dorset, a visit to one of these open gardens is the perfect way of understanding the local people or – if you are a visitor from overseas – the English. We are the most passionate gardeners in the world and the West Country, with its rich soil and mild climate, makes enthusiasts out of even reluctant horticulturists. The gardens that are open in this scheme come in every size, from manor-house grounds to the kitchen gardens of semi-detached cottages. And it's not just the gardens you'll enjoy. Almost every householder taking part in the scheme adds to the money raised by offering coffee and tea with a wonderful array of cakes.

SOMETHING OLD...

Despite its largely rural nature East Devon is well off for antique shops, often with good-quality and unusual items on sale. Enthusiasts may like to add a spot of browsing to their itineraries. We've listed the main ones below (working from Exeter in the west to Axminster in the east), but there are many others.

The Vintage Trading Post 16 Marsh Green Rd, Marsh Barton, Exeter ℘ 01392 494967 ⑪ thevintagetradingpost ☉ 10.00–17.00 daily. Huge 8,500ft^2 showroom with a changing stock of decorative, functional and collectable items including retro, art, records and militaria. Refreshments available.

Exeter's Antiques Centre & Riverside Café The Quay, Exeter ℘ 01392 493501 ⑧ exeterquayantiques.co.uk ☉ 10.00–17.00 daily. On the edge of Exeter's historic quayside. The collectable miscellany includes a tray of old postcards, carefully grouped under their many themes and often hidden by a line of deeply absorbed browsers. See page 49.

The Antiques Complex Exeter Airport Industrial Estate, Westcott Ln (adjacent to the airport). Includes **McBains Antiques Centre** (℘ 01392 366261 ⑪ mcbainsantiques ☉ 10.00–17.00 Mon–Fri except bank hols, 10.00–13.00 Sat) and **Carradale**

Farm Antiques (℘ 01392 447082 ⑧ carradalefarmantiquesltd.com), both with a wide range of antique and decorative furniture plus smaller good-quality antiques and *objets d'art*.

Topsham Quay Antiques Centre Topsham Quay ℘ 01392 874006 ⑧ quayantiques.com ☉ 10.00–16.45 daily. A historic warehouse on the quayside with three floors of antique, vintage and retro items from 65 traders. Has been featured in the BBC's *Bargain Hunt*. See page 60.

Tribal Gatherings 5 High St, Exmouth ℘ 07429 016886 ⑧ tribalgatherings.co.uk ☉ 10.00–17.00 Tue–Sat. Specialists in hand-knotted oriental rugs but they also have over 40 cabinets of jewellery, antiques and other collectables.

Sidmouth Antique Centre All Saints Rd, Sidmouth ℘ 01395 512588 ⑧ sidmouthantiques.co.uk ☉ 10.00–17.00 Mon–Sat. Vintage, antique and collectable

There are gardens opening at different times throughout the year, although more, of course, in spring and summer. Some open only for one weekend so you need to plan ahead. The NGS annual publication, the *Garden Visitor's Handbook* (known as 'the yellow book'), gives a complete countrywide list and can be bought via the NGS website, but there are separate county lists too. The ones for Devon and Dorset can usually be picked up for free at tourist offices or accessed through the website.

A somewhat similar scheme, in that it brings you into closer contact with local people, is the Open Studios fortnight which takes place

items from 25 dealers including toys, clocks, coins, postcards and militaria.

Antiques on High 26 Fore St, Sidmouth EX10 8AQ ☎ 01395 577133 ⊘ antiquesonhighsidmouth.co.uk ⊙ 10.00–17.00 Mon–Sat, 11.00–16.00 Sun. A sister company to *Antiques on High* in Oxford. As well as vintage and antique collectables, this shop stocks original creations from the Oxfordshire Craft Guild.

Fountain Antiques 132 High St, Honiton EX14 1JP ☎ 01404 42074 ◼ fountainantiquescentrehoniton ⊙ 09.30–17.25 Mon–Sat. Two floors with a big variety of items including tools, china, glass, militaria, paintings, jewellery and silver. Several other Honiton shops are also very browsable (page 88).

Dolphin Antiques Centre Beer (behind the Dolphin Hotel) ☎ 01297 24362 ⊙ mid-Mar–Oct 10.00–17.00 Wed–Mon, Nov–mid-Mar 10.00–16.00 Thu–Sun. An enticing mix of affordable antique, vintage and collectable items, including books, silverware and even local fossils. See page 174.

Allsorts 9 Fore St, Seaton ☎ 01297 22177 ⊘ allsorts.online ⊙ 09.00–15.00 Mon–Sat. A changing stock of reasonably priced antiques and collectables from pillboxes and period furniture to jewellery and copperware, crammed into four rooms. It's on a pedestrian street: closest parking is in the nearby Co-op car park.

The Vintage Shed Station Yard, Colyton (behind the tramway) ☎ 01297 599121 ⊘ hevintageshed.co.uk ⊙ 10.00–17.00 daily (summer) but may vary seasonally. Extensive stock of antique, vintage and local craft items (including records, and traditional old tools) from around 20 traders. Plentiful parking.

Old Chapel Antiques & Lifestyle Centre Castle St, Axminster ☎ 01297 639993 ⊙ 10.00–16.00 Tue–Fri, 11.00–16.00 Sat. A Grade II-listed building with two floors of miscellanea from some two dozen dealers.

The Trading Post Chard Rd, Tytherleigh EX13 7BE ☎ 01460 221330, 01460 57005 ⊘ tradingpostdevon.co.uk ⊙ 11.00–16.30 Wed, 10.00–16.30 Thu–Mon. A huge selection in many rooms operated by a variety of dealers.

annually in September in Devon (∂ devonartistnetwork.co.uk) and in early June in Dorset (∂ dorsetartweeks.co.uk). Throughout the county, artists open up their studios to show their work and to talk to art enthusiasts. Some exhibit in groups, in galleries, while others set aside a room in their homes. For art lovers it adds a hugely enjoyable element to their visit to the region.

CAR-FREE TRAVEL

Road links to East Devon and Coastal Dorset are good so most visitors will drive to their destination. Once settled in their hotel or holiday cottage, however, there is more pleasure and slowness to be derived by using public transport or pedal-power rather than joining the annual fight for a parking space or queues at a junction.

PUBLIC TRANSPORT

Exeter Airport has scheduled flights from various other UK and European airports. Exeter, Axminster and Honiton have direct rail services from London; Exeter (which offers connections to Exmouth, Topsham and Lympstone) is accessible by rail from just about anywhere in Britain, often without changes. Its bus station has services to East Devon and beyond, though timetables change regularly. The route map at the front of the *East Devon* timetable shows you all the possibilities – or use the excellent interactive map on ∂ traveldevon.info.

ACTIVE EAST DEVON

I was pleasantly surprised to meet a young, alarmingly fit-looking chap who said he'd moved to Seaton because of the wealth of outdoor pursuits available: running and cycling clubs, canoeing and kayaking, kitesurfing … Another fellow joined us and told me that Lyme Bay was the best place in the UK for sailing. And the image of Seaton is of a retirement town! Here are some of the ways to burn off your excess energy.

CYCLING

Cyclists are spoilt for choice. The quiet lanes of East Devon and the Blackdown Hills are perfect for cycling, and there are some dedicated cycle paths described in the relevant chapters.

GOOD TIDINGS

The Jurassic Coast's beautiful stretches of coastline are a huge delight for visitors fascinated by cliffs, beaches and the shore. However, lifeboats are all too often called out to rescue people who find themselves trapped by the incoming tide. These potentially dangerous and costly call-outs can be avoided by always checking the **tide tables** (available in local shops and TICs) before a seashore wander.

Non-seawise visitors don't always realise how much the extent and timing of a tide's ebb and flow vary with the phases of the moon. The fact that you could walk round the tip of that promontory yesterday at midday and return safely doesn't mean you can do the same tomorrow, even if you calculate the time difference correctly: the tide may ebb less far or rise higher, and you'll be cut off. These variations apply year-round and on every stretch of Britain's coastline.

Also be aware that the cliffs that look so massive are not necessarily stable. They can quickly crumble, particularly after extreme weather, so – however tempting – please don't climb them to escape being cut off or (if you're at the top) go too close to the edge. Better safe than sorry!

The NCN Route 2 (also known as the South Coast Cycle Route) runs from Exmouth to Budleigh Salterton along a disused railway line, and through Sidmouth and Seaton to Axminster, with an off-road section to Kilmington, and then on into Dorset. A map of this route is included in Sustrans's South Devon Cycle Map, available from ◈ sustrans.org.uk.

The Buzzard Route (NCN 52) is an 80-mile circular route, around Sidmouth, Seaton, Axminster, Honiton and Woodbury, sometimes following NCN2. Axminster, Seaton and Kilmington are on the Stop Line Way, a 70-mile cycling, walking and running route between the Bristol Channel and the English Channel (see ◈ traveldevon.info/cycle).

If you haven't brought your own bicycle, they can be hired. In the east, Soanes Cycles in Colyton (page 206) offer cycle repairs and hire, as do Colyford Cycles (page 149) and Rent-a-Bike at Cyclelife in Seaton (page 183), all including the increasingly popular electric bicycles that make all those hills far more pleasurable. Along the Exe Estuary (see box, page 35) there is Exmouth Cycle Hire in Exmouth, Darts Farm and Route 2 Bike Shop in Topsham, and Saddles & Paddles on Exeter quayside.

For a different sort of cycling, check out **Velo Vintage** (◈ velovintage. co.uk), whose cycle events are a little different, as suggested by their motto 'Time to cycle, take tea, converse and dress with style'. They run a number of cycle rides each year, usually involving a cream tea and several penny-farthing bicycles. Riders are asked to dress appropriately for the 1920s to 1950s and not to turn up in Lycra. The cycling is leisurely, often only ten miles and usually with live music along the way, plus competitions for the best-decorated bicycle and best moustache. Their website has a contact link and some delightful videos.

PARKRUN

For those who don't know, parkrun ($\oslash$ parkrun.org.uk) is a free 5km event held at 09.00 every Saturday year-round, throughout the country and abroad. Although the lead runners are anything but slow the back runners, me included, are the tortoises, just enjoying the friendly atmosphere and the chance to run/jog/walk in different parts of the county. East Devon parkruns are held in Exeter, Seaton, Exmouth and Killerton (my favourite). Come and join us!

WALKING

The East Devon Way and 30 miles of the South West Coast Path (SWCP) both traverse the region, making a long circular trip of almost 70 miles. Sections of these trails and other walks are covered under their specific areas. If you are planning to walk parts or all of the Dorset SWCP, see *Chapter 7* for further information.

If you do only one walk in East Devon make it the Otter and Ladram Bay circuit (see box, page 132). This is the perfect combination of cliff top and riverbank, and exemplifies the region.

The **East Devon Way** (EDW) starts at Exmouth and goes to Lympstone, Woodbury and Aylesbeare commons, and thence through often hillier country and picturesque villages to reach the Dorset border at Lyme Regis: a total of about 40 miles through East Devon's Area of Outstanding Natural Beauty (AONB). It complements the South West Coast Path beautifully, running inland through a mixed landscape of farmland and woodland, and country lanes carrying very little traffic. The East Devon Way is much less used than the coastal path which is both an advantage and a disadvantage. On busy holiday weekends you will meet very few other walkers, but the route – even with the excellent *East Devon Way* booklet – is sometimes confusing. Look out for the magenta arrows and foxglove logo. The East Devon Way is partly managed by the AONB but has its own excellent website ($\oslash$ eastdevonway.org.uk) where you can download the guide or choose from 13 circular walks, devised with the Ramblers. A printed version of the guide can be ordered from the website or picked up at TICs (Tourist Information Centres) in East Devon. For some highlights of the EDW, see page 114.

Each September Sidmouth holds a Walking Festival (page 154), a week of free guided walks of varying lengths and difficulties.

Walking & cycling maps & guides

The website for all cycling and walking information – and all travel information – is ✆ traveldevon.info, where you can access a map of cycle trails or download separate cycle and walking routes.

The OS maps for East Devon are the Explorer 115 and 116.

Better than any OS map are the pocket-sized, 1:12,500 (five inches to the mile), maps published by Croydecycle. At present the ones covering the region are: *Exe Estuary; Exmouth & Sidmouth Cycle Map* (at a scale of 1:30,000 plus town plans); *Budleigh Salterton* & *Otterton, Exmouth East; Sidmouth; Ottery St Mary; Beer, Branscombe & Seaton; Musbury & Axminster; Lyme Regis.* The series continues to the end of the Jurassic Coast. There is also a regional map, *East Devon, Exeter* at 1:100,000 for drivers and cyclists. All are available online (✆ croydecycle.co.uk) or from TICs (Tourist Information Centres) and other outlets.

A booklet, *Shortish Walks in East Devon*, in the popular Bossiney series, gives details of 14 walks together with clear maps. TICs generally stock booklets or details of walks in their specific area.

HORSERIDING

The many bridle paths and wide spaces of the heathlands are tempting for anyone who prefers to explore the countryside on someone else's legs. There are riding schools at Budleigh Salterton (✆ devonriding.co.uk), the Coly Valley (✆ devenishpitt.com) and Hawkchurch (Woodhouse Farm Stables; ✆ woodhouseridingstables.co.uk; see ad, XX colour section). All have access to some splendid scenery.

PADDLE SPORTS

Canoeing and kayaking are popular in the region, with the Axe and Exe again the focus of water-based activities. The Axe Vale Canoe Club (✆ axevalecc.co.uk) at Axmouth Harbour runs occasional courses and taster days. The Exeter Canoe Club (✆ exetercanoeclub.org.uk) offers similar courses.

The growing sport of stand-up paddleboarding is now taking hold in the area, being ideal for inexperienced visitors who just want to have a go. Sit-on-top kayaks likewise do not need the same expertise as normal kayaks. Paddleboards and kayaks can be hired in Exeter ($\mathcal{O}$ sadpad. com), Exmouth from Exmouth Water Sports ($\mathcal{O}$ exmouthwatersports. co.uk) and Edge Water Sports ($\mathcal{O}$ edgewatersports.com) and Seaton (Seaton Bay Watersports $\mathcal{O}$ sbwatersports.co.uk).

SURFING & KITESURFING

Although it can't compete with North Devon, surfing here is not at all bad. Exmouth and Sidmouth are the places to go.

Kitesurfing is hugely popular in Exmouth, a place which offers ideal conditions. For tuition and sessions, contact Exmouth Water Sports and Edge Water Sports (see above).

SAILING

As previously mentioned, sailing is world class in this area and it is no accident that Weymouth, on the Jurassic Coast, hosted the sailing events at the 2012 Olympics. The seascape is rarely without the colourful sails of yachts. See $\mathcal{O}$ exe-sailing-club.org, $\mathcal{O}$ sidmouthsailing.org.uk and $\mathcal{O}$ axeyachtclub.co.uk.

NATURAL EAST DEVON

The other two volumes in this *Slow Travel Devon* trilogy proudly proclaim their national parks, Dartmoor and Exmoor. East Devon may at first seem like the poor relation with no equivalent moorland to boast about, but it more than makes up for this with its variety of habitats and Local Nature Reserves and has a huge expanse of countryside recognised as an Area of Outstanding Natural Beauty (AONB). The East Devon AONB, designated in 1963, covers 103 square miles (60% of the district) and includes 18 miles of the World Heritage Site, the Jurassic Coast (page 26). Adjacent to its north is the Blackdown Hills AONB. That means that almost anywhere you go is officially outstandingly beautiful – but you don't need to be told that, you can see for yourself.

East Devon is endowed with distinctive habitats that attract specialist wildlife. Two stand out in particular: the heathlands, which include the East Devon Pebblebeds (page 118), and the estuary wetlands: the Exe and Axe estuaries are nationally important for their birdlife. The Exe (page 58) is the place to see avocets, and the Axe, at Seaton Wetlands (page 188), has a host of other waders and waterfowl.

The number of agencies promoting enjoyment of the natural world is quite bewildering. To sort out what you want to do, get hold of the booklet *Countryside Events* published by the Countryside Team of the East Devon District Council (⊘ eastdevon.gov.uk) available from tourist information centres and Seaton Wetlands or visit the AONB website (⊘ eastdevonaonb.org.uk). There is some sort of organised nature activity almost every day in the spring and summer (and winter – another guide is published each season), run by one of the numerous wildlife organisations. Partners of the EDDC include the following:

Devon Wildlife Trust ⊘ devonwildlifetrust.org. Part of a nationwide network of wildlife trusts, and active in all aspects of wildlife conservation in Devon, with an informative website.
Pebblebed Heaths Conservation Trust ⊘ pebblebedheaths.org.uk. An organisation established and run by the Clinton Devon Estates to manage the Pebblebed Heaths for the benefit of wildlife, and to promote public enjoyment and appreciation of this habitat.

BLUEBELLS

Everyone loves bluebells. It's the combination of swathes of that wonderful purplish blue with the almost translucent green of young beech leaves. Here are a few insiders' tips on the best May bluebell displays in East Devon and on Dorset's Jurassic Coast, from west to east.

Blackbury Camp ♀ SY1873192371. This wins my award for consistently offering the best display. There's parking nearby and level walking, and trees for the youngsters to climb – plus some interesting ancient history described on noticeboards (page 142).

Holyford Woods ♀ SY2316292008. This local nature reserve north of Seaton prides itself on its bluebells and has an annual Bluebell Day in early May to celebrate them.

The downside (or upside for walkers) is that there is no parking nearby. Park in the lay-by near the top of Seaton Down Hill (page 145). **The Spittles** ♀ SY3455692775. Just northwest of Lyme Regis is this little National Trust woodland of hillocks and bluebells. On a good year it's terrific because the hilly terrain gives you some unusual views of the flowers. You need a good pair of legs to climb the steep inclines.

Langdon Hill ♀ ST4119593278. Northwest of Golden Cap, the car park here (National Trust) is also the one for this popular climb so you can combine bluebells with coastal views. A broad, easy-to-walk track follows the perimeter of the woods where there is usually a good display of bluebells.

RSPB ⌂ rspb.org.uk. The Royal Society for the Protection of Birds runs birding walks, birdwatching cruises on the Exe Estuary and other local events. It has an office at Darts Farm (page 61).

THE JURASSIC COAST: NATURAL WORLD HERITAGE SITE

Mike Green

In 2001 the East Devon and Dorset coast was designated by UNESCO as England's first and only Natural World Heritage Site in recognition of its unique geology and geomorphology. It is known as the Jurassic Coast.

This stretch of the East Devon and Dorset coast runs from Exmouth to Studland, just beyond Swanage: 95 miles in distance but 185 million years of the Earth's history. Indeed, this is the whole of the Mesozoic era, sometimes called the Age of the Dinosaurs; the Mesozoic comprises the Triassic, Jurassic and Cretaceous periods. The Cretaceous and Mesozoic together ended in a bang (probably a meteorite) about 65 million years ago which brought the reign of the dinosaurs to a close.

But to begin at the beginning. The geology starts 250 million years ago (mya) with the red Triassic cliffs of East Devon, after the mass extinction at the end of the Permian era. The cliffs were laid down in desert conditions when East Devon was way down in the tropics and

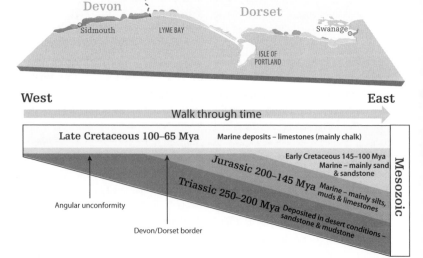

part of the super continent, Pangaea. By 200 mya, as Pangaea slowly broke apart, driven by tectonic plate movements (continental plates colliding as they drift over the surface of the Earth), Devon and Dorset started to sink beneath the sea and the Jurassic layers were laid down in marine conditions. They vary in colour from blueish grey to murky black muds with silts and grey limestones, except for the spectacular golden cliffs at West Bay. As Pangaea continued to break up and our land moved northwards, the seas became warm shallow lagoons and by 140 mya the early Cretaceous (mainly greensands – so called because of their greenish colour due to glauconite) was laid down.

The next big event, driven by tectonic plate movements, was about 100 mya and resulted in East Devon being uplifted in the west to create a tilt in all these layers. The rest of the early Cretaceous was then laid down in deepening seas followed by the Late Cretaceous limestones, the conspicuous chalk cliffs.

It is this tilt, enabling one to walk along the coast passing through all these layers of time visible in the cliffs, which makes the Jurassic Coast unique and gives it its outstanding universal value (which is a UNESCO requirement). It is the only place in the world where you can see such a complete record of the Mesozoic era.

There are numerous places along the Jurassic Coast where this geology is explained and illustrated, most notably at the Seaton Jurassic Centre (page 185). See also the box on page 154 for a geological walk along East Devon's coast.

HOW THIS BOOK IS ARRANGED

The chapter divisions are based on what we hope is a mixture of common sense, travelling from west to east, and an understanding of what most visitors want; so we have a separate, very detailed, chapter for the seaside, which is the focus of most holidays, and a section on places to eat along the A3052, a road which all visitors to East Devon will travel along.

MAPS

The map at the front of this book shows the area covered in each of the seven chapters, along with suggestions on where to base yourself for a holiday in this region. Each chapter then begins with a sketch map of the area, highlighting the places mentioned in the text or in the accommodation section. The numbers on the map correspond to those against the headings. The ♀ symbol indicates a walk or featured bus journey, and featured walks are also given sketch maps.

LISTINGS

These are usually alphabetical, unless logic dictates that they should be geographical, such as grouping places in the same town together.

FOOD, DRINK & ACCOMMODATION

We've listed some of our, and local residents', favourite pubs, cafés, and restaurants, favouring those places that are a little bit different, or convenient, or are just exceptionally good or atmospheric; we've also highlighted our absolute favourites in the box on page 11. The list is far from exhaustive, and some exploration and curiosity on your part will unearth many others.

At the back of this guide (page 256), there are some accommodation ideas for each area: a mixture of camping, glamping, self-catering, B&B and hotels. Again, the list is by no means exhaustive, and you should certainly also try places that aren't mentioned. The hotels and B&Bs are indicated by 🏠 under the heading for the area in which they are located, self-catering is 🏠, glamping, which is ever-more luxurious by ⛺, and campsites by ⛺.

For further accommodation reviews, go to ⬀ bradtguides.com/ edevonsleeps.

ATTRACTIONS

We have given contact details for these when relevant, and it is always worth checking their websites for any changes. We have generally not listed admission fees as these often change; always check beforehand to avoid an unpleasant shock. If a description does not say admission is free, you should expect to be charged.

Note that no charge has been made for the inclusion of any business in this guide (apart from advertisements).

FURTHER READING
Media: newspapers & local radio

If you buy a local newspaper while in East Devon make it the *Western Morning News* (⬀ thisiswesternmorningnews.co.uk). Published since

DOG-FRIENDLY DEVON

The beaches, footpaths and heathland of East Devon are great for dogs, and dog owners need to know which places welcome them. Claire Doyle has come to the rescue with her excellent website (⌁ doggydevon. co.uk), which is packed with helpful facts about travelling with your dog: pubs and restaurants, accommodation – and beaches. Over 100 Devon beaches are listed, with easy coding showing at a glance whether and when your pet can accompany you.

More and more places are dog-friendly these days so owners have a particular responsibility for cleaning up their dog mess, even in wild areas. A warden for one of the nature reserves sent me this plea: 'People may not realise that dog mess left on or near footpaths is detrimental to the balance of the ecosystem. Also dogs on nature reserves should either be easily controlled/recalled, or be kept on a lead, to avoid worrying livestock and the wildlife'.

1860, it is an excellent paper with lots of information and reports on local events as well as politically unbiased international news. Taking the longer view is the monthly magazine *Devon Life* (⌁ devonlife.co.uk), with in-depth articles on a range of town and country issues, and the free *Devonshire* magazine which focuses more on East and South Devon. For event listing, the *Marshwood Vale* magazine, free and available in West Dorset and as far as Seaton in Devon, lists absolutely everything that's going on in this region, as well as having readable articles of local interest.

Radio Devon (103.4MHz FM), broadcast from the BBC studios in Plymouth, is one of the most listened-to of the BBC's local radio stations. Tune in to hear traffic news as well as local-interest stories and interviews.

Source material: books

We have drawn on the information in several out-of-print books by inspirational authors. These include:

A Handbook for Travellers in Devon and Cornwall (no author credited), John Murray, 1872. Extraordinarily detailed information on how and where to travel around using horse-drawn carriages and 'post buses'.

A Tour to the West of England in 1788 Shaw, Rev Stebbing, Gale ECCO, 2010. A digitised version of Shaw's original book, in which he enthusiastically describes the places he visits and their history.

Devon Hoskins, W G, Collins, 1954; reprints 2003, 2011, Phillimore & Co. Hoskins is the authority on Devon. No place is too small or insignificant to merit an entry in the gazetteer.

Devon: A Shell Guide Jellicoe, Ann and Mayne, Roger, Faber & Faber, 1975. The erudite research and literary style that you would expect in a Shell Guide.

Early Tours in Devon and Cornwall Pearse Chope, R (ed), James G Commin, 1918; reprinted 1967, David & Charles. A fascinating look at how early travellers in Devon saw the county. The writers include John Leland (travelling 1534–43), Celia Fiennes (1695), Daniel Defoe (1724) and Robert Southey (1802).

Glorious Devon Mais, S P B, Great Western Railway Company, 1932. A warm and human account, in Mais's masterly style, bringing the scenery and the people enjoyably to life. Also *This Unknown Island*, by the same author and equally readable.

The Coasts of Devon and Lundy Island: their towns, villages, scenery, antiquities and legends Page, John Lloyd Warden. Originally published in 1895 by Horace Cox. Reprinted in facsimile by Ulan Press. Page travelled, observed, listened and wrote exhaustively about Devon. His fat book is stuffed with observations, legends and history.

The King's England: Devon Mee, Arthur, Hodder and Stoughton. Various editions since 1928. Arranged alphabetically as a gazetteer, Mee's descriptions of the places are affectionate and his style is very readable. He includes some unusual details and a sprinkling of old tales and legends. In the same series is *Dorset*.

Some specialist books on East Devon

East Devon Pebblebed Heaths Cooper, Andrew, Heaths Conservation Trust & Impress Books Ltd. A detailed description of every aspect of East Devon's unique pebblebed ecology.

My Devonshire Year: an illustrated journal of the Jurassic Coast & Countryside Pogson, Margaret L, Richard Webb Publishers. A journal of the region covered by this book, beautifully illustrated with the author's watercolours.

SEND US YOUR PHOTOS!

We'd love to follow your adventures using our *Slow Travel East Devon & the Jurassic Coast* guide – why not tag us in your photos and stories via Twitter (@BradtGuides) and Instagram (@bradtguides)? Alternatively, you can upload your photos directly to the gallery on the East Devon destination page via our website (bradtguides.com/edevon).

Seaton Jurassic or Around the Axe Campbell, Donald, Devon Wildlife Trust & EDDC Countryside Service. All aspects of the Jurassic Coast and region. Also *Geology, History and Wildlife within 5km of Axmouth Bridge* by the same author.

WEBSITES

The organisations below have informative websites covering the natural attractions of this area, with illustrated descriptions and listings of current events and activities. Their associated publications are generally available online and in TICs.

WILDLIFE TRUSTS AND PARTNERSHIPS

Devon Wildlife Trust (⊘ devonwildlifetrust.org) and **Dorset Wildlife Trust** (⊘ dorsetwildlifetrust.org.uk) are part of a countrywide wildlife trust network.

Exe Estuary Management Partnership (⊘ exe-estuary.org) has information, maps and downloadable leaflets for the whole estuary area.

Jurassic Coast Trust (⊘ jurassiccoast.org) organises events and activities throughout the World Heritage Site.

Pebblebed Heaths Conservation Trust (⊘ pebblebedheaths.org.uk) manages the internationally important Pebblebed Heaths for both wildlife and visitors.

AREAS OF OUTSTANDING NATURAL BEAUTY (AONBS)

Blackdown Hills AONB (⊘ blackdownhills.org.uk)

Dorset AONB (⊘ dorsetaonb.org.uk) Includes the Jurassic Coast.

East Devon AONB (⊘ eastdevonaonb.org.uk) Protected since 1963, East Devon's AONB covers 103 square miles including 18 miles of coast.

EAST DEVON DISTRICT COUNCIL

The **EDDC** (⊘ eastdevon.gov.uk/visit) has practical tourist information under various headings on its website, and its booklet *Countryside Events* is available from TICs.

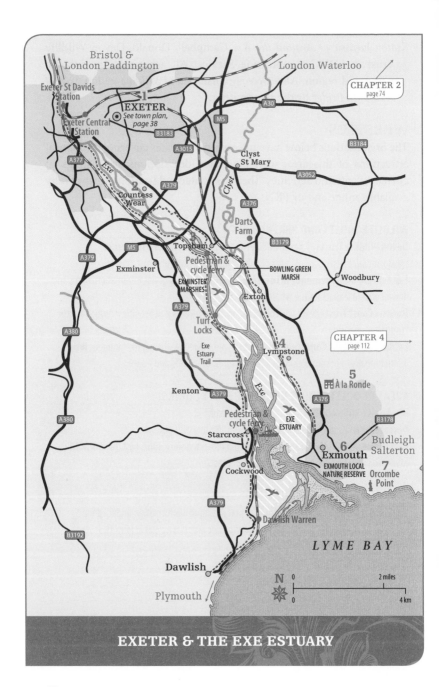

EXETER & THE EXE ESTUARY

1

EXETER &
THE EXE ESTUARY

The city of Exeter and capital of this region is situated on a gradual descent on the east side of the River Ex, whence it derives its name, according to an old verse of Alexander Neckham, once prior of St Nicholas: 'The Ex, a river of great fame, to Exeter has given name'.
Rev Stebbing Shaw, 1789

Shame on us, you may well think, for starting off a declaredly 'Slow' guide with a city! However, as cities go, **Exeter** is in fact surprisingly gentle, with plenty of open spaces and visible history encouraging a moment's pause and enjoyment. It's also compact, cupped in green surroundings, without the unappealing urban spread that commonly occurs. There are so many unexpected discoveries: the 10th-century 'Exeter Book' of Anglo-Saxon poetry; the breathtaking beauty of the great cathedral's Gothic arches; the rough texture of the old Roman wall, still as it was when strolled along by sandalled Roman feet; tiny ancient churches; twisting medieval lanes; sudden bursts of art; markets and cafés proudly selling local produce; parks and gardens bright with flowers; a poem inscribed on the pavement – the list goes on. Of course there are downsides too – the crowds, traffic, ugly post-war rebuilding, a soulless shopping area, some dreary streets – but the balance is definitely positive. Rated in surveys as one of Britain's happiest cities in which to live, Exeter is well worth exploring.

Of course Exeter's great plus is, as the Rev Stebbing Shaw mentions above, the **River Exe**; its broad estuary, stretching seaward, attracts a mass of birdlife and an equal mass of Exeter's inhabitants, enjoying its leisure potential. Watersports in the waterside towns and villages are fast growing in popularity, and the 26-mile cycle trail along its banks, from Exmouth on one side right round to Dawlish on the other, provides stunning views and some hearty exercise for both cyclists and walkers. And, while Exmouth marks the end of the estuary's eastern bank, it also marks the start of the geologically fascinating **Jurassic Coast**, a UNESCO Natural World Heritage Site stretching 95 miles eastward into Dorset.

WET-WEATHER ACTIVITIES

Royal Albert Memorial Museum (page 47)
Bill Douglas Cinema Museum (page 48)
St Nicholas Priory (page 45)
Underground Passages (page 40)

GETTING THERE & AROUND

This is an easily accessible area, by air, train, bus or car.

PUBLIC TRANSPORT

Exeter Airport, six miles away, has flights to other UK airports and to continental Europe. There are **rail links** to Exeter from just about anywhere in Britain, with direct services to/from London (Paddington and Waterloo), Bristol and Plymouth, Cornwall and Scotland. The two-coach 'Avocet Line' train to Exmouth has good views over the Exe Estuary with its extensive birdlife, and leaflets are available from TICs with recommended walks from and between its stations; while the start of the southward route to Plymouth is among the most scenic stretches in Britain, running alongside first the estuary, then the open sea and lastly the River Teign. Sit on the left for the outward journey. Exeter has two main rail stations: Central (in the centre of town) and St David's, about 20 minutes' walk away. It's worth noting that Central Station has no eating place inside but there are plenty just outside, including the Exploding Bakery, which does some of the best coffee in Exeter plus oven-fresh baking and lunchtime snacks.

Exeter's central **bus** station (about 12 minutes' walk from Central Station) should be a brand new one by the time you read this, if the remains of a Roman fort discovered on the site in September 2019 don't delay its reconstruction. Buses from here cover all parts of Devon and beyond. The number 57 runs between Exeter and Exmouth, serving the towns along the estuary. There's also an efficient network of buses within the city, stopping in either the bus station or along the High Street; the tourist information centre and the bus station have guides and timetables.

Seasonal **foot ferries** operate on the estuary to/from Exeter, Exmouth, Topsham, Starcross and Exminster: see listing on page 57, but do double-check times as some change seasonally. Stuart Line Cruises

(stuartlinecruises.co.uk) have a 'Round Robin' ticket allowing you to travel by train to Exmouth and cruise back along the estuary to Topsham for your return train to Exeter – or vice versa. The train ticket is hop-on-hop-off so you can visit Lympstone too, or even do a stretch between stations on foot along the Exe Estuary Trail.

There are three **Park and Ride** car parks on the outskirts, at Honiton Road (EX2 7NL), Matford (EX2 8FD) and Sowton (EX2 5GL), with frequent bus connections to the centre. Within the city, car parks are well signposted, but the one-way systems can be confusing. The estuary towns mentioned all have well-signed car parks.

CYCLING & WALKING

The jewel in the crown for cyclists and walkers is the wonderfully scenic **Exe Estuary Trail** (see box, below). Even cycling in the city is by no means as daunting as it might seem: Exeter (apart from the traffic hotspots) is relatively cycle-friendly, and many parts have purpose-built cycle-ways or quiet roads. Download an interactive cycle map

THE EXE ESTUARY TRAIL

From Exeter, this terrific 26-mile cycling and walking trail stretches to Exmouth along the eastern bank of the Exe Estuary, including all of the towns mentioned in this chapter, and as far as Dawlish on the western bank. Mostly flat and mostly off-road, it offers far-reaching views over the estuary, which is one of the most important birdlife habitats in Europe.

With the help of buses, trains and ferries, it can easily be broken into manageable stretches and even circular trails: buses from Exeter serve all the estuary towns, where bikes can usually be hired; the train from Exeter to Exmouth serves those on the eastern bank; and trains to Plymouth stop at Starcross on the western bank from where there's a ferry across to Exmouth. Topsham also has ferries to the opposite bank. So you can do a stretch along one side and then switch to the other; for example from Exmouth you could go via Lympstone to Topsham (six miles), crossing the Clyst Bridge; take a ferry from Topsham across the water to Turf Locks; pause for refreshment at the historic Turf Inn; and then head off to Starcross (three miles) to pick up a ferry back to Exmouth. Both ferries carry cycles.

The Exe Estuary Management Partnership (exe-estuary.org) produces an excellent series of leaflets (*Exe Explorer*, *Exe Wildlife*, *Exe Heritage* and *Exe Activities*) which are downloadable from their website or available in TICs. Also the Croydecycle *Exe Estuary Walking and Cycling Map*, scale 1:12,500, shows the whole area in great detail and with helpful notes (croydecycle.co.uk).

from ⊘ traveldevon.info/cycle, or use the very good Croydecycle *Exe Estuary Walking and Cycling* Map, scale 1:12,500, which covers the areas mentioned in this chapter.

The 40-mile East Devon Way (page 114) also starts in Exmouth, so walkers doing the whole length of the trail will be sharing some of the route with cyclists. Hardy cyclists should also check 'The Nello' (page 60), a challenging 100-mile annual charity cycle ride from Topsham over the roof of Exmoor and back. Its 20th anniversary was in 2019; see ⊘ forcecancercharity.co.uk.

 CYCLE HIRE

Exeter
There's a newly installed electric docking stand outside Central Station for **Co-bikes** (⊘ co-bikes.co.uk) , and possibly more around the city by the time you read this. More traditional places are listed below.

Saddles & Paddles 4 King's Wharf, The Quay ✆ 01392 424241 ⊘ sadpad.com ◷ 09.00–18.00 daily (closed Wed in term-time Nov–Easter). Bike & paddle sports hire (canoes, kayaks, stand-up paddleboards) plus bike sales and repairs. Helpful, knowledgeable staff.

Exmouth
Exmouth Cycle Hire 1a Victoria Rd, EX8 1DL ✆ 01395 225656 ⊘ exmouthcyclehire.co.uk ◷ 09.00–17.30 Mon–Sat year round, Apr–Oct also 10.00–16.00 Sun.
Knobblies Bike Shop 107 Exeter Rd, EX8 1QE ✆ 01395 270182 ⊘ knobbliesbikes.co.uk ◷ 09.00–17.30 Mon–Sat. Cycle repairs & sales. Also run adventurous guided bike tours over Dartmoor & Woodbury, plus half-day e-bike tours to Woodbury.

Topsham
Darts Farm EX3 0QH ✆ 01392 878209 ⊘ dartsfarm.co.uk
Route 2 Bike Shop 4 Amity Pl, EX3 0JL ✆ 01392 879160 ⊘ route2bikes.co.uk ◷ summer 10.00–17.00 Mon–Sat, check for winter changes. Cycle hire (including e-bikes), servicing and sales, plus paddleboard hire. Café/bar onsite.

STARTING WITH THE ROMANS

When the Romans rowed their great galleys up the Exe, bent on subjugation, Exeter was the capital of the Dumnonii (their territory stretched throughout Devon and Cornwall) who had named it Caerwisc or 'city of the waters'. The river at that time was said to be rich in salmon, no doubt a welcome bonus for the invaders. Renaming the town Isca Dumnoniorum and the Exe the Isca, the Romans then – inevitably – built a fortress, which from around AD55 to AD70 accommodated some 5,000 men, most of them legionnaires originating from Italy, Spain and France. After the legionnaires had been moved to sites of new Roman conquests elsewhere in Britain, Isca gradually spread beyond the fortress; a protective wall was built to enclose its wider area, together with new housing, temples, bath houses, markets and administrative buildings. Foundations of a large bath house on the green in front of today's cathedral, dating to approximately AD55, were last excavated in 1973 but then covered over; if funds can be found, work there will resume. Meanwhile Roman galleys carried cargoes of continental goods and foodstuffs up Exeter's river, and over 1,000 Roman coins have been found in the city: a surprisingly large number and a sign of active trading. Life for its residents was good – for a while. However, by the end of the 4th century (with the departure of the Romans) the town had declined and pretty much reverted to farming.

Records from the Dark Ages are sketchy. Anglo-Saxons occupied Exeter in 658 but lived peaceably with the existing inhabitants; they founded a monastery in 670, just to the west of the present cathedral. King Alfred created the town a Royal Borough in 877, and in 1003 it was 'laid level from the east to the west gate, and the whole inhabitants massacred in the most cruel manner, by Sueno the Dane and his horrid barbarians', according to the Rev Stebbing Shaw in 1789. He continues: 'It had scarce time to recruit when William the Conqueror took possession of it after a close siege and obstinate resistance'. It later stoutly resisted further attacks and sieges, including that of the Prayer Book Rebellion (see box, page 117), and by the end of the 17th century the woollen cloth trade had made it one of England's biggest and busiest cities, the Exe enabling it to trade extensively with continental Europe.

"The river at that time was said to be rich in salmon, no doubt a welcome bonus for the invaders."

Topsham also prospered, becoming an alternative port when a weir across the estuary blocked Exeter's access to the sea in the 13th century (page 58), and its attractive Dutch-style houses still recall its medieval trading status. In 1966 it became officially a part of Exeter. Happily for today's visitors, medieval growth did not erase all trace of Exeter's Roman past; even today, nearly 2,000 years later, almost 70% of the sturdy city wall survives.

1 EXETER

Tourist information: Dix's Field, Exeter EX1 1GF ✆ 01392 665700 ⌽ visitexeter.com
◷ Apr–Sep 09.00–17.00 Mon–Sat, Oct–Mar 09.30–16.30 Mon–Sat

By their nature, cities aren't Slow places and Exeter does bustle. During World War II it was severely bombed (on one night in 1942 alone, it lost almost 2,000 shops and houses) and some of the modern replacements are soulless, but attractive old buildings remain tucked away around the city centre and the old quayside has been developed into a pleasant area of traditional shops, cafés and workshops. Above all the great Cathedral Church of St Peter, started by the Normans in 1114 and remodelled in

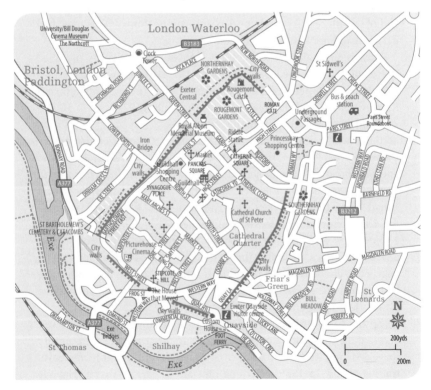

Gothic style between 1270 and 1369, is magnificent: an unmissable part of any visit. In fact there's so much of historic interest in Exeter that it needs a whole guidebook; we can only summarise some of the main sites here and leave you to make further discoveries. *Two Thousand Years in Exeter* by W G Hoskins (1960, updated 2004) gives helpful and readable background information. Of the Exeter visits suggested here, only the cathedral and the Underground Passages have an entry fee; everywhere else is free.

GUIDED & SELF-GUIDED WALKS

All the main places of interest around the centre are within walking distance of each other. Amid the inevitable bustle of a city there are small quiet lanes and attractive medieval buildings. The TICs (and website ⌀ exeter.gov.uk; use the 'search' box at the top) have details of self-guided walks round the remains of the **Roman city wall** (almost two miles), round **medieval Exeter** (just over a mile) and along a **Woollen Trail** (two miles); or you can join up with walks to the main sites led by expert **Red Coat Guided Tours**. These are free, very informative, at a relatively gentle pace and cover all aspects of Exeter's history – including its historic buildings, its ghosts and legends, the blitz and 'forgotten Exeter'. Details are available from the TICs, from ✆ 01392 265203, and from ⌀ exeter.gov.uk/guidedtours. There's no need to book: just turn up at the right time and starting point, which is generally Cathedral Close.

ON & OFF THE HIGH STREET

> The principal street and thoroughfare is very long and spacious, and to the west much improved by an elegant bridge of three large arches over the river.
>
> Rev Stebbing Shaw, 1789

The High Street is still 'long' and reasonably 'spacious', but Rev Stebbing would be hard put to recognise it today. The gleaming new Princesshay Shopping Centre dominates the northern end, and the middle is over-heavy with national chains. However, many of Exeter's attractions are either in the High Street or just round a corner, so come for a guided stroll.

If you arrive at the central bus station in Paris Street, you're handily close to the visitor information centre or TIC, from where it's only a short walk to the Underground Passages.

The **Underground Passages** (2 Paris St ✆ 01392 665887 ♂ exeter.gov. uk/passages ⊙ approx 10.00–17.30 daily with the last tour at 16.30 (earlier on Sun), but check beforehand for daily & seasonal variations, Oct–May closed Mon) are fascinating, as long as you don't mind putting on a hard hat and going down into a narrow enclosed passage. They were built in the 14th century to house lead pipes carrying fresh water into the city; Exeter is the only UK city to have underground passages of this type, and they're one of the most complete medieval water systems in Europe. During the 25-minute tour I learnt that during the 1549 Prayer Book Rebellion rebels broke into the tunnels and stole lead to make bullets, also that the joints on the old pipes used to leak a lot because the medieval builders were good brickies but poor plumbers. There's also a small museum, a ten-minute film about the passages and interactive displays.

Starting southwards down the High Street, a narrow covered alley on the right between Boots and the Halifax leads to a path through **Northernhay Gardens** (see *Parks & greenery*, page 50) towards Central Station and the Royal Albert Memorial Museum, both in Queen Street, passing the side of 11th-century Rougemont Castle and part of the city wall. There's little historic interest inside the castle now: it's partly administrative offices and partly used for art exhibitions, weddings and other events.

Continuing south, you may pass (on your right) two of my favourite traditional pavement snackeries: the Hot Sausage Company stand and a solar-powered Crêperie. The smell when the sausage-seller has a batch sizzling away on his griddle is mouthwatering, and the pancake seller is fascinating to watch. He's been serving pancakes there for more than a quarter of a century now, and spreads, flips and folds them with amazing dexterity. They taste good too.

Ahead of you on the right-hand pavement is a tall shiny statue made of stainless steel and stone: a 21ft-high pyramid with balls around the base, called the **Riddle Statue**. Made by the artist Michael Fairfax, who also created the geoneedle marking the start of the Jurassic Coast in Exmouth and the finger labyrinth in Seaton, it was unveiled in 2005 as part of a million-pound refurbishment of the High Street. On its eight panels there are ancient verses – riddles – translated by Kevin Crossley Holland from those in *The Exeter Book* (see box, page 54). They have been laser-cut into the steel in mirror writing, and their reflections can be read in the opposite panel.

Coming up on the right is **Gandy Street**, which was laid out during the reign of Alfred the Great, and marks the line that the Roman soldiers followed when they were patrolling the wall of their fortress. It's described as the Carnaby Street of Exeter – with some attractive small independent shops. There seem to be more each time I come – Seasalt clothing, Chococo, crystals, Nomadic Travel, mobile phone servicing, hairdressing, tofu, vintage and reworked clothing, jewellery, the very good Bill's Restaurant at No 32 – and now my favourite, the Recycled Candle Company (∂ therecycledcandlecompany.co.uk) at number 16. It's such a simple idea. They collect candle remnants from hotels, restaurants, pubs, galleries, churches, cathedrals and the public and recycle the wax. In the five years after starting (in 2014), they recycled over 40 tons of wax into thousands of luxury scented candles of all shapes and sizes, which are now used and sold throughout the UK. And they're beautiful. The shop is a shiny fairyland of colour, light and perfume, and the candles make such attractive gifts. I love it.

Opposite Gandy Street across the High Street is **St Stephen's Church**, one of a handful of small and very historic churches in the centre of Exeter: see box, page 42. The distinctive red stone in which several of them (and many other buildings around Exeter – you can't miss it) are built is known as **Heavitree stone** (or, more descriptively, 'bullock's blood & gravel'!) and originates from Exeter's Heavitree quarter. It dates back around 280 million years, to when the whole area was an arid desert. Violent storms and torrential rain mixed the red desert sand with fragments of rock and pebbles, and over millennia this silty mixture became compressed into the

"It dates back around 280 million years, to when the whole area was an arid desert."

distinctive red stone. Outcrops of it in the Heavitree area have been quarried and used for building since early medieval times; being coarse and rather soft, it's more suitable for chunky constructions like walls than for decorative stonework, where something like Beer stone (page 177) might be used. Look out for more of it as you walk on! (For more information, see ∂ heavitreequarrytrails.org.uk.)

Queen Street on the right leads to Central Station, the Royal Albert Memorial Museum (page 47) and a row of small independent shops and cafés. Among them, Devon Coffee (number 88) has an interesting range of specialist coffees to buy or drink, plus good local food.

EXETER'S LITTLE CHURCHES

St Martin's Church

This beautiful little church is squashed into a corner of Cathedral Close. The original church, consecrated by Bishop Leofric in 1065 and one of the oldest in Exeter, was rebuilt in the 15th century, in red Heavitree stone, probably re-using some masonry and features from the old church. To fit the small space available, the east end was built at a skewed angle and the tower was added later, on a piece of rented land. The dramatic front window (of Beer stone) and other windows date from the 14th century. Its parish area is tiny, a mere 1.75 acres (0.7ha), yet in 1821 it held 329 residents, in houses long since gone. Towered over by the so-called 'Mol's Coffee House' next door (page 53), St Martin's is now well cared for by the Churches Conservation Trust.

St Mary Arches Church

This stately little church on the street of the same name is only occasionally open to the public now – its interior, dating from around 1190, is the oldest still existing in Exeter. The layout is unique in Devon, and beautiful: two Norman four-bay arcades stand on either side of a nave, separated by massive, circular stone piers. In the early 20th century, a layer of cement was added to some of the exterior to 'protect' the crumbly local stone: but it's ugly, encourages damp and kills the church's medieval character. There's a traditional sanctuary knocker on the door, which entitled any fugitive holding it to 40 days of protection. Exeter had several churches dedicated to St Mary so they were given nicknames to distinguish them; the

'arches' here may refer to the church's own Norman arches or to former arches in the street outside.

St Mary Steps Church

The beautiful and atmospheric St Mary Steps on West Street is so named because it has – yes – steps beside it, on Stepcote Hill. The original church dating from about 1150 was rebuilt in the 15th century and little remains from the earlier period, apart from the strikingly decorated Norman font, carved from a single massive limestone block. However, the church has several treasures. Its 15th-century rood screen with 12 painted panels of saints came from medieval St Mary Major which was demolished in 1865; part is thought to be a skilful copy, but its original section is the only pre-Reformation chancel screen surviving in any Exeter parish church. St Mary Steps is best known locally for its colourful animated 'Matthew the Miller clock', installed in 1621 and said to commemorate a local miller who lived his life with very precise timing. He sits in the centre, nodding on the hour, while two guards on either side strike the quarters. Charles Dickens wrote:

Adam and Eve would never believe
That Matthew the Miller was dead
For every hour in Westgate tower
Old Matthew nods his head.

St Olave's Church

Situated on Fore Street, this Saxon church has a separate Saxon tower. Originally a chapel, it was possibly built for King Harold's mother, Gytha. St Olav was an 11th-century Viking king who converted to Christianity.

In fact Harold gave him the choice of either converting or being beheaded, so he took the predictable option – but then died in battle anyway. After his death it is said that his nails and hair continued to grow and a stream of clear water gushed out from his grave, hence the sainthood.

St Pancras' Church

This tiny church, first recorded in 1191 and located in the Guildhall Shopping Precinct, is just 46ft long by 16ft wide. Although traces of a Saxon door were discovered during repairs in the 19th century, its origins may possibly stretch back much further: to a church built by Roman Christians during the Roman occupation, which would make it one of the oldest known Christian sites in Britain. It has an impressive 12th-century font with bead moulding, and a 13th-century scalloped piscina. The location is startling: walk straight through the Guildhall Shopping Precinct to the end, battling your way past the shoppers; turn right after Sainsbury's and Primark; and you'll find it just outside, sitting serenely in the centre of what at present is a building site. It's a 'Small Pilgrim Place' (⊘ smallpilgrimplaces.org), as is the Point in View Chapel at À la Ronde (page 65).

St Petrock's Church

Devon has 17 churches dedicated to St Petrock or Petroc, who visited the area in the 6th century. This one on High Street may possibly date back to the 7th century in some form or other, although no Celtic traces remain. Part of its north wall is 12th or 13th century. Various extensions were patched on to it over the centuries, until historian Nikolaus Pevsner described its interior as being 'among the most confusing of any church in the whole of England'. Today it has been divided in two: the more recent parts are used as an office for the St Petrock's charity (⊘ stpetrocks.org.uk) which does much-needed work among Exeter's homeless. It's also a campanology centre, with permanent displays and information about local and national bell-ringing societies.

St Stephen's Church

Also on High Street, St Stephen's already existed in 1086, when it was mentioned in the Domesday Book as belonging to the Bishop of Exeter. Restoration work in 1826 unexpectedly revealed an early Norman crypt, containing some arches from a vaulted ceiling and two round limestone columns with decorated capitals: they are some of the oldest standing stonework in Exeter, and a great treasure. For reasons of structural safety the crypt has now been sealed (with them still inside) and is inaccessible. The only other known crypt of this antiquity in Devon is in Sidbury (page 140). In medieval times an extension – St Stephen's Bow – was built across an adjacent Saxon lane to give more space inside, and a low archway was left beneath it so that pedestrians could still use the lane. You can walk through it today. St Stephen's reopened in 2012 after substantial reconstruction: inside it's now a light and flexible and welcoming open space, used for community events. On its front step is written 'Be welcoming to strangers; you may be entertaining angels unawares'.

After the Queen Street turning comes the impressive **Guildhall**, where the affairs of Exeter have been run for over 800 years. One of the oldest municipal buildings in England still in use, it hosts a number of functions and events at which times it's closed to the public. Otherwise the main hall should be open on weekdays 10.30–13.00 and 14.00–16.00; check beforehand on ✆ 01392 665500 or ⊗ exeter.gov.uk/guildhall. The building itself is 14th century or earlier; the ornate frontage and portico were added in the 16th century. Apart from the council chamber's roof (14th century) and an 18th-century chandelier, the internal fittings and furnishings are Victorian. The city stocks once stood under the portico, and beneath the council chamber is an early 14th-century cellar that was once a prison known as the 'pytt of the Guyldhall'. Medieval kings were entertained in the Guildhall, and miscreants executed on a gallows outside. Rebellions were planned here and politicians chosen. Judge Jeffreys presided over sessions of the 'Bloody Assizes' here in 1685, and during the tumultuous mayoral elections of the 18th century rival mobs fought outside with fists and clubs. As late as the early 1800s, death sentences were issued here for crimes as minor as stealing a sheep or a cow, or transportation orders for such offences as stealing a purse containing 1s 6d (7.5p). By contrast, during World War II it became an occasional dance hall and the front was encased in brick to escape bomb damage. It's a great survivor, and a window to Exeter's history.

Not far from the Guildhall, roughly opposite St Petrock's church, is what's claimed to be the **narrowest street** in the world: Parliament Street, 25 inches wide at one end increasing to a maximum 45 inches. (It all depends on your definition of 'street'.)

Don't pass the Guildhall without looking down at the pavement – you could be walking on a poem, a curly line of metallic letters winding their way along the slabs:

Conjure with me: three letters of the alphabet, or two and one, or one.

Run me backwards and I would seem to be unchanged, but that would be an uphill task of course.

My name speaks of former times while I am still current: though what current can be still?

By poet Richard Skinner, the poem was first published in *The New Exeter Book of Riddles* (eds Lawrence Sail & Kevin Crossley-Holland,

Enitharmon Press 2002) and echoes the style of the riddles in *The Exeter Book* (see box, page 54).

The High Street becomes Fore Street at its junction with North and South streets, and here the **Great Conduit** once stood. Built in 1461, this was where citizens could come to collect water. The lead pipes running into the city (see *Underground Passages*, page 40) terminated here, in an ornately carved and rather church-like little building (there's a picture in the Underground Passages). The junction was called the Carfor or Carfax, from the French *carrefour* or *quatrefoix* meaning 'crossroads'.

"As late as the early 1800s, death sentences were issued here for crimes as minor as stealing a sheep."

For shops, **Fore Street** is far more interesting than the High Street, with lots of independent and quirky little businesses. Continue down it past the churches of St Mary Arches and St Olave (see box, page 42) and on your right you reach the beautiful little medieval lane called **The Mint**.

Follow The Mint along and on your left is one of Exeter's treasures, **St Nicholas Priory** (⊘ nicholaspriory.com), said to be the city's oldest complete building. After his victory at Hastings in 1066, William the conqueror founded Battle Abbey in Sussex. In 1068 he laid siege to Exeter; then gave Exeter's church of St Olave (see box, page 42) as a gift to the new abbey. Benedictine monks, sent from Battle to administer the church and its possessions, set about building a monastery with its own church; it was dedicated to Saint Nicholas in 1087. (St Nicholas – later aka Santa Claus – was a 4th-century Roman saint regarded as the patron saint of children.) The monks were just a small community – the ideal was 12 but records in the 14th century show only four – but the monastery held a respected place in the town, providing hospitality to pilgrims and accommodation for important visitors. New rooms were built on as funds permitted. Then, when Henry VIII dissolved smaller monasteries in 1536, the church and cloisters were demolished and the monks moved away. The remaining monastic buildings were sold off by the Crown, and by the early 17th century the building had become an impressive Elizabethan townhouse. A part of this is what you can see today, with a peaceful garden at its side, looked after by the Exeter Historic Buildings Trust. It's currently open on Sundays from 13.00 to 14.00 and at other times for special events, but this may vary later; check via the website or the TIC. It's a beautiful place, full of atmosphere.

ON A WING AND A COO

Heroines come in all shapes and sizes. In 2018 a blue plaque was put up in West Street to mark the former home of Mary of Exeter – a pigeon. Her owner, Charlie Brewer, was born in Exeter St Thomas in 1895 and apprenticed to a bootmaker aged 15. In 1922 he moved with his young wife to West Street, where he took up bootmaking and, as a hobby, bred and trained racing pigeons. In the 1940s he put his prize pigeon, Mary, at the disposal of the National Pigeon Service, and soon she was being dropped behind enemy lines. Despite being wounded three times and once going missing for ten days, she always returned to Exeter where Charlie nursed her back into action. She was awarded the Dicken Medal, often called the animal VC, for her gallantry and outstanding wartime service. She died in 1950, was buried in the PDSA pet cemetery in Ilford and is commemorated on the animals' war memorial in London's Hyde Park, as well as being pictured in the mosaic under the Exeter St Thomas railway bridge. Charlie, who also received a medal and used to raise money for charity by giving talks about Mary, died in 1985 aged 90. My thanks to Exeter's Double Elephant Print Workshop (doubleelephant.org.uk) for many of these details; they worked with young people locally to discover Mary's story.

Returning to walk down Fore Street, West Street on the left leads to the church of **St Mary Steps** with its animated clock (see box, page 42), and the fascinating 15th-century '**House That Moved**'. In 1961 it was doomed to demolition, when roads in the area were to be re-made and the inner bypass built, but was saved in the nick of time by being listed. In December that year a strengthening jacket was placed around it and iron wheels were set at the corners, attached to hydraulic jacks. Then gradually it was lifted and very slowly, over six days, with constant adjustment of the jacks to keep it level, was pulled on rails some distance uphill to its present position. It gives a new meaning to 'moving house'.

Cross the dual carriageway outside and then follow the pavement for a few yards up the hill, and you'll come to a footpath and steps down to the quayside.

Opposite the West Street junction (standing here you're just a stone's downward throw away from the excellent little Angela's Restaurant at 38 New Bridge Street; page 55), Bartholomew Street East leads to **St Bartholomew's Cemetery**, established in the early 19th century when Exeter's other cemeteries were full, and now a park. It also houses Exeter's massive **catacombs**, built between 1835 and 1837 against the city wall: the first cemetery buildings in Britain to be built in Egyptian style, with entrances resembling Egyptian tombs and the pointed granite gate pillars reflecting Egyptian obelisks. A dividing wall separated Anglicans from non-conformists. Burial there offered safety from grave-robbers, a threat at the time. Inside, high, arched passages stretch away into the darkness, with tiers of empty tombs at the side like compartments in a mortuary. The initial cost of a grave was 20 guineas, or about £6,000 at today's rate. Unsurprisingly, there were few takers, so this was dropped to seven guineas, but fewer than 20 bodies were ever laid to rest there. Bats live in the passages now, and the iron gates are locked if they're active, otherwise some Red Coat guided tours (page 39) do go there during the summer.

MARKETS

Exeter Farmers' Market, with local produce from all around the area, takes place every Thursday morning at the junction of Fore Street and South Street. There's home-reared meat, fish from the Devon coast, venison and all manner of fresh seasonal vegetables, as well as baking, dairy goods and some handicrafts. The **Sidwell Street Market** is an informal affair, Monday–Saturday, selling just about everything, including flowers, kitchen utensils and secondhand books. **Exeter Street Food** events ($\oslash$ streetfoodexeter.co.uk) are now popping up around the city. Three regular summer ones are: in Southernhay Gardens (EX1 1PJ $\odot$ May–Sep 11.00–20.00, last Fri of the month); The Quay, beneath the transit shed ($\odot$ May–Sep 17.30–21.00, 1st Thu); and Piazza Terracina (Quay $\odot$ Jun–Sep 16.30–21.30, 3rd Fri).

ROYAL ALBERT MEMORIAL MUSEUM (RAMM)

Queen St $\mathscr{J}$ 01392 265858 $\oslash$ exeter.gov.uk/ramm $\odot$ 10.00–17.00 Tue–Sun; entry free

The museum's imposing Gothic building was completed in 1868. In 2012 Art Fund, the national fundraising charity for art, named it the UK's Museum of the Year. It has been called 'an exquisite jewel-box of a building; a Venetian casket; one of the most appealing treasures in Britain'. Indeed its million-odd exhibits do cover an extraordinary range – ceramics, bronzes, natural history (birds, bugs, mammals, seashells), geology, World War II, a giraffe named Gerald, toby jugs, flint-knapping, the 18th- and 19th-century global explorers and many other changing exhibits. More coherently, it is predictably strong on every aspect of Devon, from the prehistoric to the present, but also includes international cultures (with some rare West African art). And the Seaton Down Hoard (page 181) is housed here. Allow plenty of time for a browse; there's a good café, if you need refreshment midway.

ENTERTAINMENTS

There have been theatres in Exeter since the 14th century, with many of its players becoming well-known national names. A disastrous fire at the old Theatre Royal in 1887 killed at least 186 people, when gas lights high above the stage set fire to some scenery. Of the three main theatres today, The Northcott up at the university hosts national touring shows and performers as well as a variety of local productions; smaller but active venues include the Barnfield in Barnfield Road and the multi-artform Phoenix in Gandy Street. Programmes are listed in the local press.

Exeter has three **cinemas**: the Picturehouse in Bartholomew Street shows independent art films as well as current releases and streamed live performances, and has a pleasant little upstairs café/bar. The multi-screen Vue in Belgrave Road and Odeon in Sidwell Street have the usual crop of national releases.

Movie buffs can have a happy browse in the **Bill Douglas Cinema Museum** (The Old Library, University of Exeter, Prince of Wales Rd, EX4 4SB ✎ 01392 724321 ⌖ bdcmuseum.org.uk ◷ 10.00–17.00 daily except bank hols & Christmas to New Year), which has a miscellany of around 75,000 cinema-related items. Some date back to the 17th century, and they cover all aspects of cinema, pre-cinema and the history of the moving image.

The eponymous Bill Douglas (1934–91) was born in the impoverished mining village of Newcraighall near Edinburgh. His childhood was financially tough but at the local cinema he could buy a ticket for the price of two returned jam jars, and from this youthful enthusiasm became a filmmaker said by critics and fans to have one of the most unique, personal and poetic visions in British cinema history. He and his lifelong film-making friend Peter Jewell assembled a remarkable collection of over 50,000 items, which on Bill's death Peter gave to Exeter University for the founding of the museum. Many more donations followed, building the collection you can see today.

The university is within (longish) walking distance of the city centre and (closer to) St David's Station; buses D and H go there from the centre. You may spot the entertaining **interactive sculpture** outside: it's entitled

EXETER FESTIVAL OF SOUTH WEST FOOD & DRINK

This vibrant annual not-for-profit event, started in 2003 and run with the support of Exeter City Council and numerous other sponsors, takes place over three days (late April or early May) in the courtyard of Exeter Castle and the surrounding Northernhay Gardens, attracting many thousands of visitors. In the Festival Cookery Theatre, the region's leading chefs entertain with demonstrations and talks, while the two food pavilions and over a hundred of the finest local artisan producers ensure that a mouthwatering array of wonderful West Country food and drink is on display – and to be eaten or drunk. There are 'Food is Fun' tepees with demos and hands-on activities, a range of other family-friendly events, sizzling street food in the castle courtyard and live music from Exeter Beats.

Increasing in scope year by year, this is a great celebration of all that is good, genuine and local about food and drink from Exeter and the whole of the South West. Let yourself be tempted!

Find out more at ⚭ exeterfoodanddrinkfestival.co.uk.

'Reflected Vision', is by artist Kenny Munro, and has been created from mirrored stainless steel, so visitors can engage with reflections both from the natural world and of themselves and their friends. For other sculptures on the university campus, see page 50.

QUAYSIDE

Tourist information: Custom House, 46 The Quay ⚭ 01392 271611 ⚭ exeter.gov.uk/customhouse ☉ Apr–Oct 10.00–13.00 & 13.45–17.00 daily; Nov–Mar 11.00–16.00 Thu–Sun

One of our favourite places, the old quayside, dating back to Roman times, has been turned into a relaxed, pleasant leisure area, with traditional workshops (unique wooden furniture, stylish metalwork, needlework, mirrors, etc) in the old warehouses and arches. You can take a boat trip along the canal, paddle off in a canoe or kayak, or hire a bike and pedal down the old towpath. Or potter off in a pedalo. On Saturdays, **parkrun** (page 22) takes place here. There are bars, cafés and restaurants with fresh local food, and antiques and curios galore; the huge Exeter Antiques Centre is well worth a browse. The **Custom House** (1680) is one of Exeter's first brick buildings, and has some beautiful 17th-century plaster ceilings by John Abbott. Celia Fiennes, on her horseback journey round Britain in 1698, called it 'the Fair House upon the Quay'. The cannons in front of it don't indicate battle;

they were brought in by boat from Glasgow, ready for shipping to the continent, but their shippers couldn't pay the necessary fees so they were abandoned – long, long ago. The visitor centre is inside; it's well stocked and helpful, and has a half-hour video on the history of Exeter. A few minutes' walk away, the recently restored **Cricklepit Mill** is home to the Devon Wildlife Trust.

The little flat-bottomed **Butts Ferry** that is hauled across the canal on a wire is the oldest wire ferry in Britain, dating from at least 1641. It was nearly retired when a bridge was built nearby in the 1970s, but a Councillor Butt saved it – hence its present name. In bad weather some years back it broke loose and drifted down to Topsham, to end up nestling cosily among six pedalos painted to resemble large black swans. Nice picture! It runs daily from Easter to October (☉ 11.00–17.00) and the crossing takes all of three minutes. Or you can use the bridge, but that's less fun. The notice by the ferry reads:

Tis yer you catch the ferry
A funny boat it be
But it gets you across the river
For only 40p.

If you don't fancy the uphill walk from the quay back to the centre, there is a bus (G), but it's only hourly, doesn't run on Sundays and the last of the day leaves on the dot of 15.30.

PARKS & GREENERY
Exeter is surprisingly green: it has five open valley parks within its boundary, plus many smaller ones closer to the heart of the city, of which **Northernhay Gardens** between the High Street and Queen Street are a good example – a pleasant, flower-filled, definitely Slow place away from the traffic where people stroll, picnic on the grass, pause on benches to read their books or newspapers and just generally relax. They were the first public gardens in England, and are the site of the annual Exeter Festival of South West Food and Drink (see box, page 49). Adjoining them are equally attractive **Rougemont Gardens**, beside the castle.

The University of Exeter
This might seem an unlikely 'park', but in fact its Streatham Campus with its arboretum, ponds and gardens is one of the most beautiful in

the country; additionally it has a unique **Sculpture Trail** with works by sculptors including Barbara Hepworth, Geoffrey Clark and Paul Mount. A pdf leaflet is available from ⊘ artsandcultureexeter.co.uk/explore/ sculpture-walk. Other pieces are inside the university buildings and generally accessible on weekdays from 09.00 to 16.00, but it's wise to confirm this (✆ 01392 661000 should pass you to the right department).

The whole trail, indoors and out, takes around two hours, depending on how long you linger; see also ⊘ artsandcultureexeter.co.uk. While you are up in the university, you could also visit the Bill Douglas Cinema Museum on the campus (page 48).

Exeter Green Circle

The Green Circle (⊘ exeter.gov.uk/greencircle) consists of five linked walks, together forming a complete circuit around the outskirts of the city. Each walk is two to three miles and the total distance is only 12 miles, showing what a compact city Exeter is. Some stretches of the circle are along quiet city streets; 'green' sections include the Alphin Brook Valley and farmland, the picturesque Hoopern Valley, the Ludwell Valley and Riverside Valley Park, climbs from the Exe Valley floodplain to the hills surrounding Exeter with far-reaching views, and the **Mincinglake Valley Park**, which before the 1970s was the city's landfill site but has been successfully transformed. Its lower part is wooded, while its upper part is meadowland rich in wild flowers, butterflies and other insects, with superb views down the Exe Estuary to the sea.

See also the Countess Wear walk on page 55, which connects with part of the circle.

THE CATHEDRAL CHURCH OF ST PETER IN EXETER

Cathedral Yard ✆ 01392 285983 ⊘ exeter-cathedral.org.uk

> **Mankind was never so happily inspired as when it made a cathedral.**
> Robert Louis Stevenson

And perhaps also never so happily inspired as when looking at one. This great building with its massive carved frontage sends my spirits soaring as soon as I step into Cathedral Yard. It's hunkered solidly there on the green, the weight of centuries pressing it into Exeter's earth, yet when you step inside the door your eye swings immediately up to the space and grace of its amazing roof: the longest unbroken stretch of Gothic vaulting in the world.

Devon's first cathedral was built in Crediton, in 909, but in 1050 the See moved to Exeter and the cathedral temporarily occupied a large Saxon Minster church in the present Cathedral Yard. The Normans started building their new cathedral in 1114 and completed it around 66 years later. Then from 1270 to 1369 it was remodelled in decorated Gothic style, and the vaulting dates from that time. When you've recovered from the impact of its size and grandeur, you can focus on small, intimate details: the individual faces of the figures on the towering frontage, animals on the choir stalls, sweet-faced angels playing musical instruments, sad swans with entwined necks, intricate roof bosses, a little 13th-century carved wooden elephant – so many, so absorbing, and such a personal glimpse into centuries of human history.

"The hole in the wall below is thought to have been for the cathedral cat, which was on the payroll."

The 15th-century astronomical clock on the North Tower is a particular treasure: a working model of the solar system as it was understood when the clock was made. The fixed golden ball in the centre is the earth, with the sun (black) and moon (black and silver) circling around it. The hole in the wall below is thought to have been for the cathedral cat, which was on the payroll at the princely rate of one penny a week. There's also a story that the clock inspired the nursery rhyme *Hickory Dickory Dock*, in which case the cat-in-residence at the time was earning its salary.

You may want simply to gaze and stroll and absorb the atmosphere, reading the explanations by the various objects, but you'll gain far more from your visit if you buy a guidebook from the well-stocked cathedral shop or take one of the guided tours. There are also tours to the North Tower (over 170 steps to climb!) and roof, but these must be booked. Allow plenty of time here, because one thing will draw you to another and the place is best savoured slowly. There are so many effigies and memorials and carvings and intricate adornments to see, all with their personal stories. (I was intrigued by a memorial to '*Margaret the Wife of Irenaeus Moe Esq of the Island of Barbados*' who '*died near this City the 25th of Oct 1770 in the 29th Year of her Age*'.) If you like your history quirky, *The Cathedral Cat: stories from Exeter Cathedral* by Nicholas Orme (available in the shop) is a good buy. The **Cathedral Café** set in the historic cloisters is a pleasant place for a break; with its friendly atmosphere and fresh homemade food. There is an entrance fee to the cathedral, but it seems insignificant compared with the grandeur of the place.

The Cathedral Close

There's history here too, in the shadow of St Peter's. Sadly, in 2016 a catastrophic fire destroyed the fine old **Clarence Hotel**. It was a dramatic scene, with flames leaping high into the night sky and reflecting from the cathedral walls. Heroic action by the firefighters saved the adjoining buildings but the Clarence was gutted. Its owners hoped to rebuild and various plans were submitted, but the cost escalated and in July 2019 they reluctantly decided to sell. The site's future isn't yet known.

The building first came into prominence around 1766. Prior to that it had been leased out to a succession of minor tenants, but more serious development started from this point. By March 1768 a French schoolmaster named Peter Berlon was advertising it as 'Berlon's Coffee-house' and later that year he announced that he had 'lately fitted lodgings, for the conveniency of those Gentlemen and Ladies who please to honour him with their Favours'. In September 1770, he described it as a 'New Coffee-house, Inn, and Tavern, Or, The Hotel, In St. Peter's Church-yard, Exeter'. This is thought to have been the first use of the word *hotel* in England. Admiral Nelson visited in 1801, and it gained its present name after a visit by Adelaide, Duchess of Clarence, in July 1827. Franz Liszt performed two concerts at the hotel, and other visitors included Beatrix Potter, Thomas Hardy, and the actors Clark Gable and Gary Cooper. Celebrity chef Michael Caines took it on in 2000 and the Clarence had been a cherished part of Exeter. Its death is sad.

The elaborate medieval building next to St Martin's Church was quickly doused in foam to protect it from the fire, and survived unscathed. There are various versions of its history. The latest one (from *Exeter Unveiled*, by Todd Gray) links its name **'Mol's Coffee House'** to a time when it was run by a woman named Mary (or Mol). The original pre-Reformation building was erected by the Cathedral authorities to house the 'Annuellars', or priests, who attended to the last wishes of benefactors to the cathedral, comforting their relatives and keeping a memorial candle lit. The Reformation saw these practices banned, and the buildings were leased out to various secular tenants.

THE EXETER BOOK (CODEX EXONIENSIS)

When the cathedral's first bishop, Leofric, died in 1072 he left Exeter Cathedral 66 books, an impressive library at that time. Among them was the amazing and ancient *Exeter Book*, the oldest of only four surviving collections of Old English poetry. He described it as 'a large book in English verse about various subjects'. It's thought to date from between 960 and 990 (earlier than Beowulf), and is written in what Dr Robin Flower (1881–1946) called 'what one may unhesitatingly describe as the noblest of Anglo-Saxon hands'.

Some pages are missing and others are damaged; it seems to have been used as a cutting board, maybe for cheese or bread, there are medieval beer stains on it, and a long burn on the last 14 pages has destroyed some of the text. It contains a great range of poetry – including 96 poetic 'riddles', longer and more elaborate than those we associate with Christmas crackers today. Some (in haunting translation by Kevin Crossley-Holland) are on Michael Fairfax's Riddle Statue in the High Street. It's in the Cathedral Library, as are many other rare volumes, and is very occasionally on view to the public; phone ✆ 01392 285983 or see ⌂ exeter-cathedral.org.uk for details.

From 1596 to 1660 the ground floor was used as a customs house (that's when the royal coat of arms on the front was added), before becoming an apothecary, a shoe shop, a haberdashery … and eventually in 1726 a coffee shop, run by Mary Wildy. Other women subsequently took it over, continuing it as a coffee shop until 1837. It then became an art gallery, a 'bookbinders, stationers and gilders' … and so on. But no more coffee. See the very informative, well-written and up-to-date website ⌂ exetermemories.co.uk/em/molscoffee.php for more information. Today it sells designer gifts, and the frontage features in any number of selfies taken by tourists.

🍴 FOOD & DRINK

As in all cities, you're surrounded by eating places, and more are opening all the time. The food scene in all of Devon is developing rapidly, and Exeter is no exception; the emphasis today is on locally sourced food, well presented. We've already mentioned a few favourites and you'll certainly find more; those below are just examples. See also the **Exeter Festival of South West Food & Drink** (see box, page 49) and **Exeter Street Food** under Markets on page 47.

In addition to those places listed below, **the quayside** (page 49) has a wide choice of places for snacks or larger meals – just stroll past and study the menus – and it's such a pleasant area to sit, eat and drink outside on a sunny day (or inside on a wet one).

Angela's Restaurant 38 New Bridge St ✆ 01392 499038 ⊘ angelasrestaurant.co.uk ⊘ 18.30–21.30 Wed–Sat but licensed to midnight. A terrific little place, just a short downhill walk from the bottom of the High Street (page 45) and well worth the detour. It serves really local, freshly cooked and beautifully presented local fish and meat, with menus adapted to the seasons, the weather and market availability. It's small and popular, so do book ahead.

The Fat Pig 2 John St, a turning off Fore St ⊘ fatpig-exeter.co.uk ⊘ food 17.00–21.30 Mon–Fri, 12.00–16.00 & 17.00–21.00 Sat, 12.00–16.00 Sun; pub hours longer. A friendly pub with good food (they take pride in their local meat, and have their own brewery/distillery) and sometimes live music; the wooden stools and benches can be a bit hard on less-than-youthful backs and bottoms. Good Saturday brunch and Sunday roasts.

The Hourglass 21 Melbourne St, on the way down to the quay from the Inner Bypass ⊘ hourglassexeter.co.uk. A characterful and friendly wood-panelled pub established in 1848, with a good selection of local ales and a changing blackboard menu. The food, from bread downwards (or upwards!), is cooked on the spot in the kitchen.

2 COUNTESS WEAR

> The country at Countess Weir, in and around the village, is full of scenic beauties and sweet Devonshire lanes, fragrant with violets and primroses, leading nowhere and everywhere, to river-banks and clover meadows, separated by thick blackberry bushes, farming boundaries and hedges to the farmstead.
>
> James Carter, *In the Wake of the Setting Sun*, 1909

Countess Wear is a part of Exeter now, and a bit short on clover meadows and Devonshire lanes, although it does have greenery, some thatched cottages and good rural and watery views across the Exe floodplain. It bridges the two parts of this chapter, Exeter and the Exe Estuary: administratively it's in the first but its heart remains in the second. It makes a pleasant, flat, five-mile circular walk from Exeter Quay, going outward along the Exeter Canal on the route of the Exe Valley Way and back along the river, connecting with parts of the Exeter Green Circle (page 51). You'll pass its old paper mill, originally built in 1284 by Countess Isabella de Fortibus as a corn mill. After being rebuilt in 1658 it began making paper from rags; then was destroyed by fire in the early 19th century and yet again rebuilt, but closed in 1885. The ruin is still there, as is another old paper mill more recently in use; paper-making was an important industry at the time. Also there's an attractive arched stone bridge, built in 1774 and originally a toll bridge charging 1d (one penny) per person, 1/- (one shilling) for a coach plus six horses, and 10d for a score of oxen. The Custom House Visitor Centre on the Quayside can point you in the right direction.

But the weir or wear is part of a much bigger story! A local poet wrote, probably about three centuries ago:

Once the haughty Isabella – she of Countess Weir renown Had a quarrel, as they tell us, with the 'cits' of Exon town

And preferring – God forgive her! – private rights to public weal In her arrogance the river from the City sought to steal

'Build a dam across the river,' cried the fury in her pride; And she built it, God forgive her; built her monument, and died.

He's writing about Isabella de Fortibus or Forz, who built the mill (page 55). She was born around 1237, the oldest daughter of Baldwin de Redvers, sixth Earl of Devon, and died in 1293. At the age of 11 or 12 she became the second wife of William de Forz, fourth Earl of Albemarle, and inherited land in Yorkshire and Cumberland on his death in 1260. They had six children, all of whom she outlived. When her brother Baldwin (seventh Earl of Devon after the death of their father) died in 1262 she inherited the title and his land in Devon, Hampshire and Yorkshire – and all of the Isle of Wight, where she mostly lived from then on. Still in her twenties she was an immensely rich woman, raking in substantial income from her various estates. In 1264 Simon de Montfort, second son of the Earl of Leicester, acquired the right to marry her (such things were formally arranged), but she refused him, as in 1268 she also refused Edmund Crouchback, son of Henry III. Her daughter Adeline married him in 1269, aged 11, but died four years later. Isabella never remarried. Then, for some unrecorded reason or grudge (history is fuzzy on this point) in 1272 (or 1282, or 1284) she built a weir across the estuary, thus cutting Exeter off from access to the shipping engendered by its prosperous wool trade with the continent. All vessels then had to unload at Topsham – which thus by the mid 16th century was the second busiest port in England. The weir didn't do the local salmon fishery much good either.

King Edward I had long coveted Isabella's estates. When she fell gravely ill in 1293 he hastily sent to her bedside a document confirming his purchase of the Isle of Wight, which she managed to seal before dying. A whirlwind of a life! But in the Exeter area she's still remembered simply as the woman who blocked the river with her weir.

THE EXE ESTUARY

The broad Exe Estuary stretching south from Exeter is a haven of birdlife, nature reserves, easy trails for cyclists and walkers, and exceptional views across the water. Strictly speaking only the eastern side comes within the area of this book, but we're including some practicalities about the western bank in this section just to help you with overall planning. The **Exe Estuary Management Partnership** (℘ 01392 382236 ⊘ exe-estuary.org) has some excellent leaflets (*Exe Wildlife*, *Exe Explorer* and *Exe Activities*), providing maps and details of walks, birds, ferries, places of interest, etc. They are available online and from tourist information centres.

 FERRIES & BOAT TRIPS

Exmouth/Starcross Ferry ℘ 01626 774770 ⬛ StarcrossExmouthFerry. Runs daily (hourly) from Apr to late Oct; carries cycles & connects with Route 2 of National Cycle Network. Also runs trips round Dawlish Bay, coastline cruises, cruises on the Exe and mackerel fishing.

RSPB ℘ 01392 432691 ⊘ rspb.org.uk. Runs birdwatching cruises from Topsham. See page 58.

Stuart Line Cruises ℘ 01395 222144 ⊘ stuartlinecruises.co.uk. A family business operating from Exmouth since 1968. Runs various cruises on the Exe and along the coast between Sidmouth and Torbay. It's a popular service; trips run year-round and extra ones are sometimes added.

Topsham Ferry ℘ 07801 203338. Ferry Road in Topsham to Topsham Lock Cottage (for Exminster Marshes). Also water taxis. Run by Exeter City Council (⊘ exeter.gov.uk). Daily in summer except Tue; weekends and bank holidays in winter. Times depend on tide; phone for details or to book water taxis.

Topsham to Turf Ferry (*Sea Dream II*) ℘ 07778 370582 ⊘ topshamtoturfferry.co.uk. From Topsham to Turf Locks for the Turf Inn, also RSPB birdwatching cruises. Carries cycles. Times/ dates variable: check beforehand.

 WET-WEATHER ACTIVITIES

Topsham Museum (page 60)
À la Ronde (page 64)
Exmouth Museum (page 67)
World of Country Life indoor activities (page 71)

BIRD RESERVES AROUND THE EXE ESTUARY

If you're walking or cycling round the estuary, you'll pass some of the best mudflats and wetland habitats in Devon.

In spring you can see lapwings and redshanks and – if you're a serious twitcher – listen for the rare Cetti's warbler; but autumn is the most rewarding time when thousands of birds, including dark-bellied Brent geese, fly from the freezing Arctic to overwinter there. As winter approaches other wildfowl crowd into the estuary to feed – look out for huge flocks of widgeon and graceful pintail ducks, as well as black-tailed godwits and shoveler ducks.

The ace in the pack, however, is the **avocet** and you have a good chance of seeing some in the winter (in spring they go to East Anglia and the Netherlands to breed), especially if you take a special RSPB cruise from Topsham, Exmouth or Starcross. The RSPB office at Darts Farm (✆ 01392 879438 ⌕ rspb.org.uk/exeestuary) has details of these. Stuart Line Cruises (page 57) also run special birdwatching trips on the estuary.

The **RSPB** has four reserves along the estuary. On the eastern side is **Bowling Green Marsh** (page 60), in the pocket of wetlands south of Topsham between the River Clyst and the Exe; in summer, Topsham Ferry (page 57) connects it to Exminster Marshes and Powderham Marshes on the western side. The smaller Matford Marsh is close to the A379 in the surprisingly green outskirts of Exeter, on the edge of the floodplain.

Other wetlands include the evocatively named **Old Sludge Beds** near Countess Wear, where old sewage waterworks have been turned into a wildlife haven and the old sewage pumphouse into a roost for bats, the extensive and accessible **Exmouth Local Nature Reserve** (page 67), one of Devon's largest, with its constantly changing tidal mudflats and sands; and Exmouth's smaller **Maer Reserve** (page 67). And all within easy reach of a major city!

3 TOPSHAM

🏠 **Globe Hotel** (page 256), **Salutation Inn** (page 256) 🏚 **Route 2 apartments** (page 256)

Topsham's position so close to the mouth of the River Exe ensured its place in history. A Roman port was established here in the 1st century AD to serve Exeter, and the present Topsham Road into the city is of Roman origin. Its town charter was granted more than 800 years ago, and its prosperity increased in the 13th and 14th centuries when a weir was built across the Exe just below Exeter (page 56); ships serving Exeter's thriving continental wool trade then loaded and unloaded at Topsham, which by the mid 16th century had become the second busiest port in England. Evidence of its medieval wealth can still be seen in the Dutch-style merchants' houses along the waterfront. These date from the early 1700s when Holland was the largest buyer of Devonshire serges. In 1966, Topsham became officially a part of Exeter yet today retains its own very distinctive character.

The main street – Fore Street – has a classy selection of boutiques and galleries but most particularly food shops, of many kinds. It's also full of surprises, like the Portuguese deli, Mercado, at number 96 (owner Sara also runs the popular Petite Cuisine café at number 80) and the gin bar at number 3 (with an impressive array of gins) that becomes a coffee house by day; it also has B&B upstairs and a secret garden at the back. Many of the tradespeople are well rooted in

"Autumn is the most rewarding time when thousands of birds fly from the freezing Arctic."

the area, for example Richard of Richard's Florists (also a greengrocer, at number 64) comes from a family that has lived on its local farm for around 500 years. For package-free, sustainable shopping there's Nourish at number 56, a zero-waste food shop (⊙ Mon–Sat) where you can fill up your own containers; and a final Fore Street surprise is the small outdoor heated swimming pool (⊘ topshampool.com ⊙ Apr–Sep) tucked away behind the main car park by the fire station and run by volunteers.

The Pebblebed Wine Cellar (Ferry Rd, 50m up from Topsham Quay) is the focus of **Pebblebed Vineyards** (✐ 01392 875908 ⊘ pebblebed. co.uk), which started in 1999 as a small community project with half an acre of vines. It now has more than 20 acres of vineyards (at Clyst St George, just to the east of Topsham) and a modern winery, and in a good year can produce almost 50,000 bottles of both still and sparkling wine. The vineyards are managed with great attention to encouraging wildlife and reducing the impact of farming on the environment, and the wines are made 'naturally' with minimum use of additives. Pebblebed Sparkling is recognised as among the best in England, and the still white, rosé and pinot noir red are pretty good too. There are guided vineyard tours (bookable, £20 per person, 16.00 Thu, 11.00 Fri, 11.00 & 15.00 Sat) from May to September, plus tastings (also tapas and pizzas) at the Pebblebed Wine Cellar (𝒫 01392 661810 ⊙ 17.00–22.00 Tue–Sat). Check the website or phone for current times.

The biannual **Topsham Food Festival** (𝒹 topshamfoodfestival.org. uk) is an exuberant programme of events and opportunities to eat, drink (locally sourced products of course) and share fun activities centred on the pleasures of the table. The next is in 2020. It includes 'Nello's Longest Table', a unique street party: last time around 2,500 people joined the five-hour celebration, with 360 tables stretching along the High Street and Fore Street down to the quay. The event commemorates Nello Ghezzo, an Italian restaurateur and chef in Topsham in the 1990s. A keen cyclist, together with food and wine writer Marc Millon he cycled from Topsham to Venice in 1997 to raise money for Force, an Exeter-based cancer support charity. Sadly he contracted the disease himself a year afterwards and died in 1999. 'The Nello', a cycle ride set up in his memory which is now run by Force (see 𝒹 forcecancercharity.co.uk), has become one of Exeter's great annual sporting events.

Along by the quay, the **Quay Antiques Centre** 𝒹 quayantiques.com) has three floors containing just about anything you can imagine, from old postcards to period costumes, old suitcases and fine glassware or silver. The **Topsham Museum** (25 The Strand 𝒫 01392 873244 ⊙ Apr–Oct 14.00–17.00, last entry 16.30, closed Tue & Fri), in an attractive group of 17th-century buildings, gives a good overview of local history and wildlife, with emphasis on Topsham's maritime history. Its River Gallery has a collection of old Exe fishing boats. Rather surprisingly, there's a Vivien Leigh room, including the night-dress she wore in *Gone with the Wind*; the museum's founder was her sister-in-law. Stroll seaward down The Strand beyond the museum and, at the end, you come to Goat Walk, a footpath (no cycling) with plentiful seats and stunning views across and down the estuary. After the bustle of the shops it's a peaceful place to sit – and leads along a lane to the RSPB's **Bowling Green Marsh** reserve with its rich population of waterbirds. A bit beyond the first gate to the reserve you'll come to a large hide beside the lane, with a good view over the marsh. After another mile or so the lane heads back into Topsham – or, if you turn right, on to the Estuary Cycle Trail leading to Lympstone.

The railway station is about five minutes' walk uphill from the town centre. A short way beyond it, on the eastern edge of town, is one of the most famous pubs in Devon: the **Bridge Inn** (EX3 0QQ ✎ 01392 873862 ⊘ cheffers.co.uk ☉ lunch 12.00–14.00 daily, plus 18.00–22.30 Mon–Thu, 18.00–11.00 Fri & Sat, 19.00–22.00 Sun), overlooking the River Clyst. Pink-washed, rambling, mostly 16th-century or earlier (there was probably a building on the site in 1086) and with a long reputation for promoting real ale, it found its niche in the 1950s or thereabouts and stayed determinedly that way. The two rooms are tiny, the licensing hours strictly last century, and food plays second fiddle to the serious matter of liquid refreshment. There's a huge selection of beer, real ale and cider, and the cold snacks available (many of them sourced from Darts Farm just along the road) are top quality. They include pies and pasties made by Chunk of Ottery St Mary as well as ploughman's lunches, sandwiches with tasty fillings, good cheeses, smoked salmon and other local products. The dinner menu currently consists of a Chunk pork pie with homemade coleslaw and English mustard, but there's a bigger choice at lunchtime. It's pleasant – and less crowded – sitting outside at tables looking across the river. Mobile phones indoors must be switched off ('a pub is a place for conversation between people, not machines') but a nod to modernity is the Facebook page (🄵 thebridgeinntopsham) where you can check which local ales will be available when you visit. Photos on the wall inside show a visit here by the Queen in 1998 and there's a delightful account of this on the website, with Her Majesty looking rather bemused. The pub has been in the same family since 1897, and I can't imagine it ever being sold. Or not crammed with customers.

Darts Farm

EX3 0QH ✎ 01392 878200 ⊘ dartsfarm.co.uk; check the website for the opening times of the store's various departments & restaurants as they don't necessarily coincide

Looking eastward along the road from the inn, you can see the complex of this tribute to good food. *The Guardian* described Darts Farm as 'finding Selfridges' food store dumped in the middle of a field'. It comprises a farm shop, delicatessen, butchers, fishmongers, specialist cider and ale house (they make their own cider), and various other retailers, all as organic as they come and top quality. Look outside and you'll see the fields where they are grown: food miles – zero. There's a good, spacious restaurant for snacks and main meals, and The Fish Shed selling fish and other seafood (lobsters, scallops …) that's either fresh, grilled or battered with crunchy chips and comes from Lyme Bay, so it's freshly caught and local. At the far end, above a Cotswold Outdoor Clothing Store, there's an RSPB shop (✆ 01392 879438 🖉 rspb.co.uk/exeestuary) with a stock of outdoorsy clothes and equipment for birders. Here you can check about the RSPB's nature walks, generally on Saturdays from April to December, and its birdwatching cruises from Topsham, which include 'avocet cruises' on Topsham-to-Turf's *Sea Dream* (page 57).

¶¶ FOOD & DRINK

Topsham's restaurants are very visible as you walk through the town; just have a browse of their menus as you pass by. One you might miss because it's tucked around a corner is the **Pig & Pallet** (10 The Quay ✆ 01392 668129 🖉 pigandpallet.co.uk ⏱ 10.00–22.00 daily); they are, as they say, 'passionate about all things meaty', and are specialists in traditional and ethical methods of butchering, barbecuing and curing meat. The charcuterie (from **Good Game** (🖉 good-game.co.uk) has really good flavour, and the menu (which rather alarmingly offers Devon Dogs, New York Dogs and even Sticky Dogs) includes vegetarian items as well as the possibility of smaller portions. We've already described the **Pebblebed Wine Cellar** (page 60).

A new arrival whose food has quickly gained a good reputation is **The Boathouse Café, Crêperie & Restaurant** (Ferry Rd ✆ 01392 670475 🖉 boathousetopsham.com ⏱ 08.00–16.00 Tue–Sat, plus 18.00–22.00 Thu–Sat). Popular with cyclists and next to a cycle sale/hire/repair shop is the friendly, licensed **Route 2 Café-Bar** (1 Monmouth Hill 🖉 route2topsham.co.uk ⏱ 08.00–17.00) with all-day breakfasts (full size, half-size or vegetarian), light lunches and home baking; and finally I can't resist mentioning Topsham's **Galley Fish & Seafood Restaurant** (41 Fore St ✆ 01392 876078 🖉 galleyrestaurant. co.uk ⏱ 12.00–14.30 & 18.30–21.00 Tue–Sat), partly because it deservedly won gold in 2017 and 2019's Taste of the West awards and partly because its pudding menu (delicious) has its own list of selected 'pudding wines'! You'll find more as you browse.

4 LYMPSTONE

🏠 **Lympstone Manor** (page 256) 🏰 **Peters Tower** (page 256)

Lympstone is a small and narrow village stretched along the waterside with a wonderfully open view across the estuary. It can trace its history from Saxon times, when it suffered raids from Danish marauders. A Roman coin found here is in Exeter Museum. A dubious claim to fame is the fact that when Thomas Becket was murdered in Canterbury

Cathedral in 1170, one of the four knights responsible for the deed was the overlord of Lympstone Manor, William de Tracey. In the 18th and part of the 19th centuries it had a prosperous boat-building industry, but then seems to have fallen on harder times: the clock tower (or 'Peters Tower') near the shore, erected in 1885, is 'in memory of Mary Jane Peters, to commemorate her kindness and sympathy for the poor of Lympstone'. Rather surprisingly it contains holiday accommodation run by the Landmark Trust.

On the shore of the estuary in front of the waterside houses there are washing lines strung between tall posts. When the tide is low, householders can walk out to them to hang out their washing; then the tide comes in and the washing flaps colourfully above the water, to be retrieved once the tide has receded and the mudflats can be walked on again. A practical use of natural resources.

The village has a convenience store, four pubs and a café (Susannah's Tea Room). We had our tea at The Swan, near the harbour and railway station, sitting outside in the sun. An example of extremely fast food that is also satisfactorily Slow is that of Jason Ingham (⊘ inghamfisheries. com), who has restored an old fishing boat, the *Compass Rose*, and now fishes regularly off Lyme Bay. When he returns to Lympstone with his catch he texts his customers to tell them what's available and when his small store opposite Peters Tower will be open, so they can head off promptly to buy fish that is truly 'just off the boat'.

Lympstone's big excitement was the opening in 2017 of **Lympstone Manor** (Courtlands Ln, Lympstone EX8 3NZ ✆ 01395 202040 ⊘ lympstonemanor.co.uk), the historic Georgian mansion in 28 acres of grounds that celebrity chef Michael Caines has turned into a 21-bed country house hotel. It was only at planning stage when we wrote the last edition of this guide, but for this update (tucking my dusty little runabout next to a shiny Bentley in the car park …) I could go and see it for myself. It was worth the wait! Upstairs, where each of the rooms is named after an estuary bird and decorated accordingly, the views stretch from Powderham Castle in one direction to Exmouth and the sea beyond. It's beautiful and very, very classy, with every effect skilfully judged. There's a lot of impressive art around, with a sculpture trail running through the grounds and good modern

"When the tide is low, householders can walk out to them to hang out their washing."

paintings inside. The prices are not, of course, run-of-the-mill, but nor are they unreasonable for the amount of luxury on offer.

Of course, it goes without saying that the food is top-class – Michael Caines predictably bagged a Michelin star less than three months after opening. There are three restaurants overlooking the estuary and a world-class wine cellar. The 10.8-acre vineyard is still very young, but will eventually provide the hotel's own exclusive wine; meanwhile guests and visitors can see it on guided tours. And on a summer's day you can enjoy a traditional afternoon tea out on the lawn.

In terms of 'giving something back' the hotel has its own recycling sector and also supports a number of small charities where help can make a big difference. Like I said, skilfully judged. I'm sure it will do well.

¶¶ FOOD & DRINK

Globe Inn ✐ 01395 263166 ⚲ globelympstone.co.uk ⊙ 12.00–23.00ish daily, kitchen 12.00–15.00 & 18.00–21.00 w/days & all day at w/ends. Same owners as Pig & Pallet in Topsham (page 62) so seriously good meat.

Lympstone Manor See page 63.

Susannah's Tea Room The Strand ✐ 01295 487220 ⊙ 10.00–17.00 daily. A small, friendly, family-run place with cream teas, good home baking, soup, snacks, etc.

Swan Inn The Strand ✐ 01395 270403 ⚲ theswaninn-lympstone.co.uk. Food and hot and cold drinks served all day every day (hours may change seasonally). A friendly, hard-working place, offering good, traditional pub food (and cream teas) with a local touch.

5 À LA RONDE

Summer Ln, Exmouth EX8 5BD ✐ 01395 265514 ⊙ end Jan–beginning Nov 11.00–17.00 daily; National Trust. Summer Lane is a short, single-track lane just off the A376, roughly two miles north of Exmouth; the East Devon Way runs past & the South West Coast Path is less than a mile away.

This fascinating 16-sided house, owned by the National Trust since 1991, was built for two artistic spinster sisters, the Misses Parminter, in the 1790s. They'd just brought back all manner of souvenirs from an extensive Grand Tour of Europe, and these are on show, along with later acquisitions; for example the walls of the 'Shell Gallery' are studded with almost 25,000 shells, so fragile that they're only viewable on closed-circuit television. Immediately intriguing from outside, with its unexpected shapes and angles, the house is even more surprising inside: the decoration and furnishings (refurbished in the 1990s) reflect the sisters' enthusiasm for blending materials such as feathers, shells, découpage, seaweed, stones, glass – and more. They enjoyed cutting out silhouette pictures, some very fine, and painting on shells. The walls of the rooms are packed with paintings, etchings, miniatures and photos, and there's some beautiful furniture. Shelves and cupboards overflow with trinkets and memorabilia, from an Inuit family modelled in wood and sealskin to stuffed birds and rare old books. Really, there is nothing like it! The rooms are small and can't comfortably hold many visitors, so at busy times you may need to wait for the crowds to disperse. There's a café with tempting baking, a shop with souvenirs, and the wagon shed has been transformed into a small pre-loved bookshop with some good-quality secondhand books. The volunteer staff in the rooms are charming, always ready to help but never pushy, and clearly love the place.

In the days without electricity, a circular house was practical: as the sun moved round it, so did the sisters, switching from room to room; although the second-floor rooms had no natural light until dormer windows were installed after the sisters' death by the house's only male owner, the Rev Oswald Reichel (1840–1923), who also installed the outside laundry.

The grounds have meadows, an orchard and fine views over the Exe Estuary; you can play croquet and other sedate garden games. Further up the lane is a small chapel with some almshouses, which the sisters endowed as a charity named 'Point in View', specifying in their wills that only spinsters might live there. This ruling has been relaxed today and they're open to individuals of any gender or marital status; the chapel is a simple, peaceful place with memorials to the sisters inside and can be visited. It's a 'Small Pilgrim Place' (⊘ smallpilgrimplaces.org), as is St Pancras' Church in Exeter (page 43). There's a small car park, and traffic in the single-track lane means it's safer to drive there from À la Ronde than to walk. Note that there's no footpath across the fields from the main house.

6 EXMOUTH

Å **Exmouth Country Lodge** (page 257)
Tourist information: 45a The Strand, EX8 1AL ✆ 01395 830550 ⊘ visitexmouth.org
⊙ 10.00–16.00 Mon–Sat, bank hols variable

> Bathing at Exmouth is good, but the curious old bathing machines, those round houses on wheels divided into compartments, are one by one disappearing. There are ordinary bathing machines, and tents may be used almost all along the extensive shore.

So a guidebook described it 90 years ago, and Exmouth's wonderful long, sandy shore is still its greatest asset, although bathing machines have been replaced by the likes of surfing, windsurfing and kitesurfing. Signs of the dignified Victorian resort still remain in stretches of the promenade and a few roads, but the centre has been pretty much modernised: the central square is now a lively pedestrian precinct with seating and space for cycles and is dubbed the 'café quarter' by locals. It even has an outdoor ping-pong table. Nearby Manor Gardens (off Alexandra Terrace, EX8 1BB) are more peaceful for sitting and have interesting plants, some of them sub-tropical. They were once the grounds of an old manor; the house was demolished in 1894. The iron railings now around the gardens were only installed in the mid 1990s, the original ones having been uprooted for their metal content during World War II. Exmouth claims to be Devon's oldest seaside resort. Before the 1700s it was just a simple fishing town with a small harbour, from which Sir Walter Raleigh (born just a few miles away in East Budleigh, page 134) sailed on many of his voyages. Later, when France became an undesirable gateway to continental Europe because of the revolution, some fashionable holidaymakers switched to Exmouth for its attractive views and supposedly medicinal waters. The journey wasn't easy. In 1768 a coach, the 'Exmouth Machine', left Exeter for Exmouth daily at 08.00, but travellers from London would already have endured an 'express' two-day coach journey (a bone-shaking innovation: it had taken four days in 1760) and an overnight stop in Exeter. Consequently only the most determined tourists came from so far afield, and there are contemporary reports of Exmouth residents being irritated by rowdy weekend holidaymakers from Exeter. Change was in the air, however, in the form of that new-fangled invention – the railway! It reached Exmouth in 1861, and in the first five days after the line opened it carried 10,000 passengers. Property prices increased overnight, and the little town was plunged into mass tourism.

"Change was in the air, however, in the form of that newfangled invention – the railway!"

The story of Exmouth and its people is told in the **Exmouth Museum** (Sheppards Row, off Exeter Rd ⊘ exmouthmuseum.co.uk ☉ Apr–Oct 10.30–12.30 Mon, Fri & Sat, 10.30–16.30 Tue–Thu). Set in a 19th-century building that was the Council Stables, it has rooms of period memorabilia including a Victorian kitchen, antique lace and commemorative china. For children there are quiz sheets and a 'Find the Cat' trail.

The town has other historic connections. Lady Nelson shared a house with her son here, and Lady Annabella Byron – married to the 'mad, bad poet' Lord Byron – stayed here with her daughter Ada, later to become **Countess of Lovelace** and work with the irascible Charles Babbage on his mathematical machines that were the chunky forerunners of today's computers. Ada Lovelace (1815–52) is now sometimes known as the first computer programmer: her notes on Babbage's creations were far ahead of their time. Her image has appeared on Microsoft authenticity stickers, and in 1979 the US Defense Department named an early, secret software programme 'ADA' after her. Now she's even the heroine of a graphic novel, *The Thrilling Adventures of Lovelace and Babbage* by Sydney Padua, published in 2015.

As part of a project to celebrate the millennium, blue plaques were attached to Exmouth's historic buildings – and there are more than 33 of them! A leaflet is available from the TIC (page 65) so that you can follow this Heritage Trail. Another entertaining way to see Exmouth is on the little hop-on-hop-off **Land Train** (⊘ 07597 358659 ⊘ exmouthlandtrain. co.uk ☉ May–early Oct) that chugs sedately around the town, starting at the Maer Road car park. Schedules are available online or from the Tourist Office.

Nature reserves

Exmouth's **Local Nature Reserve** (LNR) on the estuary, a massive area of tidal sand and mud managed by East Devon District Council, is one of the biggest LNRs in Devon, and a globally important area for overwintering waders and waterfowl. Walking out over the sandbanks at low water offers you the chance to get away from the town and explore a watery wilderness, looking inward to the shore rather than outward from it. The reserve is easy to reach from the train and bus stations, and the A376.

There's also the smaller **Maer Reserve**, set back behind sand dunes on the eastern part of the seafront. Insects thrive in its warm sandy soil and many unusual solitary bees and wasps make their nest tunnels there. Once a part of the sand dunes, it's now an open area of scrubby grass with small flowers, popular with local walkers and dog walkers and safe for children.

7 Orcombe Point

The cliffs here are the location of the 'geoneedle', 16.4ft high, that marks the start of Exmouth's biggest 21st-century claim to fame: as the westernmost gateway to the Jurassic Coast World Heritage Site (⏀ jurassiccoast.org; page 26). Follow the two-mile promenade and sandy beach eastward from the harbour (a lovely stroll) and when the paved promenade ends, take the steps that zigzag up the cliff. At the top, keep right and follow the coast eastward; after ten minutes or so you'll see the pointed geoneedle ahead. Commissioned from artist/sculptor Michael Fairfax, who also made the Riddle Statue in Exeter's High Street and Seaton's finger labyrinth (page 183), it was unveiled by the Prince of Wales in 2002. It is constructed from a variety of different stones, representing both the major building stones to be found on the Jurassic Coast and the sequence of rocks that form this part of the coastline. The top is capped with stainless steel which reflects the surroundings. Approach the geoneedle from the Exmouth side and you'll see various flat natural stones set into the turf: a game of 'Jurassic Coast Hopscotch', using stones taken from the different geological eras. Jump from one to another (go on, recapture your childhood!) and with each jump you'll be moving through millions of geological years.

Back in Triassic times, the red rock of the cliff below the geoneedle was part of a bare, baked desert – remember that as you gaze seaward from the storm-swept headland, rain trickling down your neck and this book a soggy lump in your pocket. A good way to see the coast today is on one of the Stuart Line Cruises (page 57). The boat stays close to the shore; as it passes the end of the beach and rounds Orcombe Point, the dramatic cliffs appear, freckled by the white of seabirds roosting in the nooks and crannies. Keep an eye out for cross bedding in the cliff face and differently layered and coloured rocks.

Active Exmouth

Exmouth can proudly claim to be the region's cycling centre. It has several cycle-hire and repair shops (page 36), and makes an excellent

EXMOUTH'S MUSSELS

Mussels are pretty amazing animals. A full-grown adult can filter 18 litres of water an hour; a female may produce between five and ten million eggs in a year; and the River Exe could produce 8,000 tonnes of mussels a year for our dinner tables. However, the founder of the award-winning **Exmouth Mussel Company**, Myles Blood Smyth, prefers to hold it at 2,000 tonnes a year to ensure a sustainable future for the shellfish. 'We collect the mussel seed from areas that would otherwise be destroyed', Myles told me, 'and spread it among the yachts, where it's safe. Mussels grow incredibly fast, but we leave them for two years, until they reach the ideal size of 55mm.'

He describes the Exe Estuary as perfect for farming mussels. The water is exceptionally clean, yet rich in nutrients such as plankton and algae, and the mussels are an essential part of the estuary's biodiversity; many birds depend on them or their seed. When the mussels are ready to be harvested they are eased from the riverbed using a hydraulic elevator so there is no damage to the surrounding environment or other species.

Exmouth's mussels are served in many of Devon's best restaurants, but you can also buy them direct from the company; check out their website under 'products'. As Myles says confidently: 'Try them and I don't think you'll ever want to eat mussels from anywhere else.'

The Exmouth Mussel Company The Pierhead, Exmouth EX8 1DU ✆ 01395 277720
🖱 exmouthmussels.com ⊙ 07.00–16.00 Mon–Fri, 08.00–13.00 Sat

start or end point of the **Exe Estuary Trail**. A booklet *Exmouth Cycling Guide & Map* is available from the TIC or can be downloaded from 🖱 cycledevon.info, and the Croydecycle *Exe Estuary Walking & Cycling Map*, scale 1:12,500, shows the whole trail in great detail. The ferry from Exmouth to Starcross across the estuary can carry cycles, as can the 'Avocet Line' train to/from Exeter. The first stretch of the trail, from Exmouth to Lympstone, is a gentle 2½-mile ride just to get you started; in common with most stretches it's equally pleasant for walkers, with good views across the water.

It is also the beginning of the **East Devon Way** (EDW) so walkers arrive at the station all set for the first leg of their 40-mile hike.

Watersports have hit Exmouth in a big way; you'll find sailing, kitesurfing, windsurfing, kayaking, paddle boarding, jet skiing, rowing, yachting, swimming and snorkelling, none of them particularly Slow but still part of a holiday. The combination of two miles of sandy beach, heading into the estuary of the River Exe and sheltered in the arch of Lyme Bay, makes Exmouth a perfect water playground. If you're a beginner and need coaching it's a good place to learn to kitesurf, windsurf and paddleboard. The 'duckpond', as it's known locally, is a sheltered area of the estuary which is perfect for beginners. For more advanced watersporters the area around Pole Sands, where the River Exe meets the open sea, is an ideal (if sometimes challenging) place to catch the wind.

And a big development is pending. In summer 2020 a large state-of-the-art watersports centre, **Sideshore**, is scheduled to open on Queen's Drive, covering such activities as paddleboarding, kitesurfing, power-kiting and more. It will contain a restaurant run by Michael Caines, the sea-front road is being realigned to accommodate it, and it will have direct, sloped access to the beach. Once established, it should have global appeal, and bring a whole new range of visitors and attractions to Exmouth. Check its progress on ⊘ sideshore.co.uk.

 WATERSPORT INSTRUCTION

Edge Watersports The Pierhead, Exmouth Marina EX8 1ER ✆ 01395 222551 ⊘ edgewatersports.com. Edge is run and owned by Steph & Eric Bridge who between them have over 30 years' experience of teaching watersports; they hold multiple world and national titles in kite racing and freestyle.

Exmouth Watersports ✆ 01395 276599 ⊘ exmouthwatersports.co.uk. An experienced team of watersporters and instructors, priding themselves on good customer service. Multiple activities. Also has a campsite (Exmouth Country Lodge; page 257).

Walking from Exmouth to Lympstone: the start of the East Devon Way

This is a pleasant walk, hugging the estuary, and giving you the opportunity to have a meal in delightful Lympstone before taking the equally enjoyable Avocet Line train back to Exmouth. It's also the first part of the first leg of the East Devon Way (EDW).

If you want a straightforward walk without having to think too much, just follow the Exe Estuary Trail (EET) from the station, keeping the railway to your left. Some of it is on roads, but they have wide pavements. However, you are sharing this route with cyclists so you need to keep alert. Quieter and more scenic is the footpath that runs on the left side of the railway line.

For the footpath option, park in the estuary long-stay car park and walk up Royal Avenue, close to the estuary, to its end and continuation as the EDW. After about half a mile the path crosses the railway to join a road over a bridge and along to Lower Halsdon Farm, keeping close to the right side of the railway. Shortly after joining the EET a footpath (not the EDW) branches off to the left, crosses the railway, and runs on its left-hand side to Sowden Lane which leads into Lympstone. At one point you are walking along the narrow sea wall, but on the whole it's easy to follow and not difficult. The views of the estuary are better than on the official EDW and you're not competing with cyclists for space.

The World of Country Life
Sandy Bay EX8 5BY ✆ 01395 274533 ⏚ worldofcountrylife.co.uk ⏰ Mar–Nov 10.00–17.00 daily, plus half term & some w/ends in Feb

This place is big: it incorporates an extensive museum of rural life with animal displays aimed at children, plus a separate falconry demonstration run by Hawkridge Birds of Prey. It needs at least a half day to see and experience everything and entry isn't cheap, but as a family day out it's probably the most interesting and rewarding in the region. The indoor section has something for everyone: 1920s clothing (including lingerie, which is always popular with kids), old-fashioned toys, and a great display of vintage cars and motorbikes, some half-size, and steam engines. I marvelled at the multiple matchstick models of Exeter Cathedral, perfect in every detail.

Exhibits that particularly caught my attention were the donkey panniers, a reminder of the role that donkeys played in the early part of the last century when they were essential for carrying produce such as potatoes up the steep paths from the 'plats', cultivated areas on the cliffside. Advertisements included one for Wincarnis, a tonic wine which cured most things including brain-fag and mental prostration and was recommended by 10,000 doctors (who counted?).

In the animal section, kids can stroke rabbits, bottle-feed lambs, coo over baby animals and – more unusually – take a goat for a walk. Then there's the Deer Train: the resident red deer and llamas race up to it to be fed as it potters through the spacious grounds. I could see for myself why llamas make such good shepherds, keeping away predators; although in this instance they were targeting a well-aimed kick at the fleecy food competitors sharing their field. The sheep come into their own – or their offspring do – at the Lamb Grand National. Those youngsters can really run, and jump, when there's a reward at the end.

BUTTER BIKE

Jeni Reeve has always loved peanut butter, but it was during a spell in New Zealand that she learned what pure, unadulterated peanut butter tasted like. 'So when I came back home, the choice was to make my own or go hungry. I wanted a proper roasted, savoury peanut butter, without any added sugar and certainly without any of the added oils or other mystery ingredients'. She started selling her homemade peanut butter at the Exeter flea market, and soon got repeat orders that needed to be delivered. 'They were all dotted around Exeter, so I jumped on my vintage Phillips and soon got a name for myself as "the peanut butter lady on the bike" and that was it, Butter Bike was born!' She still offers delivery in central Exeter by bike, but as a one-person business she uses a courier for orders further afield.

Jeni also sells her peanut butter online, to various retailers, at a wide range of farm shops in Devon and at food fairs around the county where her enthusiasm attracts new fans and the five varieties can be sampled. I met her at the River Cottage Festival, and can confirm that she's on to a good thing.

Check out her website ⊘ butterbike.co.uk.

The **Hawkridge Birds of Prey** organisation (⊘ 01395 279443 ⊘ hawkridgebirdsofprey.com) is a separate concern within the WOCL grounds and included in the price. They have a wide variety of hawks and owls, and even a bald eagle. As well as the flying displays you can book in advance for a bird-handling experience – anything from an hour to a full day.

FOOD & DRINK

Like so much of Devon, Exmouth is becoming an increasingly foodie destination. It claims to have 40 pubs (I haven't counted) and even more restaurants and other eateries. These stand out from the crowd but there are many more.

Bumble and Bee Manor Gardens, EX8 1BB (page 66) ⊘ bumbleandbee.co.uk ⊙ Apr–Sep 09.00–17.00 daily, Nov–Mar 09.30–16.00 Tue–Fri, 09.00–16.00 Sat & Sun. Award-winning tea room in pleasant gardens just a couple of minutes from the town centre: breakfasts, soup, sandwiches, light lunches, local baking, cream teas – the lot. Entertaining website, too.

River Exe Café and Restaurant ⊘ 07761 116103 ⊘ riverexecafe.com ⊙ Apr–Sep, booking essential. This is something of an adventure: we can't give you an address because it's moored in the middle of the estuary, a purpose-built restaurant on a barge! Unique location, terrific food (strong on fish, naturally) and fabulous views. If you haven't a boat you get there by Puffin Water Taxi; they depart from Exmouth Marina, from the visitors' pontoon outside the Point Bar (EX8 1XA). The River Exe Café has an arrangement with them and will tell you the times and details when you book your meal. Obviously the boats are weather-dependent (and the estuary can get quite choppy if it's stormy) so on the day of your booking do check that they're running.

Rockfish Pier Head, EX8 1DU 🖉 01395 272100 🖒 therockfish.co.uk/restaurants/exmouth ◷ 12.00 –21.30 daily. Opened by top chef Mitch Tonks in 2016. Next to the town slipway, overlooking the beautiful Exe Estuary. Great seafood; fresh mussels from the estuary and other local fish are prepared simply by either crisp frying, grilling or cooking over charcoal. Has a log burner for colder days.

EAST DEVON & THE JURASSIC COAST ONLINE

For additional online content, articles, photos and more on East Devon and the Jurassic Coast, why not visit 🖒 bradtguides.com/edevon?

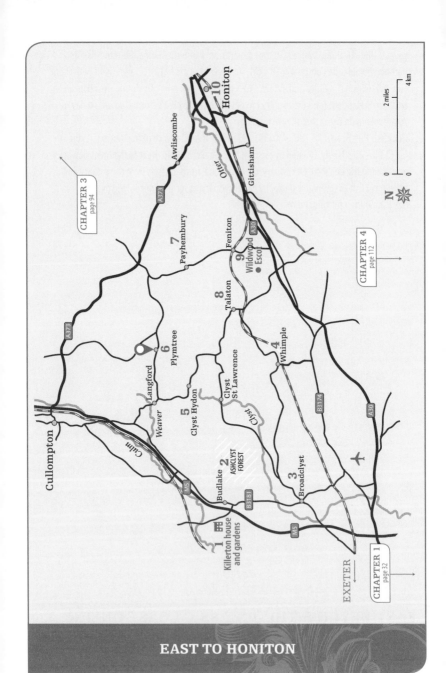

EAST TO HONITON

2
EAST TO HONITON

After dining at an excellent inn, we proceeded over vast hills surrounded with beautiful vales; from the top of Honiton hill the landscape may vie with any part of this Kingdom.

The Rev Stebbing Shaw, 1788

Away from the seaside and accompanying holiday crowds, this is the heart of East Devon, a gentle landscape of rolling hills, spacious views, narrow lanes almost hidden by the wayside flowers, little churches and welcoming pubs. It is a region for walkers and cyclists looking for solitude, or brave drivers who are comfortable on the single-track lanes. The M5, A30 and A373 form a triangle around this area, with the latter two roads meeting at Honiton, one of East Devon's most important inland towns.

WET-WEATHER ACTIVITIES

Killerton House (page 76)
Plymtree church (page 81)
Allhallows Museum, Honiton (page 90)
Beehive Centre & art galleries, Honiton (page 90)

GETTING THERE & AROUND

Most people will drive in from the M5, but public transport isn't bad, with regular buses serving the countryside west of Honiton including the delightful number 694 (see box, page 91). It is also served by the train line from London Waterloo to Exeter, with stations at Honiton (page 87), Feniton and Whimple (page 80), so bus- and train-assisted walks are a good option for those who dislike driving on narrow lanes. Roads between main towns are generally good; more remote ones may be single-track and/or twisty.

SELF-POWERED TRAVEL

This is a good area for cyclists who are looking for gentler hills than Devon usually offers – and you rarely meet a car. Walkers are well served with a network of footpaths. The OS map for the region is ✳ OS Explorer Map 115 (note that there is no Croydecycle map of this area).

THE KILLERTON ESTATE

🏠 **Killerton Estate Holiday Cottages** (page 257)

The M5 passes over this vast estate, which the Acland family owned from the reign of Elizabeth I. The last Acland was Sir Richard, who gave the whole estate, which includes Broadclyst village, Ashclyst Forest and Killerton, to the National Trust in 1944. Killerton House and Park lie on the west side of the M5, Budlake a short walk away on the east and Broadclyst, also on the east side, is over a mile from the house.

1 KILLERTON HOUSE & GARDEN

EX5 3LE 🖉 01392 881345 ⊘ garden daily; house, Old Post Office, Marker's Cottage & Clyston Mill: times vary, check National Trust website; National Trust

Killerton Estate was given to the National Trust by Sir Richard Acland, a committed Socialist. Although the house is Georgian, the interior was redesigned in 1900 and a new entrance added in 1926 following a fire, so it now represents the way of life of an aristocratic family between the wars.

The apricot-coloured **house** (⊘ 11.00–17.00) with its swathes of wisteria and other creepers has a welcoming look, and inside are shifting and often topical exhibitions. For instance in 2019 the theme was woodland, to commemorate the founding of the Forestry Commission in 1919 by Francis Acland to deal with the shortage of timber following World War I. Permanent pieces of interest include a Broadwood piano in the drawing room made in 1802, which is the oldest surviving piano made by John Broadwood and Sons. It is now too fragile to be played. Sir Thomas Acland's wife Lydia was obviously keen on music: her organ dominates the music room. In the library see if you can spot the joke titles of the fake books that conceal a drinks cupboard. These include *Hard Nuts to Crack, Authors not Generally Known, Sermons on Hard Subjects*, and two reference books: *Crabb on Fishes*, and *Hobble on Corns*.

Upstairs there's a collection of clothing from the 18th to 20th centuries and a film and display of shoe-making, but more interestingly Killerton collaborates with the Exeter School of Art at Exeter College to design themed clothing, which is also displayed here in a shifting exhibition. There were some wonderful wood-themed designs when I was there.

The best part of Killerton is undoubtedly the **garden**, all 20 acres of it, with huge lawns sloping down from a multicoloured copse that, in the spring, is ablaze with rhododendrons and magnolias. There are numerous large and rare trees dotted around, including a magnificent Lucombe oak, a hybrid Spanish oak created by William Lucombe at his Exeter nursery in 1762 and brought here three years later.

Don't miss the **Bear's Hut**, so named because, so they say, Gilbert Acland kept a pet bear here when he was a child. This delightful thatched summer house was originally built by Sir Thomas Acland for his wife Lydia and called Ladycot. Each tiny room is made from different materials. The floors are sections of logs, cobblestones, and – extraordinarily – hundreds of 'knuckle bones' from deer. Evidently the Aclands ate a lot of venison. The 'deer room', now closed off but you can look over the half door, has a ceiling of deer hide, and the two other rooms have woven matting decorated with fir cones. Finally there's a very beautiful stained-glass window made from fragments of 16th-century Flemish glass.

The chapel, built in 1841, is also worth a visit, especially late in the day when the sun is streaming through the stained-glass window and lighting up the pews.

There are several places for **refreshments**. Near the entrance is The Stables coffee shop for hot drinks and cakes (you might want to avoid this on Saturday mornings when it will be full of sweaty parkrunners including, at times, one of the authors). The Dairy Café in the garden (it opens later, at 11.00) serves snacks, and the bistro-style Kitchen Restaurant does proper, high-quality lunches from 12.00 (page 79).

On the third Saturday of the month a **farmers' market** is held near the car park with a wide range of tempting produce.

Budlake Old Post Office

A short walk away across a field is this piece of nostalgia for those who remember the 1950s. It is now a museum, but appears as a shop caught in a time warp: its shelves display biscuit tins with the new Queen's portrait, Brasso and Bluebell polish, Creamola rice pudding, Sunny Spread and Izal extra-strong toilet tissue. In the little garden is a pigsty, with instructions not to feed your pig with paper, soap or rhubarb leaves, and a cosy side-by-side privy. Recordings of local people talking about the old days can also be played.

2 ASHCLYST FOREST

This ancient forest is also part of the massive Killerton Estate so under the care of the National Trust but lies a couple of miles from the house, on the eastern side of the M5. Access is up a lane leading from the B3181, and there is a choice of four parking places, each with an information board showing the walking circuits: the longest is 3½ miles. The paths have been surfaced, making them suitable for running as well as walking, there are benches where you can have a rest and listen to the birds, and the woodland is a rewarding mix of conifer and various species of deciduous tree. It is perhaps this mixed habitat that makes the forest such a haven for butterflies: enthusiasts come from far afield in search of white admiral, silver-washed fritillary, and purple hairstreaks.

3 BROADCLYST

It's surprising to find such a picturesque and peaceful village so close to Exeter. There are thatched cottages galore, including the delightful cob-and-thatch medieval **Marker's Cottage**, notable for its cross-passage screen dating from 1530, and **Clyston Mill** (○ summer 13.00–17.00 Sat–Wed) which still produces flour. Both are now cared for by the National Trust as part of the Killerton Estate.

The **church** is tucked away next to the Red Lion pub, its 16th-century elegantly pinnacle, tall tower providing a landmark for miles around. The interior is splendid: large, light and stuffed with monuments. The oldest, a knight in 14th-century armour tucked away in the sanctuary near the altar, is probably Sir Roger de Nonant. He has a toothy lion gazing at him adoringly, and a cluster of attentive cherubs. On the north side of the sanctuary is a small monument to Henry Burroughs, who founded the village almshouses, along with his wife Elizabeth. Then there's Edward Drewe with his splendid moustache and ruff, together with his wife who has a rather sweet, bear-like dog at her feet. Drewe was Queen Elizabeth's legal officer and the Recorder of Exeter, a position he agreed to on the proviso that if the Queen needed him in London he would have to go. And go he did. His son inherited the estate and sold it to the Aclands. Sir John Acland lies in an elaborately carved monument by the north wall, propped on one elbow, with his large family above him.

Every capital is different, with intriguing faces and foliage, and includes a mason's joke. One carving represents a Staffordshire knot, a pun on the name of Bishop Stafford.

The rood screen has gone but the door to it remains, now isolated on the north wall. Opposite are photocopies of large fragments of parchment from an illuminated missal used in 15th-century worship, which were found ignominiously providing the cover for a church warden's account book.

▌▌ FOOD & DRINK

The Kitchen Killerton House. A limited menu of baked potatoes, salad and burgers cooked to a high standard, along with some tempting desserts. Inside or outside seating in this splendid garden. See page 77.

Red Lion Broadclyst ✆ 01392 461271 ⬥ www.redlionbroadclyst.co.uk. A traditional 16th-century inn located in a quiet spot next to the church. It's dog-friendly, open all day at weekends, and has an extensive menu of typical pub food and local real ales. Their Sunday roast (Sep–Nov) is particularly popular, and there's always a good choice of vegetarian and vegan options.

FROM THE M5 TO HONITON

In the triangle of countryside between the M5, the A30 and the A373 are some of the most charming and overlooked villages in East Devon, each with its own pub, church and feeling of community. Honiton lies at the eastern apex and the River Clyst meanders through the western part, lending its name to several of the villages. The circuit below is just a sample of what is there to be discovered.

NOURISHMENT FOR BODY & SOUL: A PUB AND CHURCH TOUR

Well off the tourist trail, drivers and cyclists can enjoy a relaxing circuit of some choice villages with pauses for a drink, a meal, and a piece of history. I've chosen Whimple as the start/end point because of the train station, so cyclists can bring their own bicycle. The full circuit is about 15 miles, and is perfect for cycling, with gentle hills and very little traffic along the narrow lanes.

4 Whimple

EX5 2SS

With its train links to Exeter and London, this is a popular commuter village but has several attractive houses (plenty of thatch), a post office/shop, two pubs and a heritage centre.

The well-tended **St Mary's Church**, with its silver-leaved weeping pear tree donated by the WI to commemorate the Queen's Silver Jubilee, holds some surprises: eight 16th-century painted panels of saints discovered when the pulpit was replaced and now incorporated into the tower screen at the back. One 'saint' is Henry VI – depicted without a halo since he hadn't yet been canonised; Henry VIII, his grandson, was not keen on paying the Pope a very large sum of money for this service. Henry achieved sainthood later by popular acclaim, having led a devout life and apparently suffered a violent death. Here he stands in front of a prison, representing his time in the Tower of London, richly dressed, with a white hart at his feet showing his allegiance to the White Rose in the War of the Roses.

Other saints include St Roche, patron saint of the plague, displaying his plague sores and accompanied by the faithful dog that brought him bread when he retreated from the world, expecting to die of the disease. St Sebastian is also here, absolutely riddled with arrows. St Apollonia displays the extracted tooth that makes her the patron saint of dentists, and St Sidwell, whom we meet again at Plymtree; here she carries her head and the scythe that removed it from her body.

Uphill from the church, next to the New Fountain Inn, is the **Whimple Heritage Centre** (✆ 01404 822499 ⌂ whimple.org ☉ Apr–Sep 13.00–15.00 Wed, 10.30–16.00 Sat & bank hol Mon) run by the dynamic Whimple History Society. In addition to the changing displays of historical photos and village memorabilia, the Whiteway's Cyder room is also here. The Whiteway family established their cyder factory in1896 on a site conveniently located near the station.

"St Apollonia displays the extracted tooth that makes her the patron saint of dentists."

Apples were brought here by goods train from orchards in Honiton, Broadclyst and Ottery St Mary, all of which were on the railway in those days. Photos, documents and artefacts show how Whiteway's became the most famous cider-producer in England. Whimple holds a popular Wassail festival each winter.

5 CLYST HYDON

EX15 2NT

This village is notable mostly for the excellent pub, **The Five Bells** (page 83). However, St Andrew's Church deserves a look, particularly as it was instrumental in giving the pub its name. The inn used to be next door to the church but the rowdy boozers so upset the vicar that he asked them to move. Which they did, but kept a churchy name to annoy him. Unusual in the **church** are the box pews, including a square one so parishioners (most likely the inhabitants of the manor) could sit with their back to the preacher, ignoring the goings on.

The church now has six bells.

6 Plymtree

EX15 2JU

The church of St John the Baptist is the star of this tour and one of the best in East Devon for its painted saints in the screen panels: 34 of them in excellent condition and dating from the late 15th century. In the Middle Ages this church was a stopping place for pilgrims bound for Glastonbury from the Devon ports; Glastonbury's Joseph of Arimathea is one of the saints depicted.

The **church** is satisfactory as soon as you enter the graveyard and see the thousand-year-old yew tree, and look up at the ancient stone carving of the Virgin and Child on the western face of the tower (to the left of the clock), which survived having missiles hurled at it, presumably during the Reformation. When the statue was restored in 1993, the workmen found stones, a wooden top and a leather-stitched ball lodged there.

As you push open the beautiful old oak door the immediate impression is of light and harmony; the windows are plain glass, letting in the Devon sunshine, and highlighting the carved, worm-eaten bench ends. There are some floor stones including one that commemorates Abraham Webber who died in 1660 aged 84, which reminds us that longevity isn't new – it's just that disease usually came along to dispatch people before they reached their four-score years. There's also a memorial to a couple from the same era who had passed their golden wedding anniversary. Before we come to the screen there's a remarkable Flemish alabaster carving, dating from the early 1600s, of the Resurrection. It is done in extraordinary detail, with every embellishment of the Roman soldiers' armour picked out (some are asleep, another shielding his face in horror and one in the foreground, with a glorious Father Christmas beard, tumbling to the ground in astonishment). Jesus himself looks a bit fey, rising up amid what appear to be a mass of intestines but I suppose are clouds. A few cherubs are helping him on his way.

So, the fan-vaulted, gilded screen. The carving is intricate, as it always is, but it's the painted saints and biblical characters that draw our attention. There is Mary holding out the baby Jesus who seems only too eager to reach the gifts offered by the Magi. There's the Annunciation with a rather fierce-looking archangel Gabriel and a suitably submissive Mary, and Mary Magdalene who is the only portrait that has been deliberately damaged – her eyes have been gouged out. Other saints include St Margaret, re-emerging from the mouth of a monster/whale, St Michael standing triumphant over a pathetic little dragon, a very gloomy looking St Roche making too great a fuss over quite a small plague sore, and St Sebastian – always easy to recognise with his arrow-pierced body. Less well known is St Sidwell or Sidwella, who was an Exeter lass commemorated in both the cathedral and a street and church named after her. She, like her sister St Urith, was scythed to death by farmers led on by her wicked stepmother. Her head was lopped off whereupon, as so often happens, a spring gushed forth and became a holy well (her name is a corruption of scythe-well).

"Her head was lopped off whereupon, as so often happens, a spring gushed forth."

The village itself has a very good **community shop**/post office, which sells absolutely everything including alcoholic drinks. This is the place to take your refreshment (there are two chairs outside for the purpose, and glasses will be provided) since the pub, the **Blacksmiths Arms** at the time of writing, only open during the day at weekends, though it opens each evening at 18.00 to serve good food.

7 Payhembury
EX14 3HZ

You can tell what a thriving community this is from its website (⌂ payhembury.org.uk)! It's a quiet village of whitewashed houses with a community shop and post office, **Payhembury Provisions**, and a pub, **The Six Bells** (not to be confused with the Five Bells in Clyst Hydon; opposite). The **church** has a fine wagon roof with gilded bosses, angels playing instruments on the chancel roof, and a carved pulpit cover which is raised and lowered by pulleys.

In the churchyard is a magnificent yew, split into four trunks and thought to be almost as old as Christianity.

The hembury part of the name comes from the hillfort north of the village (page 102). Worth a visit when you are in the area.

8 Talaton

EX5 2RL

This somewhat sprawling village comes into its own in the vicinity of the church, where there's a cluster of picture-postcard thatched cottages. **The Talaton Inn** (✐ 01404 822214) provides a wide range of local beers, good food (including a £5 lunch) and open fires in the winter.

The **church** of St James the Apostle has probably stood here, in some form or another, since Norman times, and it's worth walking round it to appreciate the many gargoyles and carvings around the 15th-century tower, which were restored in the 1990s. These include biblical figures – saints, the evangelists, and the Virgin and Child – and some splendid mythical creatures. One's attention is particularly drawn to the goat-like *yale*, a beast able to swivel its horns in any direction, springing away from the wall.

As you enter, note the original sanctuary ring which, if touched by a fugitive, secured his freedom from arrest. Inside there is a beautiful wagon roof, a gilded screen, old carved oak bench ends, and numbered pews with doors. There is also a rather charming illustrated framed document, painstakingly done with beautiful calligraphy, which was presented to Philip Pyle, a church warden, 'to mark their appreciation of his valuable services in the successful augmentation of the ring of five bells in the church tower of Talaton into a ring of six by the addition of a new treble.' He also received a set of decanters. It is signed by 70 names and dated Easter Monday 1891. Such was village life at the end of the 19th century, although I bet there was a back story to this.

After Talaton it's a short journey back to your starting point at Whimple.

▯▯ FOOD & DRINK

The Five Bells Clyst Hydon EX15 2NT ✐ 01884 277288 ⌂ fivebells.uk.com ☉ 12.00–14.30 & 18.00–21.00 Tue–Sat (Sat also open pm for drinks), 12.00–15.00 Sun. Everything a Devon pub should be: a 16th-century thatched inn, once a Devon longhouse, reached along narrow

Bus, train, walk, eat: a car-free circuit

✻ OS Explorer map 115; start: Greenend Farm ♥ ST050027; 6 miles; easy

This is the complete package: the best of East Devon's transport and food – and church – tied together with a gentle six-mile walk through farmland. You'll need boots, if you have them, for the frequently muddy bit, although if you leave the right of way for a short stretch you'll stay dry.

Though the walk itself begins on the outskirts of Plymtree, the trip starts and ends in **Honiton**, with one of Devon's most scenic bus journeys to get you in a tranquil mood. You end up in **Whimple** before taking the hourly train or bus back to Honiton.

The 694 bus (see box, page 91) to Plymtree leaves Honiton at 08.45, if you want to eat at the end of your walk, or at 12.15 which drops you in Plymtree at 12.52. Lunchtime, but do take a look at the church and its painted saints before heading for your treat of a meal at the upmarket Five Bells (page 83) in Clyst Hydon. The walk proper begins at the **end of Green End Lane** (1). You'll see the footpath sign on the left just before Greenend Farm. The path runs diagonally across some pasture to a metal kissing gate and the next field where you turn right, skirting the edge of the field and keeping the hedge on your right, past a big oak tree and through a wooden gate. Head across the field to a stand of poplars and the next gate. This field is usually sown with crops, so turn left and follow its boundary to reach a little footbridge over a stream at the far corner. Continue to keep the hedge on your left, crossing another footbridge, into another meadow, keeping the pylon on your left. Head across the field towards the farm buildings, keeping an eye out for the footpath sign, and follow the farm track to a metal gate and over a stile.

At the junction of three paths, turn right through the gate and across a footbridge, then diagonally across the corner of the field to another footbridge. You are now approaching **Clyst Hydon**, so keep following the footpath signs until you emerge on to a lane that leads to the church (2). Walk through the graveyard and emerge on to a lane (note the Victorian letter box) that leads to Clyst St Lawrence and the **Five Bells**, which is well signposted. By the time you reach the pub/restaurant you will have walked two miles and deserve your gourmet lunch (note, the pub is closed on Mondays).

The next part of the walk is four miles, and takes you through some very beautiful wildflower meadows (at least in the spring) and then more farmland to Whimple. We went wrong on this section so remember that there is a footpath sign on every gate. If you don't see the sign you're not on the right path.

Keep walking in the direction of **Clyst St Lawrence**; you'll see the footpath on the left (3), crossing a cow pasture, shortly after leaving the pub. Walk diagonally to the right, keeping the hedge in sight so you don't miss the little metal gate and footbridge at the corner. Keep the fence on your left down the next field, through another gate and across the first of two wildflower meadows, heading for a stately line of oaks on the left. After this gate it's downhill, keeping the hedge on your right, following footpath signs until you emerge in Clyst St Lawrence (4), less than two miles from Clyst Hydon. This is a tiny village, with just a few very beautiful thatched houses and an appealing little church with a disproportionately tall tower that is, sadly, usually kept locked.

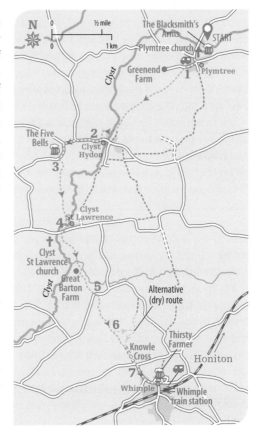

Head towards the **bridge over the River Clyst** and the church, keeping an eye out for your next footpath, which is through a farmyard opposite a red-brick barn. Beyond the farm buildings the path leads straight across an arable field to a metal farm gate. The next field is also sown with crops but a blue bag has been helpfully tied to the branches of a tree to show the location of the kissing gate and footbridge over a ditch. Then cross the meadow aiming for a thatched house set in a poplar grove. The footpath runs to the left of this house, and over a stile into the track leading to **Great Barton Farm**. Follow this to the lane (5) where you turn left and almost immediately right on another footpath.

Keep the hedge on your left, following the edge of the field since the next stile and footpath sign is almost hidden in the hedge and easy to miss. In the next field pass between the pylons ▶

Bus, train, walk, eat: a car-free circuit (continued)

◄ and through another gate to a green road/track, which you follow until it takes a right-angled turn to the left (6). You are now faced with a dilemma. The footpath, signed, is over a stile straight ahead. It is narrow, and even after a dry spell, challengingly muddy. But it is the right of way. Your alternative is to continue along the track when it makes its turn to the left. This bypasses the mud and very shortly brings you out on to the green road that leads to **Knowle Cross**, just north of Whimple. But it is not a public right of way.

From Knowle Cross it's half a mile to Whimple and its two pubs (page 80) (7) where you can rehydrate or eat lunch while waiting for your train or bus back to Honiton. Trains mostly leave at around 44 minutes past the hour every two hours (but check the timetable); and bus number 4 currently leaves at 51 minutes past every hour from 09.51 to 17.51 (Mon–Sat) and at 43 minutes past every three hours on Sunday. Again, check the timetable for changes.

---

lanes, offering award-winning fine dining as well as traditional but beautiful pub classics and one of Devon's best Sunday roasts. They serve (very) local beers, ciders, gins and soft drinks. Affordable lunch deals and a children's menu available. Dog friendly.

Jack in the Green Rockbeare EX5 2EE ✆ 01404 822240 ⬦ jackinthegreen.uk.com
⊙ 10.00–15.00 & 17.30–23.00 Mon–Sat, 10.00–23.00 Sun; food served 11.30–14.00 & 18.00–21.00 Mon–Sat, 12.00–21.00 Sun. The name suggests a rural idyll but it's on a main road with a new housing estate nearby. Nevertheless this unpretentious pub/restaurant, close to the M5 and A30, is probably the best in East Devon. There is a relatively affordable two-course 'Totally Devon' menu that, as the name implies, is all locally produced, and a five-course tasting menu for a treat. If neither takes your fancy you can go for the wide à la carte choice and the option of traditional – and cheaper – 'pub grub'. The head chef is Matt Mason who has been there for many years.

9 WILDWOOD ESCOT

EX11 1LU ✆ 01404 822188 ⬦ wildwoodescot.org ⊙ daily

Just north of the A30, this hybrid of garden, adventure playground and small zoo showcasing native and formerly native British animals is perfect for a day out with the family. It is run by the Wildwood Trust and what I liked about the place was the unstructured activities available for gutsy children. There are rope swings and a zip wire, and plenty of freedom to roam in the woods. Or try the Drop Slide which is a scary 19ft. There are very few warning signs: the charity sensibly expects parents to take responsibility for their children, and the policy works. It is also a place where young children can get back to nature, sleep in a yurt and experience – among other things – a swamp walk. 'The water was up to here!' one excited eight-year old told me, pointing to her chest. In a reconstructed Saxon village kids can learn how to build a shelter, light a fire and live as their very early ancestors did. These school visits and activities need to be booked in advance.

There is always something new here. Animals now include otters, red squirrels, boar, lynx, wildcat, red fox and wolves in spacious enclosures, as well as a variety of birds of prey that take part in falconry demonstrations.

The **Coach House Café** provides snacks if stamina starts to falter.

10 HONITON

🏠 **The Pig at Combe**, Gittisham (page 257), ⛺ **Deer Park Tree House**, Weston (page 257)
Tourist information: Allhallows Museum, High St ✆ 01404 44966 🌐 honitonmuseum. co.uk 🕐 Easter–Oct 09.30–16.30 Mon–Fri (16.00 in Oct), 09.30–13.00 Sat (12.30 in Oct). A new TIC and tourism website (the old 🌐 honiton.com is defunct) are under discussion at the time of writing.

> Honiton is a neat market town situate on the river Otter; the country around it is beautiful. The present condition of this town is indebted to a dreadful fire, which broke out on July 19 1747, and reduced three parts of it to ashes, to the great distress of several hundred industrious inhabitants. The houses now wear a pleasing aspect, and the principle street extending from east to west is remarkably paved, forming a small channel well shouldered up on each side with pebbles and green turf, which holds a stream of clear water with a square dipping place opposite each door; a mark of cleanliness and convenience I never saw before.
>
> The Rev Stebbing Shaw, 1788

In a very different and far more ancient landscape than the Rev Stebbing Shaw's, Honiton's earliest known inhabitants were the Honiton hippos, dating back around 100,000 years. Their bones, now in Allhallows Museum (page 90), were found in the 1960s when a bypass was being built. Following them, about 25,000 years ago, Stone Age peoples made their flint tools on the banks of a river running close to today's Dowell Street, and populations increased steadily through the ages. There is little record of the Dark Ages, but by the 13th century Honiton was one of the main centres of Devon's weaving and woollen cloth trade; then from the 16th century became widely known for lacemaking. Pottery has also featured, since at least the 17th century; originally it was a coarse type of earthenware, then the Honiton Pottery was started in the High Street in 1881, using clay dug from the ground behind the pottery. The business passed through various owners and finally ended production in the 1990s.

Honiton was also the eighth stop for a change of horses on what is now known as the **Trafalgar Way**. On 4 November 1805, following the Battle of Trafalgar, the schooner HMS *Pickle* landed at Falmouth with the urgent news of Nelson's death and England's victory against the French and Spanish. It had to be transmitted forthwith to the Admiralty and King George III, so the *Pickle*'s captain, Lieutenant John Richards Lapenotière, set off on a breathless 271-mile journey to London by post-chaise. It took him 38 hours and at least 21 changes of horse, and cost altogether 46 pounds, nineteen shillings and one penny, which was around half a year's salary for an officer of his rank and equivalent to £4,500 today. His coach changes in Devon were in Okehampton, Crockernwell (Dartmoor), Exeter, Honiton and Axminster, the last three costing £1/17/6d, £2/14/0 and £1/11/7d respectively. Coaches and horses didn't come cheaply! Lapenotière delivered his dispatches to the Admiralty at 01.00 on Wednesday 6 November; the news was quickly passed to the king and the PM, and appeared in newspapers later that day. As part of the battle's 200th anniversary celebrations, Lapenotière's route was named the Trafalgar Way. For further information, see ⌀ thetrafalgarway.org.

"It is well known for its antique shops, of which there are enough to delight any browser's heart."

Even today the busy, modern town of Honiton holds echoes of the past; it is well known for its antique shops, of which there are enough to delight any browser's heart. More than 80 antique dealers are said to trade in and around town, and a week-long antiques festival takes place in November. If you enjoy antiquarian and secondhand books, don't miss High Street Books (150 High St ✆ 01404 45570) with its strong travel and exploration section, and further down the hill Graham York Rare Books (225 High St ⌀ www.gyork.co.uk) which also has art and some intriguing ephemera. Both are normally open Tuesdays to

HONITON LACE

In the late 16th century it took three days to transport products to London by coach but this did not inhibit the starting of the lace trade in Honiton: from marketing its cloth the town already had the necessary transport and organisation, the lace was just a very fine form of weaving so the skills were easily transferred, and flax for the thread was already grown in the Axminster area.

'Honiton lace' has since become a guarantee of quality worldwide. It was greatly in demand during the 17th and 18th centuries, both at home and abroad; in fact, at the end of the 17th century, over half of Honiton's inhabitants were earning their living from lace, with children as young as five or six working long hours alongside the adults.

There was no factory: it was literally a 'cottage industry', with so-called manufacturers employing women in Honiton and the wider area to design and make the lace in their homes, for very little pay; the employers then sold the finished product. Often these 'manufacturers' owned local shops, and paid their workers with tokens that could only be spent there.

In 1669 the Grand Duke of Tuscany rather sweepingly observed of Devon that 'there is not a cottage in all the county where

white lace is not made in great quantities', and indeed some of these cottages making 'Honiton' lace were in many parts of the area: the Honiton lace trimmings on Queen Victoria's wedding dress and her veil, for example, were made in Beer. Victoria's first daughter's christening robe was also of Honiton lace. The original robe, which has been worn by members of the current royal family, is carefully preserved; since 2008 a replica has been used, notably at the christenings of Prince George, Princess Charlotte and Prince Louis.

In the early 19th century machines began producing a cheaper version of what had been made so painstakingly by hand, and the lacemaking industry declined, with many families losing their main source of income.

Today lacemaking by hand is no longer a lucrative trade but the 400-year-old tradition is kept alive, worldwide, as a hobby. Honiton lace is still treasured for its exquisite quality, finding its way into such places as parliamentary ceremonies and Princess Diana's wedding, and in 2013 Honiton's Pat Perryman, then aged 74, was awarded the British Empire Medal in the Queen's Birthday Honours for services to the heritage of lacemaking.

See also Allhallows Museum (page 90).

Saturdays 10.00–17.00, are much larger than their frontages suggest and cover a wide and infinitely browsable range of subjects.

The High Street is long, wide and lined with a mixture of old buildings and (mainly) small, busy shops, both traditional and modern. Weekly street markets are held here on Tuesdays, Saturdays and most Thursdays. Among traditional food shops, Complete Meats of Honiton offers a top-quality range of local meats, deli and cheeses, while Fishmongers in New Street has shiningly fresh local fish, game, cooked dishes and treats ranging from oysters to Arbroath smokies. At the Pottery Shop & Milkshake Bar (30 High St ⌀ honitonpottery.co.uk) you can make and/ or paint your own piece of pottery, fortified by hot and cold snacks and 45 flavours of milkshake.

The **Beehive Community & Arts Centre**, opened in 2014, provides a venue for films, live theatre, music, dance and exhibitions. Art galleries include the **Thelma Hulbert Gallery** (Dowell St ✆ 01404 45006 ⌀ thelmahulbert.com) with a changing programme of exhibitions and other events in the eponymous late artist's attractive Georgian home; and in another Georgian house the stylish **Hybrid Gallery** (51 High St ✆ 01404 43201 ⌀ hybrid-devon.co.uk) presents original displays of British figurative art by a relatively small but select group of both established and emerging artists. Both galleries are open Tuesday to Saturday.

ALLHALLOWS MUSEUM OF LACE & LOCAL ANTIQUITIES

High St (next to St Paul's Church) ✆ 01404 44966 ⌀ honitonmuseum.co.uk ◷ Easter–Oct 09.30–16.30 Mon–Fri, 09.30–13.00 Sat. Closes 30 mins earlier in Oct.

The comprehensive collection of Honiton lace in Allhallows Museum is one of the best in the world (it's beautiful!) and receives visitors from far afield. The finest examples, carefully protected, are astonishingly delicate and intricate, in so many shapes and patterns. Historic old lacemaking tools are on display too, as well as resources (tools, patterns and materials) for present-day lacemakers. Demonstrations of lacemaking are given during summer months, and you can even try your hand at making it yourself.

The museum itself is historically interesting, too. It's the oldest building in Honiton, dating from before 1327, and was first a chapel and then a school (Allhallows) before being opened as a museum 50 years ago. The miscellany of non-lace displays include a fine furnished doll's house from around 1840, ancient documents, the history and archaeology of the town and local area, children's toys, war memorabilia and more. Space is also given to Honiton pottery (page 88), which was made in the area for more than 240 years.

There are quizzes, puzzles and lacemaking activities for the children. One display case has mementos of the old Allhallows School; it began in

A MEANDER ON THE NUMBER 694 BUS FROM HONITON

Bus-pass users know what a delectable experience a country bus can be, but for even for fare-paying passengers this 1½-hour ride is a bargain. The 694 is little – it has to be to fit down the Devon lanes – and ours was driven by Charlie who knew most of his passengers by name. This is the shopping bus, bringing non-drivers from the little villages in the 'Western Triangle' to Honiton and Cullompton, and since it starts and ends in Honiton, all you have to do is sit there. There are currently two a day, but only on Tuesday, Friday and Saturday, leaving Honiton at 08.45 (from Dowell Street) and 12.15 (from the Congregational Church).

The bus was almost full when we boarded at 12.15 and the shoppers had clearly had a successful time. One woman struggled on with an enormous roll of carpet, another had a curtain rail, and there were many bulging shopping bags. The first stop was **Feniton**, a pretty village away from the station. Roll of Carpet got off, calling over her shoulder 'You can see what I'm going to be doing this afternoon!'

'Next stop please, Charlie', said another as we headed for **Payhembury** along single-track lanes where approaching cars had to reverse into gateways to let it pass. Even on this single-decker we were high enough to see over hedges and watch the landscape slowly unfold; and were momentarily taken aback when the bus drew gently to a stop diagonally across the road. 'All right, Mary?' the driver asked as his elderly passenger climbed carefully down and headed for her front gate. 'I always do that', he told us afterwards. 'It keeps her safe from the traffic.' **Plymtree** came and went, as did the single-track lanes as we approached Cullompton, by which time we were the only passengers. The journey here had taken an hour. The return to Honiton was along roads which – gasp! – were wide enough for two cars to pass, and was relatively ordinary apart from the delightful scarecrows in **Awliscombe** and nearby villages, which make their appearance each spring in various inventive shapes and poses.

Before disembarking we chatted to Charlie. 'You must love driving a bus when you know most of the passengers.' 'Oh yes, I used to drive a bus in London.' Charlie paused. 'I haven't had so much fun in all my life. The characters!'

these premises in the Middle Ages, probably as a chantry school where priests taught boys to read Latin so that they could sing in the choir, then moved to Rousdon near Lyme Regis in 1938 before closing in 1998.

FAIRS & FESTIVALS

The first recorded Honiton Fair was in 1221, a bustling mêlée of livestock, local wares, the usual scattering of showmen and the town crier in full voice. Nearly eight centuries later, the present town crier still opens

Honiton Fair annually on the Tuesday following 19 July, striding his way up the High Street carrying a long flower-garlanded pole with a golden glove tied to the top. At 12.00 he rings his bell and shouts three times:

> **Oyez! Oyez! Oyez! The glove is up! The fair is begun! No man shall be arrested! Until the glove is taken down! God save the Queen!**

Then follows the ancient and apparently inflation-proof 'Hot Pennies' tradition of throwing hot pennies (ouch) from the upper windows of some local pubs to the waiting crowds. At the dress rehearsal beforehand, sweets are thrown. Hot Pennies reaches its 800th anniversary in 2021, and some serious merrymaking is already being planned. There should be details on local and social media beforehand – search for 'Honiton hot pennies'.

The following Saturday is Charter Day, marking the signing of the market charter some 750 years ago, when people dress in medieval costume and merry-make appropriately.

On 1 August (the same date every year) is the **Honiton Agricultural Show** (⊘ honitonshow.co.uk), said to be one of the largest in the country, with primped and pampered pedigree livestock (sheep, goats, cattle …) and row upon row of trade and demonstration stands. Just about everything that's local is represented, and various displays and events are held in the main ring. Also in August, the two-day **Honiton Hill Rally** (⊘ honitonhillrally.co.uk, described as a 'carnival of country life') features a range of vintage vehicles including steam engines, tractors, cars, military vehicles, fire appliances and motorcycles. There are also horses, displays of traditional farming techniques and rural skills, and working demonstrations of corn cutting, ploughing, baling, threshing and combining by the vintage machines.

⨏ FOOD & DRINK

In town

The Holt Pub, Restaurant & Smokehouse 178 High St ⊘ 01404 47707 ⊘ theholt-honiton.com ⊙ pub 11.00–15.00 & 17.30–23.00 Tue–Sat, kitchen 12.00–14.00 & 18.30–21.30. An award-winning pub with good-value bar food, fine wines, a full range of Otter beers and a superior restaurant, serving a carefully selected menu of 'great tastes and flavours from all over the world' ranging from tasty international tapas to local roasts and very good bubble & squeak. Friendly efficient service. Also holds cookery & breadmaking classes. Park in Dowell Street car park, a short walk away.

The Yellow Deli 43–47 High St ☏ 01404 378023 ⌖ yellowdeli.com/england ⊙ 12.00–23.00 Sun, 07.00–23.00 Mon–Thu, 07.00–15.00 Fri. Very recently opened after a long period of renovation, this cheery, American-style place has several branches in the US, also in Spain, Japan and Argentina, but only the one in Britain. It serves breakfasts, sandwiches (pick & mix from a variety of fillings), soup, salads and desserts, with all breads baked freshly on the premises; and looks set to become a popular addition to Honiton's food scene.

Zest Café 9 Black Lion Court ☏ 01404 43777 ⊙ 09.00–15.00 Tue–Sat. Located in the centre of Honiton's shopping area, near the junction of High Street and New Street, this clean, quiet, family-run café is convenient for a drink or light lunch while you explore the town. Food (wraps, pasties, specials of the day …) is freshly cooked and well presented; my asparagus baked with Parma ham and a perfectly cooked poached egg on sourdough was delicious and very good value, washed down with Luscombe's apple juice. The coffee's good too.

Out of town

Hare & Hounds Putts Corner EX10 0QQ ☏ 01404 41760 ⌖ hareandhounds-devon.co.uk ⊙ 10.00–23.00 daily (22.30 Sun). A landmark at the crossroads on the Honiton-to-Sidmouth road. Particularly proud of its deservedly popular carvery (with veg alternatives), available lunchtime and evening Monday to Saturday and all day Sunday, with concessions for senior citizens on weekday lunchtimes and Monday to Thursday evenings. Indoor and outdoor seating, and ample parking. The large rock outside is the 'Witches' Stone', said to roll down to the River Sid in the dead of night for a drink or a wash, and to dance to the sound of the bells at Sidbury church – thereby giving a new meaning to 'rock and roll'.

The Pig at Combe Gittisham EX14 3AD ☏ 01404 540400. One of six Pig hotel/restaurants (page 257) with the trademark combination of relaxed dining and superbly cooked food in gracious surroundings. Pricey, so come here for that special treat.

SEND US YOUR PHOTOS!

We'd love to follow your adventures using our *Slow Travel East Devon & the Jurassic Coast* guide – why not tag us in your photos and stories via Twitter (@BradtGuides) and Instagram (@bradtguides)? Alternatively, you can upload your photos directly to the gallery on the East Devon destination page via our website (⌖ bradtguides.com/edevon).

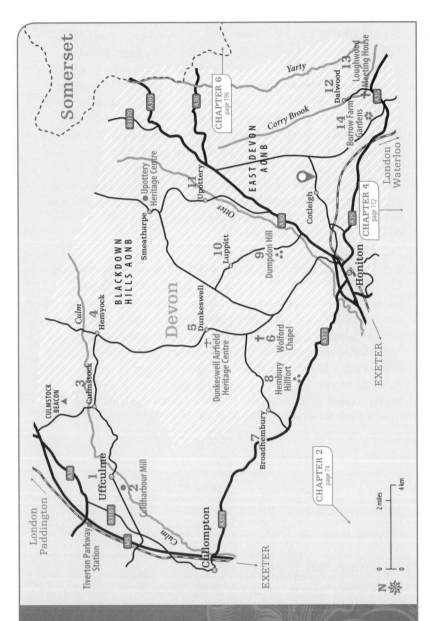

THE CULM VALLEY & THE BLACKDOWN HILLS

3

THE CULM VALLEY &
THE BLACKDOWN HILLS

> The hills that here divide the valleys of the Otter and the Yarty ...
> involve several steep "pitches" up and down which the motorist must
> perforce go at a pace that enables him for once to view the landscape
> o'er and not merely the perspective of the hedge in front of him.
>
> From *Wanderings in Wessex* by Edric Holmes, 1922

Few tourists come to this peaceful part of inland Devon, but curious Slow
visitors looking for something different appreciate the rural landscape
of this river valley and the Blackdown Hills, dotted with farms and
thatched-cottage villages, and lack of well-publicised 'attractions'. It's no
coincidence that some of the best glamping and self-catering places are
situated here, and our earliest ancestors found this fertile region much
to their liking; there are two Iron Age hillforts.

 ## WET-WEATHER ACTIVITIES
Coldharbour Mill (page 97)
Dunkeswell Airfield Heritage Centre (page 100)
Upottery Heritage Centre (page 106)

GETTING THERE & AROUND

The M5 and A30 allow easy access for drivers, but the only bus going
to some of these villages is the number 20 from Seaton to Taunton via
Honiton, which stops at Dunkeswell, Hemyock and Culmstock. The
railway from Paddington to Plymouth and Penzance calls at Tiverton
Parkway (an exceptionally hassle-free station just off the motorway,
with good parking) and cycles can be carried on the train.

SELF-POWERED TRAVEL
I met a couple in Culmstock who were exploring the Blackdown Hills by
bicycle from their base in Taunton. 'It's lovely – as long as you've got the

legs for it' they told me. Indeed, though there are few more rewarding areas in terms of constantly changing views and little traffic, and the region is easily accessible via Tiverton Parkway railway station so cyclists can bring their bicycles from afar. Walkers are equally well served, with tempting Public Footpath signs encouraging them to create their own route, with the help of ❋ OS Explorer Map 128 (but note that there is no Croydecycle map of this area).

THE CULM VALLEY

The River Culm squiggles its way down from the Blackdown Hills, becoming broader and more leisurely near Culmstock before joining the Exe above Exeter. It gives its name to several villages in the area, a quiet and relatively little-known part of the county, despite its proximity to the M5.

1 UFFCULME

This is a fairly ordinary small town just off the M25 and the church seems fairly ordinary too – until you look more closely: it has one extraordinary feature, the **Walrond Chapel**, which was being used as a store room when I was last there, but I hope temporarily. Here is the tomb and effigies of (probably) four generations of Walronds, mostly called William. The Walronds lived in Bradfield, a couple of miles south of Uffculme, in a mansion that is still standing. On top of the tomb are three half-sized figures, posed as if for some medieval photograph, and on the front are two busts or reliefs, the left-hand one of an absolutely furious-looking old man. Brightly painted and costumed in their Elizabethan finery, these effigies would be eye-catching anyway, but look at the right-hand relief. Is it a moustachioed man wearing a woman's gown and bonnet? Or a woman with long wavy hair to whom a flamboyant moustache has been added? Or just a man in normal period dress or armour, who happens to look slightly feminine?

"On top of the tomb are three half-sized figures, posed as if for some medieval photograph."

Trying to untangle the people involved only complicates matters. One source says the 'moustachioed lady' is Ursula, wife of one of the Williams, on whom a moustache was later (and inexplicably!) added, while another believes, equally improbably, that the figure was originally a man to whom woman's clothing and headwear were later added. Probably Arthur Mee, writing in *The King's England* in the early part of the last century, comes closest to the mark by describing it as 'a young man open-eyed in wonder'. Take your pick!

The reports agree that the man reclining on a windowsill above them all is the youngest William. He is full size, in armour, eyes closed, his red lips upturned into a smug smile and his gloriously bewigged head resting on his hand looking, as Arthur Mee says, 'as if he were taking an afternoon nap on the battlefield.'

2 COLDHARBOUR MILL

EX15 3EE ✐ 01884 840960 ⊘ coldharbourmill.org.uk ☉ 10.00–16.00 Mon–Fri

This restored woollen mill to the west of Uffculme, built in 1799 by Thomas Fox and modified in 1865 to accommodate steam power, is partly a museum and partly a working mill producing a range of yarns and woven goods which are sold in the shop. There's a self-guided tour of the mill that introduces you to the process of machine carding and spinning, and includes the original water wheel, powered by the River Culm, which was built in 1821. The signage is good and the sheer scale of the weaving process is impressive, but try to get to the mill on one of its monthly steam-up days when the old steam-driven engines are powered up.

On display is a tartan that owes nothing to Scotland: the Devon green tartan. The sign explains the significance of the colours: two greens for the moors and meadows, grey for Dartmoor's tors, white for the grazing sheep, and rust-red for soil and cattle.

Don't miss the combing shed downstairs which shows how a sheep's fleece becomes a skein of wool. There are some surprising facts here – such as the name for a coil of combed wool: a cheese.

If you've never been quite sure what puttees are, visit the exhibition on the first floor; manufacture of these was one of Thomas Fox's specialities. The adjacent Fox Gallery has World War II memorabilia.

3 CULMSTOCK

The village is famous for having a yew tree growing from its church tower, but not much notice is taken of it otherwise. However, we found it to be just the way a Devon village should be: attractive in an unpretentious way, with the river forming a central focus, an old bridge, an unusual pub, and the excellent **Strand Stores, Café and Deli** (✆ 01884 840232 ☉ 07.30–19.00 Mon–Sat, 09.30–12.30 Sun). A list on the wall shows the local suppliers, and the shelves are stacked with homemade preserves, cider and beer from local breweries and a good range of wines. The hot snacks and cakes on offer in the café are also produced on the premises and are exceptionally good (try the flapjacks!) and there are special evening meals from time to time. Before departing, head for the piano-themed loo: it's as original as the shop!

The Culm Valley pub, just across the bridge, is heralded by a splendid totem pole. It was carved from a single trunk of oak by Fiona Gray, in memory of her father. An equally eye-catching wood-carved dragon guards the car park, his wings prudently removed, so publican Dave Harris told me, because they were too much of a temptation to climbing children. But do go inside – the food is particularly good.

Then there's the **church** with its yew tree – and that's all we can tell you since it's kept locked. Apparently the yew started growing soon after the spire was taken down in 1776, and it is a matter of village pride to keep it alive – during particularly dry summers villagers have carried up buckets of water so that it doesn't dry out. The reason it's small for its age is that the constricting masonry has a 'bonsai' effect. In 1835 the father of R D Blackmore (of *Lorna Doone* fame) became curate at Culmstock, and Blackmore lived there from the age of ten; he mentions the tree in his novel *Perlycross*, which is set in the area.

"The beehive-shaped hut there was built in the reign of Queen Elizabeth I to act as a lookout."

There are some lovely walks around here, including a very steep climb up to **Culmstock Beacon**. The beehive-shaped hut there was built in the reign of Queen Elizabeth I to act as a lookout and warning against attack by the Spanish Armada. A chain of such beacons stretched across the county, and if the enemy entered the English Channel a watchman would light the first beacon, triggering the lighting of the next and so on. This was the signal for all able-bodied men to arm themselves and gather in the church to await instructions. The roofed structure gave shelter to the watchman in this exposed place, but there was a hole in the roof for the beacon pole, and slits at each side providing views of the neighbouring beacons of Upottery and Blackborough. The chain of beacons was lit for the 400th anniversary of the Spanish Armada in 1988, and for the Queen's Golden Jubilee. There is a similar beehive hut on Shute Hill (see box, page 202).

THE BLACKDOWN HILLS

The Blackdown Hills is a sparsely populated Area of Outstanding Natural Beauty (AONB) divided between Devon and Somerset: a farming region, untroubled by tourism. The River Otter cuts it roughly in half from its source at Otterhead Lakes in Somerset, while Cory Brook and the River Yarty combine in the eastern section to join the Axe near Axminster.

To appreciate the deep lanes hemmed in by banks of wild flowers or beech woods and sudden views of patchwork fields with villages cradled in the valleys, you really need to see it the Slow way by bicycle, but it's not called the Blackdown Hills for nothing.

There are very few level stretches. Motorists will proceed with caution along the single-track lanes but there is little other traffic.

"It's not called the Blackdown Hills for nothing. There are very few level stretches."

The active Blackdown Hills AONB team (⌀ blackdownhills.org.uk) produces an informative leaflet and a good website listing events in the region, including guided walks and suggested cycle rides. Their office is St Ivel House, Station Road, Hemyock.

4 HEMYOCK

⋏ Kingsmead Centre (page 258)

The village is nothing special visually but makes up for this with its active community. One initiative that is particularly welcome to the Slow movement is the bimonthly **Repair Café** held in the village hall. A team of volunteers repair all sorts of things: electrical, ceramics, clothing, jewellery, computers, furniture, bicycles ... you name it, there will probably be someone on hand to repair (or sharpen) it. In our throw-away society, what a great message of sustainability. See ⌀ blackdownhills.org.uk/repaircafe.

The castle, now in ruins, is a rare example of a moated medieval castle. During the Civil War it was used as a parliamentary prison. It is in private hands but can be visited on open days, generally held on Bank Holiday Mondays. Check the website ⌀ hemyockcastle.uk.

5 DUNKESWELL

⚠ The Nest, Tree House (page 258) **🏠 The Old Kennels** (page 257)

This unassuming village has some pretty thatched houses, a church with a fascinating Norman font and an **airfield** that played a prominent role in World War II and is now Devon's venue for skydivers who get to see the Blackdown Hills from 15,000ft up. The **Aviator** restaurant here does a Sunday carvery, and a sister museum to the one at Upottery displays photos of the part Dunkeswell played in the Battle of the Atlantic. The **Dunkeswell Airfield Heritage Centre** (EX14 4LG; same opening times as Upottery) makes an interesting addition to a skydive with its photographic displays, films and memorabilia. A must for World War II enthusiasts.

Before leaving the village, take a look at the font inside the **church of St Nicholas**. Carved around 1200, this almost competes with that of Luppitt (page 103) although the carvings have deteriorated and a clumsy repair makes the obscure even more obscure. Among the people there's a gloomy bishop, a severe king and a charming man and woman. He has his arm round her and they are holding hands. But it is the 'scaly elephant' that is the most interesting. I must admit that I would not have recognised it as an elephant if I hadn't read about it, but the interesting information sheet on the font tells us more. The first elephant was brought to England in 1255, so this could be the first depiction of a beast described but not seen. But why scaly? Apparently the Roman author Pliny confidently described the scales and their purpose: 'To crush the flies that settled on it; an unlikely piece of biological engineering.' Below the elephant are (possibly) waves and a monster's head. So the speculation is that this illustrates the belief that elephants gave birth underwater to protect their calves from dragons. Who knows? Like all such carvings, the mystery is all part of the pleasure for the viewer.

"I must admit that I would not have recognised it as an elephant if I hadn't read about it."

The ruined 13th-century Cistercian **Dunkeswell Abbey** (EX14 4RP) lies a few miles to the north of the village at a hamlet appropriately named Abbey. At the time of writing the history of the place remains something of a mystery but this is due to change. A Lottery grant will enable a reconstruction of the abbey to be displayed, along with other information that will make a visit much more rewarding. At present it is a tranquil place accessed through a white gate and narrow footpath. The little **church of the Holy Trinity**, adjacent to the abbey, is currently locked.

Close to the abbey is the **Old Kennels** (⌀ theoldkennels.co.uk), which runs a large number of top-class arts and crafts courses and has accommodation (page 257).

6 WOLFORD CHAPEL

EX14 4QL

If you're Canadian and feeling homesick, or have always wanted to visit Ontario but never got round to crossing the Atlantic, you can find a corner of a Devon field that is forever Canada. The Wolford Chapel and its land were given to the people of Ontario in 1966 and the Maple Leaf flies proudly over the little chapel every day. The reason is that the first Lieutenant-Governor of Canada, John Graves Simcoe, is buried here, along with his large family. Simcoe was only 52 when he died but he achieved a great deal in his lifetime, particularly in the four years he was in Upper Canada, now Ontario. From 1792 to 1796 he set up and ran a modern government in the territory that influenced the development of the province for years to come. A very informative leaflet about the chapel and John Graves Simcoe is available in the chapel, along with a scrapbook of cuttings and photos, and a guest book. It's all beautifully cared for. The chapel is well signposted and reached down a quiet country lane – a track, really – and is full of peace and birdsong.

7 BROADHEMBURY

Broadhembury is the only village in this region which attracts substantial numbers of coach parties, and understandably so: it's very pretty. The Drewe family built this typical estate village, with its rows of cream-coloured thatched cottages abutting the road, the lack of front gardens more than compensated for by the profusion of roses and creepers up the walls. The exceptional preservation of the village is largely due to the wealth of Julius Drewe, who built Castle Drogo near Dartmoor and bought half of Broadhembury, including its inn, in the early part of the 20th century. He built the substantial Broadhembury House, which is still lived in by his descendants. The original manor, the Grange, was built in 1603 by Edward Drewe, legal officer of Queen Elizabeth, who is buried in Broadclyst church (page 78).

This is a classic English village with a church, a pub and a post office-cum-shop-cum-tea room. The large **church** of St Andrew is impressive, with a splendid organ, capitals carved with vines and foliage, and an intriguing font decorated with eight figures including Paul, Peter and John the Baptist. As you would expect, the Drewes are well commemorated here: one of them kneels uncomfortably at a desk, wearing an Elizabethan ruff, and there's a splendid memorial to Francis Drewe who died in 1675. The descendant who wrote the inscription has gone way over the top:

> If vertue could the just and loyal save from ye dishonours of ye darksome grave, then hadst not thou most happy soul so soon left us in teares and to the Angels gone, but walls of flesh we see cant long confine souls truly noble, and like thine, Devine.

The much-mourned gentleman died at 71, so had lived his threescore years and ten.

Genealogists will find the family trees interesting, with the Drewes of the Grange and their connection with Dunster Castle in Exmoor and the Hills of Kerswell Priory displayed.

The **post office, shop and tea room** are concealed behind a discrete doorway in one of the terraced cottages opposite the church, and pack everything you need into a small space.

8 Hembury Fort

The hembury part of Broadhembury's name, and that of Payhembury (page 82), comes from this hillfort that lies a few miles to the south. Hembury Fort is a scheduled monument and considered the finest hillfort in Devon. To ensure that it survived as such, the Hembury Management Team was created to preserve and manage the site. They have put up informative signs and their excellent website ($\hat{\otimes}$ hemburyfort.co.uk) tells you of recent and future plans.

Excavations show that the fort was in use well before the Iron Age, with flint tools from the Mesolithic period discovered. The earth defences were built in the Iron Age but subsequently the Romans made use of it, and signs of metal working suggest that they may have had a centre here for repairing military ware.

A path climbs steeply up to the fort from the A373, connecting with other footpaths, and leading to splendid views from the high point.

FOOD & DRINK

The Drewe Arms Broadhembury ✆ 01404 841267 ⌂ thedrewearms.co.uk ⏱ 12.00–23.00, food served 12.00–14.45 & 18.00–20.45 Mon–Sat, 12.00–20.45 Sun. A medieval thatched pub with loads of character and an impressive menu with a Mediterranean feel from Chef Damian Luque Garcia. Mouthwatering options include crab linguini with chilli, spring onion, dill and lime butter, and pan-fried John Dory.

9 DUMPDON HILL

📍 ST178040

A mile west of the A30 is this Iron Age hillfort, dating back over 2,000 years. There is very little left of the fort, though you can make out some earth ramparts, but the view from the hill is stupendous: Devon's patchwork of fields and little clumps of villages stretch before you in all directions. The walk up to and around the fort is infinitely rewarding, especially in the spring when the hillsides are a purplish haze of bluebells. The highest point is marked by an OS trig point. There are more paths than are shown on the National Trust map at the car park, so it can get confusing. Take a photo of this map before setting out.

Just south of Dumpdon Hill is **The Rough Nature Reserve**, an area of marshland looked after by the Devon Wildlife Trust. There are bog-loving plants here, including orchids, and several rare species of butterfly, but it's heavy going for non-enthusiasts.

10 LUPPITT

The village consists of a few houses strung along the deep valley and a tiny pub, but **St Mary's Church** is sheer delight. It sits high above the village (the car park even higher) with benches in the graveyard so parishioners and visitors can enjoy the view. You may need a rest after working on the Millennium Puzzle Bench, which has a brain teaser on each of its exposed sides: a novel and intriguing memorial.

Once in the church the first thing that strikes you is the cruciform design set off by the dark timbered wagon roof of the nave and transepts, which are said to date back to the 14th century. It is both beautiful and extraordinary. How did they get the oak timbers to curve like that? Presumably by using the ship-builders' traditional knowledge of 'grown knees' where the timber is selected from the natural curve of a lower branch or root of the oak. A list of names on a door on the north side shows the soldiers in World War I who came safely home – a nice change from the usual Glorious Dead (who have their own memorial in the graveyard).

The pride and joy of the church is the font. It was unearthed from a bank near the church boundary in 1890, is thought to be about a thousand years old and, to the unschooled eye, looks delightfully pagan. It is four-sided, with a grotesque bearded head at each corner. On one side a very cross-looking dragon is locked in toothy combat with another head on what could be its tail, hotly pursued by a determined man with a spear. The official explanation is that it's a double-headed monster (an amphisbaena) that represents the evils of

The Daffodil Walk

OS Explorer 116; start: near Cotleigh, north of Wilmington ST215023; 2½ miles; easy to moderate; uneven underfoot, may be muddy, some steep steps

Although an enjoyable and varied walk year round, with a combination of woods, lanes and meadows, this is a circuit to do in the early spring when you will be treated to a Wordsworthian display of wild daffodils. It was suggested and described by Jan Uden who leads Seaton's U3A walks.

Parking is on the verge just beyond the bridleway signed Court Place Farm and Little Hayne. Continue down the lane, steeply downhill between banks lush with vegetation, and just before the bridge over the Umborne Brook go through the farm-type gate on the left. (There is a stall here for produce in season.) Take the track straight ahead towards the old cottage, ignoring the turning signed 'Pigeons', past a chicken run and an ancient boat. Skirt left round a timber store and follow the footpath signs to the right over a footbridge. The narrow path ascends the edge of a terrace, and through the bushes you may catch glimpses of the cottage garden, at one time a plant nursery. There is a rather unexpected dip, followed by an ascent up a steep flight of wooden steps. For a while the path follows the field boundary, then crosses a small footbridge (in summer there may be stinging nettles), traverses a stony section and then takes some steps going down.

Now you are in delightful Court Wood, at first high on the hillside looking down on the brook, and later undulating, first almost at river level, then higher. At an earthen boundary bank, the wires to one side of the stile have been cut, so you may walk round to two more short flights of steps. When the path dips low, the river plain presents a primitive scene. Carcasses of trees lie where they fell, and giant water-loving plants rise from the mud. A dinosaur would not look out of place! In spring, you may notice one or two small wild daffodils duplicity. I prefer to retain a sense of wonder and puzzlement. Then there are some violent goings-on with a club, a huge nail and a severed head (probably a martyrdom). The next is a hunting scene, although it's not easy to know what animal is being hunted; a boar, maybe, or a huge rabbit.

Finally the carver seems to have run out of inspiration and there is an abstract design that looked to me to be a giant tapeworm, though the official description is that it's the tree of life. Whatever it's all about – and indeed, whether it is even a font, rather than a secular vessel – it's a mysterious and delightful piece of work and thrillingly old.

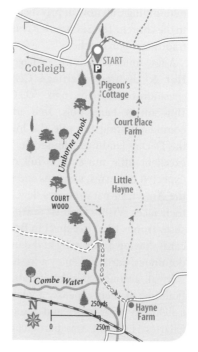

at the edge of the fertile alluvium, along with wood anemones and yellow archangels in bloom. After a little while you come to a ford, regularly used by tractors; follow the (wet) path to the left, alongside the brook. In March, the slopes to the left are ablaze with a host of golden daffodils.

Next comes a steady incline, up a broad track, to emerge on Haynes Lane. One of the houses here usually advertises local honey for sale. Turn left along the lane, and then go left through the farm gate, signed Bridleway. The path traverses a back garden, past some exotic poultry, through a second gate into a field where you follow the hedge round to the next gate. After rain, the gateway may be muddy, as may parts of the next field. Keep by the hedge until it bends sharply, at which point head for the next field gate to the right of the house that's just visible in the trees. The well-defined track leads past the house, turns left through yet another gate and on to a long straight stretch leading past Court Place Farm and back along the surfaced track to your parking place.

11 UPOTTERY

⚑ **Grey Willow Yurts**, Smeatharpe (page 258) 🏠 **Twistgates Farm Cottages** (page 258)

> Upottery taketh name of the river Otter, which riseth at Otterforde
> in Somersetshire, having its adjunct up in that it is the highest
> place where its spring maketh itself a river.
>
> Extract from *Chorographical description of Devon* by Tristram Risdon, 1714

The village's history, and that of its manor house, stretches back to William the Conqueror, but the splendid buildings that we see today are the legacy of Henry Addington, Viscount Sidmouth, who briefly – and unpopularly – served as prime minister (1801–04) before a ten-year spell as an ultra-conservative home secretary. A prudent marriage brought considerable wealth to this already prosperous man, as is evident in this spacious village with its stone-built manor house and outbuildings, all now in private hands, and the memorials to the family in the church. The Sidmouth Arms, also stone-built and spacious, serves traditional pub lunches.

A few miles north of the village, in Smeatharpe, is the **WW2 Nissen Hut & Upottery Heritage Centre** (EX14 9RD ☎ 07778 857722 ◌ southwestairfields.co.uk ◷ Good Friday–end Oct 11.00–16.00 Thu–Sun & bank hols; free admission but donation appreciated), commemorating the role the local airfield played in the lead-up to the D-Day landings. Housed in part of the original Nissen hut, this excellent little museum is full of intriguing displays as well as the expected uniforms, weapons and photos – some taken moments before the American paratroopers flew to Normandy, showing the strain on their faces. Visitors can sit down and watch a US Army film made to show troops what to expect in Britain. We see cheerful families playing cards, having a sing song and dancing, while the chaps in the pub play dominoes, darts and enjoy a freshly pulled pint.

By all accounts the Americans were generous and popular visitors, building, at their expense, a village hall for the locals, and organising a field day with glider and aeroplane rides. The commanding officer, Charles H Young, was particularly fond of this little spot in Devon, though he wrote in his diary (tongue in cheek) 'England seems to be a wet, gooey place, where people have colds, look unhealthy, wade in mud and drive around on the wrong side of narrow little roads'. Charles Young's family loaned the historic photos on display here.

Displays include the home front, rationing and the mixed experiences of Britain's evacuee children. Although Operation Pied Piper (as the evacuation was called) is now considered a success, it was also reported more negatively 'A quarter of the population of Britain would have a new address ... The result can only be described as typically British wartime shambles.'

12 DALWOOD

The narrow, unsignposted lanes around Dalwood, in the southeastern Blackdown Hills, are not designed for car drivers who don't know where they're going but are perfect for walkers, so leave your car in the Loughwood Meeting House car park (see box, page 108) and continue along the lane to this quintessential English village a mile away. It is not particularly pretty but has everything a village needs: a community shop that hopes soon to have raised enough money to add a coffee shop, a church, a village hall and an outstanding pub (page 110). And a vineyard (page 108). The red telephone box is now a seed and plant exchange centre. All this, plus the meandering Corry Brook, a tributary of the Yarty, and miles and miles of open rolling countryside.

The church of St Peter is described by Hoskins as 'of no great interest'. That's perhaps true of the interior, although I liked the way that the carved capitals were at eye level because of the low roof, but there are some good gargoyles (is that a tortoise?) and some interesting nuggets of information in a little typed leaflet about the church and village. The yew tree, for instance, is given a very specific date: 1745; schoolchildren would have their lessons in its shade in the summer. Near the south door is a headstone in the shape of a cross with a touching story to it. I quote from the leaflet:

> It is in memory of a son of an Aide-de-Camp to the Duke of Wellington who was later to become Prime Minister of Portugal. He was what, in those days, was termed a 'natural' – rather backward we would probably call him in these times. His father, having such a lofty position to fill, could not entertain his presence at the royal court, so his family arranged for the Edwards family, the retired postmaster of Dalwood ... to care for him until his death.

The lettering on the tomb is worn and covered in lichen so it's hard to make out the inscription. I could read that the boy's name was Pedro and that he was the sixth son. It's an appealing story.

The inclusivity of present-day Dalwood is reflected in the welcome notice on the church door. No-one, but no-one, is excluded.

13 LOUGHWOOD MEETING HOUSE
National Trust

With the suppression of Catholicism following the Reformation and the disruption of society in the Civil War, England was ripe for the emergence of non-conformist beliefs in the 17th century. The Baptists could only risk worshipping in secret in remote locations, and their Meeting House at Loughwood, built around 1653, is certainly remote. The little thatched building, tucked into the side of a hill, is now in the care of the National Trust, and is utterly delightful. Inside is completely simple, as you would expect, with plain box pews and a gallery for musicians, complete with music rests. On the wall is a memorial to the Rev Isaac Hann who died in 1778 at the ripe old age of 88, with a charming epitaph. Part of it reads:

DALWOOD VINEYARD

It all began with a casual remark in 2008 from one of a group of pub skittles players: 'Did you know the Romans grew vines on Danes Hill?' This hill already had historical importance, being one of the chain of hilltop beacons that would be lit to warn of a Spanish invasion in Elizabethan times (page 98). A few acres of sloping southwest-facing land happened to be available and an idea was born. 'We had no knowledge, no experience, just enthusiasm' Mike Huskins, the group's spokesman, told me during an alcohol-fuelled tour of the vineyard, which now produces award-winning wines. For me, too, who knew nothing about wine production or the complexity of wine tasting it was an eye- and tastebud-opener. Who knew, for instance, that the reason you drink sparkling wines from a tall glass – a flute – is that the shape makes you tip back your head so the wine hits the acid receptors at the back of your tongue rather than the sweet ones at the front 'which make even a good bubbly taste like Lucozade'? I didn't. England's new-found enthusiasm for growing vines prompted a rueful remark from a winemaker in Bordeaux as he conceded that Dalwood was doing pretty well: 'You haven't got history holding you back'.

Dalwood doesn't do the grapes-into-wine process – it would be financially unfeasible with only a small acreage of vines – so the grapes are sent to the winemaker Brooksbanks Barrs in Somerset. I wondered how much they should be credited with the success of the Dalwood wines. 'Well, there's a saying,' said Mike. 'You can make great wine from great grapes; you can also make crap wine from great grapes, but it's a hell of a

Wit sparkled in his pleasing face
With zeal his heart was fired
Few ministers so humble were
And yet so much admired.
Ripen'd for Heav'n by Grace divine,
Like autumn fruit he fell;
Reader think not to live so long,
But seek to live as well.

The meeting house is not easy to find – indeed the visitor's book, though full of appreciative comments, has complaints about this, so here's how you get there. It's on a narrow lane leading to Dalwood from the A35; the sat nav code is EX13 7DU but this only takes you to a point on the A35 near the turn-off, which is indicated by a very discrete National Trust sign; a better landmark is the lone-thatched cottage by the turning. If you are driving from Honiton the turning, on the left, is too sharp to negotiate safely, but you can turn round shortly

job to make great wine from crap grapes.' So Dalwood's five founders, all of whom fit in their vineyard work with other jobs, can take full credit for their success. Their first award was in 2015 with the bronze medal in the Decanter World Wine Awards ('Problem was, we quickly sold out of the whole batch') and in 2019 they won the silver medal in the English Independent Wine Awards (EIWA).

Careful thought was given to the varieties of vines grown. 'Pinot noir is the oldest cultivated vine in the world, and susceptible to every disease going, but it adds a little bit of style,' Mike told me, 'like fancy laces in a pair of shoes'. They also grow madeleine angevine, seyval blanc and solaris, which are more able to deal with the West-Country climate. The vineyard is not irrigated. 'Vines have very deep roots; irrigation encourages shallow roots.' And of course some years are better than others 'but our ethos is to react to the year. We never blend years. Nor do we use pesticides – we are 80% organic'.

Dalwood wine is entirely in keeping with this community-minded village, and is closely linked with its wonderful pub, the **Tuckers Arms** (page 110). The 2019 launch of the latest wines in the pub was attended by 70 people, the long tables filling up every possible space. Harvesting is a community effort (the reward of a bottle of wine and a meal at Tuckers being payment enough) and the wine is sold in several local outlets including, of course, Dalwood Community Shop.

For information on local stockists, the latest news and to arrange tours of the vineyard visit dalwoodvineyard.co.uk or phone Mike on 07909 545426.

afterwards in a lane/bridleway. If coming from Kilmington look for a sign for Studhayes Cross and a broad lay-by on each side of the road. The turning to Loughwood is on the right, one mile beyond this.

It's worth the search. There's a picnic table so you can enjoy the peaceful surroundings, and friendly cows in the adjacent field. The building is never locked.

¶¶ FOOD & DRINK

The Tuckers Arms Dalwood EX13 7EG ✆ 01404 881342 ⌂ thetuckersarms.co.uk. A thatched, 12th-century pub with low beams, horse brasses, flagstone floors and a generous fireplace. But the building plays second fiddle to the warm welcome diners receive from the staff, and the delicious food. Tracey and Craig McGowan have been running the Tuckers Arms for ten years and can take credit for it being the hub of the village community. The menu is not particularly extensive, just very good. My salmon and crayfish salad was perfect and I wish I'd had room for their trademark Tuckers Belly Welly, a combination of belly of pork and a puff-pastry Wellington with a lot of extras. And they serve Dalwood wine by the glass, as well as many locally brewed ales.

There is space for only five cars in the pub car park; park where you can but don't block driveways.

14 BURROW FARM GARDENS

Dalwood EX13 7ET ✆ 01404 831285 ⌂ burrowfarmgardens.co.uk ⊙ 1 Apr–31 Oct 10.00–18.00 daily

This tranquil, landscaped garden set in 13 acres, with far-reaching views of the surrounding countryside, was bought by John and Mary Benger in 1959, and they soon realised that if they were to create a garden here it would need to pay for itself; it opened to the public in the mid 1960s. Mary trained as a landscape designer at Bicton ('in case my back gave out') but still does much of the gardening herself. 'I like it to look as though we cut the lawns and don't do anything else,' she told me. 'But of course we do!' The gardening writer Noel Kingsbury agrees. 'Such an expert balance between nature and intention.'

"It is an exceptionally peaceful place for just wandering among the different features."

It is an exceptionally peaceful place for just wandering among the different features amid a blaze of different colours, and pausing in the coffee shop for a cream tea if your stamina sags. Each area has its own character, none of it too manicured or artificial: the natural woodland garden created in an old Roman clay pit, the millennium 'rill' garden, open lawns, borders, ponds surrounded by moisture-loving plants, shade, sunlight – allow plenty of time here, because it's so pleasant just to stroll. As well as the coffee shop there's a picnic area, and ample parking; and, before leaving, you can stock up with plants from the nursery or gifts from the shop.

In the summer Burrow Farm Gardens hosts a variety of open-air plays, usually Shakespeare but sometimes other classics.

UPDATES WEBSITE

You can post your comments and recommendations, and read feedback and updates from other readers online at ⌀ bradtupdates.com/eastdevon.

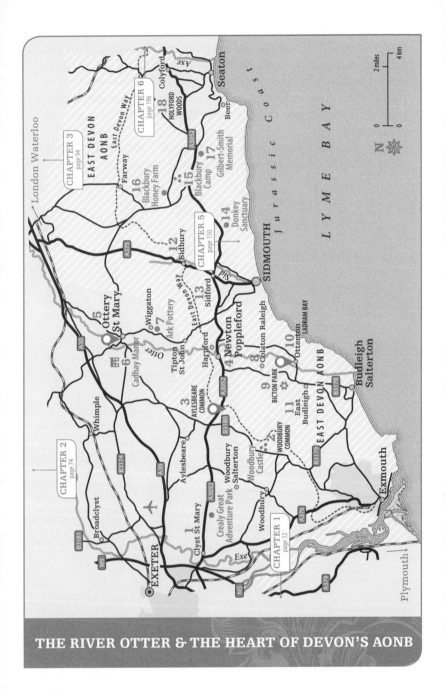

THE RIVER OTTER & THE HEART OF DEVON'S AONB

4

THE RIVER OTTER & THE HEART OF DEVON'S AONB

> A characteristic of what are known as the East Devon holiday resorts is that each has a hinterland, well watered by some river and therefore rich in foliage and flowers. In no county in England are there valleys to excel those of Devon, down which those myriad streams chant their lays.
>
> Ward Lock guide to Devon, 1930–31

The rivers which run down to those holiday resorts have, for centuries, been an obstacle to the passage of vehicles along the ancient road from Exeter to Axmouth and beyond, now the A3052. The clue is in the names. Newton Poppleford, or pebble ford, marked the ford across the River Otter, and Sidford crossed the smaller so less challenging Sid. Traffic now passes smoothly over the bridges and the rivers are the focus for recreational walking, with the Otter standing out as having the best riverside walks.

Over 60% of East Devon has been designated an Area of Outstanding Natural Beauty (AONB). This includes not only the Jurassic Coast but the heathland and gentle hills enfolding small villages which lie inland. Meandering through this region is the East Devon Way (EDW), whilst the River Otter bisects it north to south and the A3052 runs east to west, providing access to the seaside towns and villages.

 ## WET-WEATHER ACTIVITIES

Cadhay Manor (page 127)
Bicton Park (page 131)
East Budleigh church (page 135)
Ottery St Mary church (page 124)
Ottery St Mary Heritage Museum (page 124)

GETTING THERE & AROUND

The A30 and A35 whizz motorists towards Dorset on dual carriageways, leaving the A3052 as the trunk off which branch all those little lanes, tracks and footpaths. The iconic X53 Jurassic Coaster bus, which used to run from Exeter to Poole, now leaves from Axminster; bus timetables and routes seem to change on a yearly basis so check the latest timetable at ◈ traveldevon.info. Suffice to say that most of the places described can be reached by bus, even if it only runs a couple of times a week.

SELF-POWERED TRAVEL

The quiet lanes of this region – or almost any region of East Devon – are an invitation to **cyclists**. One of the most alluring rides in this exhaustingly hilly area is the 2½-mile level lane known as **The East Hill Strips**, which runs along the escarpment to the east of Ottery St Mary. Mind you, you have to get up there (personally I would put my bike on the car and drive up, but real cyclists are made of sterner stuff). The lane up from Sidford to White Cross, the southern end of the Strips, is pretty steep, but once on the level the road is pure delight, with gentle cycling through beech woods above gorgeous views over the Otter Valley.

The OS Explorer map for the area is number 115, ❋ *Exmouth & Sidmouth* (1:25,000), but Croydecycle has produced a cycle map, ❋ *Exmouth & Sidmouth*, at a scale of 1:30,000 (page 23) with lots of information specific to cyclists. For walkers at 1:12,500 (5ins to the mile) is ❋ *Sidmouth*, which covers Weston, Salcombe Regis and the Donkey Sanctuary, as well as Sidford and the River Otter up to Tipton St John; ❋ *Budleigh Salterton & Otterton* takes care of that region and the southern stretch of the River Otter, and ❋ *Ottery St Mary* the area around this town and the northern parts of the river. With these excellent maps you can safely devise your own walks.

Highlights of the East Devon Way

The greater part of this 40-mile route runs through the AONB so you can enjoy some of the highlights of this chapter on foot. I've done quite a bit of it the ideal way, with a good companion (and one who carries the picnic), using two cars. Here are my favourite sections: Lympstone Common to Woodbury Castle (2½ miles), then on to Newton Poppleford, 8½ miles in total. Sidbury to Farway would be a strong contender were it not for the punishingly steep hills, so I've devised an easy circular walk to take in the best bit (see box, page 139). The next section, Farway to Colyton, is mainly lanes so ideal for the winter or after very wet weather, and the two villages, Farway and Northleigh, are lovely. And then you're into *Chapter 6*.

All in all, like any long-distance trail, the EDW has its rewarding bits and its hard slogs, not to mention ankle-deep mud. When planning which sections to walk, bear in mind that the commons are largely level and dry, and networked with paths so circular walks are easy to plan, whilst the in-between bits can be very hilly and hard work but reward you with splendid views and variety. Take heed of the contour lines on your OS map. In farming country, mud – especially around gateways used by cattle – is an all-season problem even after a dry spell.

CLYST ST MARY TO NEWTON POPPLEFORD

The Pebblebed Heaths or commons are the main feature of this section, particularly inviting for walkers, especially in the spring when the gorse is in blossom or late summer when the heathers – both ling and bell heather – come into their own.

1 CLYST ST MARY

This community only a few miles from Exeter still has a thoroughly villagey feel despite pressure to expand. It is notable for its pub, its history, and its 12th-century bridge, the oldest in Devon and for 700 years part of the route from Exeter to London.

The village played a prominent part in one of Devon's more bizarre wars, the Prayer Book Rebellion of 1549 (see box, page 117). During the siege of Exeter some 6,000 of the rebels gathered here to take on the powerful government forces, an act that was doomed to failure. Accounts vary as to how many were killed in the fighting, or drowned in the river, but it is thought to be at least a thousand with many more taken prisoner; and the village was burned to the ground – except for the inn. Standing in the small village street today, it's hard to imagine the clash and clamour of such a battle. Of the prisoners, it's said that 900 of them, bound and gagged, had their throats cut 'in ten minutes', provoking a retaliatory attack at Clyst Heath in which many more died.

Arthur Mee, in *The King's England: Devon*, claims that the insurrection was inadvertently started by Walter Raleigh, Sir Walter's father, who reprimanded a woman walking to church with a rosary, advising her to give up her superstitious practices. She continued to church and told her story. Raleigh barely escaped with his life when the rebels caught up with him at Clyst St Mary. A good story, even if it doesn't fit with other accounts.

FOOD & DRINK

The Half Moon Inn Frog Ln, EX5 1BR ℰ 01392 873515 ⊘ thehalfmoonclyst.co.uk ⊙ food 12.00–14.00 & 18.00–21.00 Mon–Sat, 12.00–15.00 & 17.00–20.00 Sun. A terrific pub in every way. It has the traditional Public Bar for beer and games, and a quieter Lounge Bar where the exceptional food is served. It's perfectly cooked, beautifully presented, and – oh joy! – they offer 'regular' and 'small' portions, so those with a smaller appetite (and there are plenty of us around) can save enough room for the delicious puddings. Here are puddings your mother used to cook: jam sponge, treacle tart, and a divine lemon posset (which she probably didn't cook). They also serve delicious Granny Gothards Ice Creams and Sorbets (the ices come in 145 flavours) from a Somerset farm with happy cows. Just off the M5, yet traffic-free and rural. Could you want more?

CREALY GREAT ADVENTURE PARK

EX5 1DR ℰ 01395 233200 ⊘ crealy.co.uk ⊙ variable opening times (check website), closed Nov except w/ends

There's nothing slow about this place, with over 60 'heart-stopping rides' but of course families love it and it's part of East Devon. In addition to putting your body through something resembling a car crash, you can pet a variety of animals and tuck in to large quantities of ice cream.

2 WOODBURY, WOODBURY COMMON & WOODBURY CASTLE

The **villages** of Woodbury and Woodbury Salterton are unremarkable, but the latter does have an attractive, and popular, thatched and flower-bedecked pub, The Digger's Rest.

Woodbury Common, to the east, is the generic name for a large area of pebblebed heaths comprising Colaton Raleigh Common, Woodbury Common and Bicton Common, part of the 2,800 acres of mainly heathland owned by the Clinton Estate. The strategic height of this heath has given it more than one place in history. Napoleon is said to

THE PRAYER BOOK REBELLION

As part of the Protestant reforms instigated under the boy king Edward VI, the familiar prayer book in Latin was declared illegal and, from Whit Sunday 1549, churches in England were required to adopt the new *Book of Common Prayer* in English. Resistance to this was particularly strong in Devon and Cornwall, as people saw their traditional methods of worship under threat. At Sampford Courtenay (near Okehampton) parishioners persuaded their priest to retain the Latin version; the authorities moved in to enforce the change and in the consequent fracas a local man was stabbed with a pitchfork.

Devon and Cornwall's villagers in their thousands, generally armed with no more than farm implements and staves, then rose in support and marched to Exeter, laying siege to the city for five weeks and demanding the withdrawal of the English version of the prayer book. But despite their fervour the rebels were no match for the large and well-armed military force of almost 9,000 men sent by the king to quell them; battles and skirmishes (including at Fenny Bridges, Woodbury, Clyst St Mary and Clyst Heath) saw them gradually vanquished. By the time the conflict ended some 4,000 from both Devon and Cornwall had died – and to little purpose, since when Edward's half-sister Mary (a devout Catholic) succeeded him in 1553 she legalised the Latin version again anyway.

have been deterred from invading Devon by General Simco's army and it has been used for military training in both world wars, and is still to this day by the Royal Marines. In 2015 they erected the Gibraltar Stone on Bicton Common to commemorate the 'Royal Marines ... who, since 1940, have trained here at Woodbury Common and gone on to serve their Crown and Country around the Globe'. The chunk of actual Gibraltar rock was donated to mark the 310th anniversary of the Battle of Gibraltar.

For most people the heath serves a more peaceful purpose, being networked with tracks so it's easy to do a circular walk or ride. The underlying pebbles make it tough on the feet, however, so it's best to wear boots. In 2015, Dartmoor ponies and beef cattle were introduced as part of the heathland management and are proving a success. Ponies and cattle have different feeding habits, so between them deal with the invasive silver birch saplings, young bracken, gorse and bramble, as well as keeping the grass short and creating fire breaks. Gorse management is important since it is the favoured habitat of the Dartford warbler, so the browsing of young gorse is beneficial by creating a bushier growth.

THE PEBBLEBED HEATHS

Dr Sam Bridgewater, Nature Conservation Manager
with Kim Strawbridge, Site Manager

Clinton Devon Estates ⊘ clintondevon.com

Providing extensive vistas across to the sea, East Devon's Pebblebed Heaths are counted among the most important conservation sites in Europe. The core area of this beautiful wildlife reserve is owned by Clinton Devon Estates and managed by the Pebblebed Heaths Conservation Trust (⊘ www.pebblebedheaths.org.uk).

The Pebblebed Heaths lie predominantly to the south of the A3052 and comprise a number of contiguous commons that historically were attached to local parishes. From south to north these include Dalditch, Withycombe, East Budleigh, Bicton, Woodbury, Colaton Raleigh and Hawkerland Commons, with Mutter's Moor an outlying area close to Sidmouth. North of the main road are Aylesbeare, Harpford and Venn Ottery.

The pebble beds that underlie the heaths to a depth of 30m were formed during the Triassic era around 240 million years ago when a great river flowed down the sandstone mountains of the megacontinent of Pangaea (page 26). The resulting soils are free draining, acidic, sandy and of low fertility, ideal for supporting heathland. Although the heaths were once predominantly woodland, thousands of years of human use have created the open landscape dominated by gorse and heather that we recognise today. In centuries past the commoners obtained the bare necessities of life from this landscape: timber and turf for fuel; gorse for fodder; grazing for cattle. Their activity helped forge the mosaic of habitats we see today, which supports over 3,000 species, 10% of which have conservation designations. These

Like other so-called castles in the region, **Woodbury Castle** is not a castle as such but an Iron Age hillfort, and a scheduled monument at that. To understand the fort you need to imagine the region denuded of trees (the beeches that make this such a

"Gorse management is important since it is the favoured habitat of the Dartford warbler."

pleasant place are relatively recent), 600 feet above sea level with a commanding view over the strategic Otter and Exe estuaries. It was built between the 6th and 4th centuries BC and was probably a stronghold of the region's chiefs. It originally had double ramparts and a ditch, reinforced by timber palisades, and possibly some roundhouses. In 2019 new interpretation boards were set up to show how the fort might have looked when inhabited.

include the iconic Dartford warbler, nightjar, southern damselfly and the silver-studded blue butterfly.

Heathlands need to be managed to maintain the rich diversity of habitats and age structures that support its wildlife. In the absence of management much of the site would revert to woodland and the rare European habitats and the specialist species they support would suffer as a result. The heaths are also an important cultural landscape forged by human hand and are much valued by those who live in the area. Of particular significance is Woodbury Castle, an Iron Age hillfort positioned on the high point of the heath. This scheduled monument has recently undergone restoration to ensure its survival into the future; interpretation boards illustrate how this site would have been used by these ancient people.

Management of the site essentially recreates the practices of the commoners of old, with controlled burning, grazing and scrub clearance all useful tools deployed to maintain this ecosystem in a healthy condition.

The Pebblebed Heaths are a fantastic place to walk, ride or cycle. The heaths are open access with cycling and horseriding also allowed on many tracks; more information is available on the website, with downloadable maps and guidance to help visitors enjoy their visit. Please note that camping, fires/barbecues and use of drones are not permitted, and dogs should be under close control during the bird breeding season (March to August) to protect ground-nesting birds. The Pebblebed Heaths Conservation Trust promotes the responsible use and appreciation of this site and frequently arrange talks, activities, working parties and educational visits. In particular, a week-long festival celebrating its history and wildlife, Heath Week, takes place in July each year (see website for more information).

These days the castle is popular with families, with steps making access up and down the steep banks much easier. It's a beautiful place, especially in the spring when the beech trees are clothed in translucent green. It is worth walking round the perimeter of the castle, rejoining the EDW at its northern end (use the EDW booklet here, not the OS map – the Way has been rerouted).

3 AYLESBEARE COMMON

Although a pebblebed heath, this common is not managed by the Clinton Estates but is an RSPB reserve. It's smaller than Woodbury, with more variety, and is classified as southern lowland heathland, a very rare habitat and perhaps the best place in Devon to see the Dartford warbler. Thirty species of butterfly have been recorded here, the ponds are great places for observing dragonflies and damselflies, adders and slow worms warm themselves in the clearings, and the interpretation boards ensure that you are kept well informed. Ponies and cattle have been here for longer than at Woodbury and are doing their job in keeping the scrub and bracken in check (although the latter also needs to be dealt with mechanically). In short, it's a great place, easily accessed by bus, and with some good walks.

4 NEWTON POPPLEFORD

🏠 **Southern Cross Guest House** (page 258) ⛺ **Hunger Hill Yurts** (page 258)

Known affectionately as Newton Pop, this is one of those places people drive through on the A3052, smile at the name (a *popple* is a smooth, rounded pebble) then forget about, a fact that irritates its residents. And indeed, Newton Poppleford is an attractive large village with some

---

A bus-assisted walk along the EDW, Aylesbeare Common & Harpford

❄ OS Explorer 115 plus East Devon Way guide; start: Joney's Cross car park ♀ SSY057898; 4 miles; easy (mostly surfaced tracks & lanes, no steep inclines)

This is a wonderfully easy and enjoyable walk taking in a combination of heath and woodland and ending in one of the area's best pubs. I recommend the use of public transport to allow a linear route but it can easily be adapted as a circular walk.

Park or take a 9 or 9A bus to the Aylesbeare Common car park at Joney's Cross (if you're going by bus, it's a request stop). Cross the A3052 and take the surfaced track across **Aylesbeare Common**, ablaze with gorse in the early part of the year, with easy walking, good interpretation signs, and everything that makes our commons special. The EDW goes straight across but if you divert to the left you pass a couple of ponds which are great for dragonflies. At the opposite end of the common you'll veer right, passing **Woolcombes Farm**, and continuing along a green lane through some woodland, always easy walking on a clear track, to **Benchams Cottage**.

The track forks to the right just beyond the cottage, and you cross another bit of heathland, **Harpford Common**, the most easterly of the Pebblebed Heaths, before joining a lane. You can cut the walk short here and walk into **Newton Poppleford**, but to extend the walk through some varied scenery, make a sharp left turn over a stile and across a field and continue on the footpath to **Court Barn**. Turn right on the lane here, continuing to the T-junction and cross the

---

cob-and-thatch cottages including arguably the oldest toll house in the county (1758) on the western edge. This once collected money from the horse-drawn vehicles making their way carefully over the pebbly ford. Before you reach the toll house (if coming from the west) you are greeted by a family of wooden bears; nearby, in Woodley's yard, is a red phone box with an antique clock face set into it. Two Newton Pop brothers are responsible for these curiosities, the clock man, Ken Woodley, also being tasked with keeping the church clock in perfect working order.

Newton Poppleford is said to be where the King Alfred daffodil originated; in fact the daffodil industry was once the village's biggest employer.

The village has a welcoming tea room (page 146), a fish and chip shop, and a general store. It's a good centre for a variety of walks, being the nearest town to Aylesbeare Common and having a convenient free car park (with toilets) behind the church.

road, passing through the gate and diagonally to the left. Follow the field edge round to the right, cross a stile and go ahead through the orchard and to the River Otter which you cross on a footbridge to arrive at **Harpford church**, tucked behind a wall at the road junction. To the right is the main part of the village, a cluster of white thatched cottages, exceptionally pretty even by Devon's high standards. Turn left up the lane and then right at **Peeks House** to follow Knapps Lane, bearing right down the track that leads through **Harpford Woods** where there are some splendid oak and beech trees. The EDW branches off this track to the left, but you continue straight ahead along the bridleway to emerge on the road just above the **Bowd Inn** (page 147). It's an ideal place for a meal or drink while waiting for the bus back to your car.

OTTERY ST MARY & AREA

⚑ **Cuckoo Down Farm Yurts**, West Hill (page 258) 🏠 **Mazzard Farm Holiday Cottages**,
East Hill (page 258) ⚑ **Knightstone Farm Glamping Safari Tent** (page 258)

The River Otter splices this region lengthwise, providing some good
walks and giving its name to several villages including the largest,
Ottery St Mary, which has a circular walk all of its own, the Ottery St
Mary Heritage Trail. Descriptive leaflets are available in the Heritage
Museum and Public Library. The poet Samuel Taylor Coleridge was
born and spent his childhood in Ottery (see box, page 126) and the
town makes the most of this claim to fame. The Coleridge Memorial
Project (⚲ coleridgememorial.org.uk) has published a delightful leaflet,
downloadable from its website, with details and background stories of
a nine-mile Coleridge-linked walk, and two shorter ones outside the
town. Another popular walk is down the River Otter to Tipton St John
(page 123). Further afield are Cadhay (page 127) one of East Devon's
very few manor houses open to the public, and the family attractions
of Wildwood Escot (page 86). The Otter Valley Association (⚲ ova.org.
uk) holds guided walks, talks and other events; it's a charity aimed at
promoting and conserving the area's natural environment, architecture
and local history.

5 OTTERY ST MARY

🏠 **Tumbling Weir Hotel** (page 258)

Tourist information: Silver St, in Public Library ⚲ 01404 813838 ◷ 10.00–13.00 Mon,
Wed & Fri (may change, depending on availability of volunteer staff)

At first acquaintance the grandeur of the cathedral-like church doesn't
really fit this fairly ordinary little Devon town, but Ottery punches above
its weight. Its history stretches back many centuries (the town mill was
recorded in Domesday and in medieval times it was an important
market centre) and it enjoys various literary connections including, of
course, Samuel Taylor Coleridge. It has a community market (held in
the Institute Hall on the last Saturday of most months) selling a terrific
range of produce and baked goods; a good free news magazine, the
Ottery Gazette; and a very worthwhile Heritage Museum (page 124).
A car park at the back of Sainsbury's helpfully offers two hours' free
parking, which is unusual in the centre of Devon towns. Local lunch/
tea places for a restoring cuppa include the traditional and welcoming

A bus-assisted walk up the Otter

❋ OS Explorer 115 or, better, the Croydecycle *Ottery St Mary* map; start: Ottery St Mary Hind St car park ♀ 2½ or 5 miles; easy

Agood path runs along the west bank of the River Otter from Ottery St Mary to Tipton St John but, though the return up the east side of the river looks fine on the OS map, it is partially closed due to flood damage with a long diversion down a lane, so a return trip is less rewarding. By making use of the 382 bus, which runs every two hours, you can get the best walking (and pubbing) and be in varied scenery the whole way.

It's always easiest, with a bus-assisted walk, to bus first and walk back, so catch the 382 in Ottery's Broad Street (stop B). Depending on how energetic you feel, you can take it to **Tipton St John** and potter back up the Otter in 2½ miles, or continue to Bowd, on the A3052, for a more varied walk. If you get off at Tipton St John, walk past the village store and take the path just before the river. Beyond the cricket pitch a bridge takes you to the west side of the river where you pretty much hug its bank until Ottery.

If getting off at **Bowd** (where you can also give up all ideas of walking and have a carvery lunch instead; page 147) you'll head up the lane a short distance, keeping an eye out for the bridle path on the left through Harpford Wood. This joins the waymarked East Devon Way (turn left) which you follow to the village of Harpford, past St Gregory's Church, and across the river where you turn right towards Tipton St John. Bowd to Tipton St John is about 2½ miles, and if you time your arrival in Tipton right you can enjoy a good lunch at the **Golden Lion** (⊙ 12.00–14.00 & 18.15–20.00).

Seasons in Silver Street (⊙ 09.00–17.00 Mon–Sat) and child-friendly **Tickety-Boo** in Mill Street (⊙ 08.30–17.30 Tue–Sun), which has good coffee. For evening meals see page 127.

Near the river is a unique 'tumbling weir', in the form of a circular hole in the middle of the stream, allowing water to sluice down to a tunnel and then to the river. The mill stream used to supply power to the nearby factory, which was built in 1789 to spin worsted thread for the wool industry and later converted to silk manufacture for the East India Company. There are some attractive old terraced cottages, and small alleys or lanes running between the houses. The **Curious Otter Bookshop** (10 Mill St ✆ 01404 814469 ⊘ beautifulnotebooks.co.uk ⊙ 09.15–16.00 Mon–Sat) has a good stock of Devon-related books and (as the website suggests) particularly beautiful notebooks of all kinds, also available by mail order. A new arrival in town is **FillFull**, a zero-waste shop (2 Mill St ✐ 01404 811144 ✐ fillfull.co.uk ☉ 10.00–17.30 Mon–Wed & Fri, 10.00–20.00 Thu, 09.00–17.30 Sat). It champions plastic-free shopping, and stocks gluten- and dairy-free foods, gifts, cosmetics and household staples.

The **Heritage Museum** (The Flexton ✐ 01404 812795 ✐ otteryheritage. org.uk ☉ Apr–Sept 10.00–16.00 Tue–Sat) celebrates the rich social and cultural history of Ottery St Mary, stretching back 2000 years. It's well worth a visit. The carefully assembled exhibits are rotated because there's simply too much material to display all at one time; they include local literary connections like Samuel Taylor Coleridge, Ottery's internationally famous tar barrels tradition

"Outside in the churchyard, the old town stocks seem ready and waiting for some future miscreant."

(see opposite), the story of St Mary's Church through the ages, the town's role in the English Civil War, bronze-age settlements and the Romans – as well as more prosaic concerns like the coming of Switchgear to Ottery and its early postal and telegraph services. Although it's quite an onslaught of information it's well presented, and deserves a careful browse. I spotted a quotation (I think slightly adapted) from Aleksandr Solzhenitsyn: 'Recording of history extends our short time on earth by carrying from man to man the whole complexity of other men's lifelong experience with all its burdens, colours and flavour'. It's true.

Just below the Heritage Museum is the **public library**, home of the TIC. Outside it are interpretation boards and an interesting bench shaped like an open book, designed and created from Scottish oak by furniture maker Angus Ross. Two quotations are on it: 'Poetry – the best words in the best order' and 'Nothing is so contagious as enthusiasm'.

The **church of St Mary** is what draws most visitors to the town. The manor of Ottery was given to the cathedral of Rouen by Edward the Confessor, and wrested back in 1334 by Bishop Grandisson who set about rebuilding the church, modelling it on Exeter Cathedral. It was added to in the 16th century and in the Victorian era and repainted in 1977. The most conspicuous feature is the two monuments to the Grandissons who lie on each side of the aisle under elaborately carved canopies. Sir Otho de Grandisson was the bishop's younger brother. He died in 1359 and lies there in full armour, with his luxuriant moustaches draped over his breastplate. He has the knight's usual lion at his feet, symbolising strength, although it has lost its head. His wife, Lady Beatrix, has been defaced -- presumably during the Reformation – and looks as uncomfortable in death as she probably was in life: her hair is incorporated into a square headdress which has the effect of a pair of blinkers; this, along with the high collar of her dress, must have ensured that she faced life looking straight ahead at all times. Two little dogs nuzzle each other at her feet, their liveliness contrasting with their poor inanimate mistress. Another notable monument, although carved in marble 500 years later, is to Jane Fortescue, Baroness Coleridge. The carving is very fine, and it's interesting to see that her feet rest on an otter rather than the usual dog.

All visitors will pick out their favourite things from the detailed church guide. Don't miss the little medieval encaustic tile showing a spear-wielding knight on a charger behind the altar screen, and the very cute elephant's head with human ears on one of the capitals opposite the entrance. The astronomical clock is also impressive for its age (perhaps as early as the mid 14th century) and its complexity. On the south wall is a brass memorial to a young soldier who died in action in Afghanistan – in 1880.

Outside in the churchyard, the old town stocks seem ready and waiting for some future miscreant.

The church clock has poetic inclinations. After its daily strikings of eight o'clock, noon and four o'clock, the bells briefly chime out the tune of the 'Old Ottery Song', written in about 1910 by Bernard, second Lord Coleridge. Should you wish to sing along, here are the words:

Sweet-breathing kine, the old grey Church,
The curfew tolling slow,
The glory of the Western sky,
The warm red earth below.

O! Ottery dear! O! Ottery fair!
My heart goes out to thee.
Thou art my home, where e'er I roam -
The West! The West for me!

Ottery's blaze of glory comes each 5 November (Guy Fawkes night) when it holds its annual Tar Barrel Ceremony in which flaming tar barrels are carried through the town streets on the shoulders of brave young men – and, these days, women.

THE COLERIDGE FAMILY

Although of humble origins, the poet's father, the Rev John Coleridge, was headmaster of the local grammar school (King's School) and vicar of St Mary's Church in Ottery St Mary from 1760 until his death in 1781. He married twice and had a total of 13 children. By the time the youngest, **Samuel Taylor** (named after his godfather), was born in 1772, his father was already in his mid 50s and his mother, a farmer's daughter, was 45. John Coleridge seems to have been an affectionate and well-meaning father and vicar, but decidedly eccentric. He insisted on reading the Bible in Hebrew to his flock of farm labourers, saying that it was 'the language of the Holy Ghost'. John Taylor's memorial stone is at the entrance to the Lady Chapel in St Mary's.

The young Samuel grew up in and around the church, but took refuge from bullying by reading adult books, so that he had 'all the docility of the little child but none of a child's habits. I never thought as a child, never had the language of a child'. He acted out scenes from the books 'on the nettles and rank grass of the churchyard'. The religious subplot of the *Rime of the Ancient Mariner* reflects his upbringing. He used to sail paper boats by a small stream that runs through the town, and a visit to Pixies' Parlour (a small cave cut into a limestone cliff) inspired his poem *Songs of the Pixies*. Coleridge is a great boon to local tourism; the tourist information centre has several leaflets on his life and association with Ottery. In Canaan Way, by the long-stay car park, granite 'Poetry Stones' were installed in 2012, with his poem *Kubla Khan* engraved on them.

The whole south transept of St Mary's Church is given over to Coleridge memorials, including the questionable mosaic tiled walls and the stained-glass window. These were the gift of Lord John Duke Coleridge, the eldest son of John Taylor Coleridge and a great nephew of the poet. He sensibly chose law and politics as his career path and rose to become Lord Chief Justice of England as well as a baron. It is his wife, Jane Fortescue Coleridge, whose marble memorial lies in the church. The otter was part of the family's heraldic device.

This is said to date from 1688, and continues despite apparently flying in the face of health and safety issues. Less inflammatory is the annual Pixie Day in midsummer, when local children dress up to re-enact the 'Pixies' Revenge'. Legend relates that long ago the Devon pixies and Ottery inhabitants lived more-or-less peacefully together apart from the occasional pixie prank; however, when the bells of the new church were first rung in 1454 the pixies objected forcefully, invaded the town and captured the bellringers, bound their hands with fairy cords and hid them in a cave. But the Ottery people fought back, rescued the bellringers, and the pixies fled in disarray. You can still visit their cave: it's one of the walks described by the Coleridge Memorial Project (page 122).

¶¶ FOOD & DRINK

The Rusty Pig Yonder St, EX11 1HD ℘ 01404 815580 ⚲ rustypig.co.uk ⊙ 09.30–16.00
Tue & Sun, 09.30–23.00 Wed–Sat. And now for something a little bit different. There is
one large social table, where convivial conversation is guaranteed, smaller tables for more
intimacy, and no menu; the owner Robin and chef Rob cook whatever seasonal produce they
have found. For meat eaters they have a nose to tail ethos, using every part of the animal,
and do a splendid cold charcuterie. They favour local smallholdings above large farmers, and
choose naturally reared animals that are slaughtered locally, minimising stress.

The Tumbling Weir Hotel Canaan Way ℘ 01404 812752 ⚲ tumblingweirhotel.co.uk. The
restaurant here serves fresh, locally sourced food overlooking the hotel garden. Happy to
provide half portions for children.

The Volunteer Inn 1 Broad St ℘ 01404 814060 ⚲ volunteerinnottery.co.uk ⊙ hours vary,
daily. Traditional pub grub, well served, in the centre of town.

6 CADHAY MANOR

🏰 **Cadhay Manor** (page 258)
EX11 1QT ℘ 01404 813511 ⚲ cadhay.org.uk ⊙ May–Sep 14.00–17.30 Fri only, plus late
spring & summer bank hols; see ad, 2nd colour section

This is a proper stately home in that it is certainly stately, and also a home.
From Saturday to Thursday the house is used as luxury self-catering, but
the rooms and gardens are open to the public on Fridays in the summer.

The house, located a few miles from Ottery St Mary and close to
Wildwood Escot (page 86), was once the seat of the De Cadehayes and
dates mainly from the mid 1500s when Robert Haydon inherited it and
did much of the interior work. He was no doubt financed by his wealthy
wife, Joan, who was the daughter of Sir Amias Poulett, principal Keeper
of Mary Queen of Scots for the last years of her life. The Haydons (of
course) supported the Royalist side in the Civil War and celebrated
the Restoration a little too extravagantly, so they were driven by debt
to sell the house in 1736, by which time it was in poor condition. It
became the property of Major Barton William-Powlett in the 1900s, and
it is his descendant, Rupert Thistlethwayte, who now owns the place.
The William-Powletts are significant in the history of Cadhay, being
descendants of William Paulet whose cousin married Robert Haydon.
The Paulet Coat of Arms can still be seen over two of the fireplaces.

So, Cadhay is a memorial to the astute politics of William Paulet, who
held high office under each of the Tudor monarchs whose statues are
arrayed so proudly around the grand courtyard. He seems to spring

from the pages of *Wolf Hall* (indeed, Authors Mantel did some of her research for *Bring Out The Bodies* here), having switched allegiance between Protestant and Catholic as often as necessary to remain in royal favour for over 50 years. When asked the secret of his success in keeping both his position and his head, he is said to have responded (in Latin) 'I am sprung from the willow not the oak'.

Although the courtyard, with its statues dated 1617 of Henry VIII (with a rather surprisingly slender waist), Edward VI, Mary and Elizabeth, is the main feature of a Cadhay tour, there is much of interest in the house itself: huge stone fireplaces, intriguing portraits, and a magnificent Great Hall with a hammerbeam roof of curved timbers. There are also some very beautiful pieces of modern furniture made by Rupert Thistlethwayte. The portraits of note include Sir Isaac Newton who was connected to the family, and Mary Reibey whose 18th-century adventures included running away from home at 14 dressed as a boy, being arrested (as a boy) for stealing a horse, and being sentenced to death but instead transported to Australia. On the convict ship she met and fell in love with Thomas Reibey. They married and became successful merchants. Her portrait appears on the Australian $20 bill.

Even without a tour of the house, the gardens are gorgeous, with lakes and blossom and hidden corners, and a walled kitchen garden displaying enviably vigorous fruit and vegetables. The grounds are mainly the work of head gardener, Dave, who started here shortly before Rupert Thistlethwayte inherited the house. 'The place was derelict,' he told us. 'I had to begin from scratch.' We asked him which part of restoring the garden he liked best. 'All of it!' And you can tell.

"The gardens are gorgeous, with lakes and blossom and hidden corners."

Teas, with yummy home baking, are served on Friday afternoons.

7 ARK POTTERY
Wiggaton EX11 1PY ℰ 01404 812628 ⌂ arkpottery.co.uk ☉ 10.00–17.00 daily (double-check on website out of season)

The pottery's well-established studio and gallery are in the old barn of a historic thatched Devon longhouse, set in an idyllic country garden. It's signposted from the A3052 and in Wiggaton, less than two miles from Ottery St Mary. Tea/coffee is available, and sometimes cream teas outside in the garden on sunny days.

The small gallery and studio are crammed with home-produced ceramics, from quirky animals to stylish tableware and distinctive 'cracquelle ware', whose innovative glazes and inlaid coloured veins mean that each piece is unique. There are also cards and work by other local artists (as well as – when I visited – some very good homemade blackcurrant jam). Visitors of all ages are welcome to have a go on the pottery wheel, helped by potter Angela Glanville, and to take their creation home. If you'd like to do this it's wise to check availability by phone beforehand. As Angela explained to me, it's particularly a hit with children: 'They're so proud of what they have made, and it's really good that they can see the lump of clay become a recognisable thing. I tell them: if you don't break it, pottery will last even longer than you.'

"The River Otter continues its way south, bringing character to the villages to its west."

THE SOUTHERN OTTER

The River Otter continues its way south, bringing character to the villages to its west and giving the town of Budleigh Salterton a nearby birdwatching attraction to add to its beach. The region is also known as the birthplace of Sir Walter Raleigh who has left his mark indelibly on the villages with which he is associated.

From Newton Poppleford the B3178 heads south to Budleigh Salterton and Exmouth, paralleling the river and giving access to some special places and the best circular walk in East Devon. Even better than driving is the **footpath** which runs, most of the time, close to the river all the way to Budleigh, making this a perfect bus-assisted walk. Bus number 157 runs reasonably frequently between the two towns, and the ❀ *Sidmouth* Croydecycle map shows the first part of the route from Newton Poppleford to Otterton, with the ❀ *Budleigh Salterton & Otterton* one covering the rest of the riverside walk. The bus goes to Colaton Raleigh and Otterton so you can break your walk at either village.

8 COLATON RALEIGH

This pleasant village with some cob-and-thatch houses is proud of its rather tenuous Raleigh connection: Sir Walter may or may not have been christened in the chapel of Place Court, a nearby manor. However,

BEAVERS IN THE RIVER OTTER

Mark Elliott, Devon Wildlife Trust

The River Otter in East Devon is the best place in England to see wild living beavers. The river is the setting for an interesting project to see if the native Eurasian beaver can be returned to lowland England.

There have been reports of beavers on the river since as early as 2007, although where they originated is a bit of a mystery. However, when they were found to be breeding in 2014, government officials decided to remove them. Following a campaign by local residents to keep their unusual neighbours, the Devon Wildlife Trust stepped in with a solution that involved health testing and then re-releasing the beavers.

Working closely with the major local landowners, the Clinton Devon Estate and beaver expert Derek Gow, the animals were rounded up and screened for disease prior to their re-release in March 2015. The River Otter Beaver Trial, with partners the University of Exeter, is now studying how the beavers recolonise, and what impact they will have on its wildlife and water, and on the farming and tourist businesses in the area.

Beavers are largely nocturnal, making them hard to spot. During long summer evenings they can sometimes be seen along the stretch of river between Ottery St Mary and the sea. Walking south along the public footpaths from Ottery St Mary or either direction from Otterton Mill are good options, but please respect the landowners by sticking to the footpaths and leaving gates as you find them.

The area is also famous for otters, which can also be seen, if you are very lucky, in exactly the same way. You will stand a much greater chance of seeing them if you are very quiet, keep as still as possible and are not accompanied by a dog.

When you are in the area spending money with local hoteliers and eateries, do get into a conversation to explain you are here to see the beavers, so that the DWT can begin to appreciate how much extra business the beavers bring to the area. If you do see the beavers, make a note of the time and place, and also the colour of any ear tags, and report them to the Devon Wildlife Trust (𝌆 devonwildlifetrust.org).

the village does have its own place in history: it is mentioned in the Domesday Book as having 20 villagers, eight smallholders and six slaves. In 1066 it was owned by Earl Harold (King Harold II), and passed to King William after Harold's defeat at the Battle of Hastings.

You may miss the village, tucked away down a side road close to the river, but you won't miss their excellent village store, which is on the main road. **Woods Village Shop** (owned by Alison and Jerry Woods) is one of those shops that Devon is so good at, specialising in the things that local people want to buy, including local produce. The Woods family have also branched out into brewing their own cider, Woodsys Cider, and have an outside table where you can enjoy a glass of it, or a mug of coffee.

9 BICTON PARK

🏯 **The China Tower** (page 258)
EX9 7BG 📞 01395 568465 🖥 bictongardens.co.uk 🕙 summer 10.00–18.00 daily, winter 10.00–16.30 daily

These splendid gardens are a mini-Kew with glass houses for different climates – arid, temperate and tropical – plus a palm house which is actually older than Kew's. It was built in the late 1820s, and is composed of 18,000 individual flat panes of glass.

The place has a rich history, and it's well worth studying the display board at the entrance that highlights events and characters of the last 1,300 years. The most prominent landowner was Lord John Rolle who died in 1842. He married Louisa when he was 72 and she 28. Despite the age difference they seem to have been a devoted couple and were instrumental together in creating much of what we admire in the gardens today. Lord Rolle caused consternation by falling down the steps at Queen Victoria's coronation at the age of 82, an event commemorated in a contemporary painting reproduced here.

Another historical record is the list of rectors and their patrons in the church, starting with Edward I, patron of Robert Cavernseye de Rockingham in 1280, and continuing to the first Rolle patron, Sir John Rolle in 1677, and then from 1926 Baron Clinton.

The spacious formal gardens are always rewarding, featuring plants from different parts of the world – Mediterranean, American – each with its own area, and a mixture of formal and informal plantings. There are some truly enormous trees, including a Grecian fir which at 138ft is the highest ever recorded, and some very ancient ones: the wisteria is thought to be over 200 years old.

A list of rules for gardeners dated 1842 makes entertaining reading. Infringements included smoking a pipe at work, coming to work on Monday in a dirty shirt or with untied shoes, swearing or 'in any way mutilating or defacing the above rules'. The fines were deducted equally from the pay of all workers at the end of the year and put 'to some useful purpose'. The rules were enforced by the head gardener, James Barnes, who is credited with being the forerunner of today's celebrity gardeners,

The Otter & Ladram Bay: a walk from Otterton

✳ OS Explorer 115 or, better, Croydecycle *Budleigh Salterton & Otterton*; start: Otterton; about 6 miles (less than 3 miles for the shorter loop); easy

The length of this walk can be varied; at its shortest it takes in the famous view of Ladram Bay's sea stacks, a short section of the South West Coast Path and a bit of river before returning to Otterton, but for the full reward, follow the coast path (along one of its gentlest stretches) to the mouth of the Otter then return to Otterton along either side of the river.

There are usually plenty of parking spaces along Otterton's wide Fore Street. Continue east through the village, bearing right on Bell Street and left on Ladram Road. Turn right on Piscombe Lane, which soon becomes a stony track. Turn left at the junction and follow the footpath to the coast and **Ladram Bay**, one of the most photographed views in Devon; the orange-red Triassic sandstone has been eroded into lumps and chunks like pieces of fudge dropped in the sea. Turn right along the coast path and, if you're taking the **short route**, follow it for about half a mile until you see the footpath leading back to Otterton. When you join Stantyway Road turn left and take the track to Colliver Lane which leads to the river. Cross the footbridge and follow the left bank back to Otterton.

For the **longer walk**, keep going along the South West Coast Path for 2½ miles to the Otter Estuary Nature Reserve. It's a really lovely stretch of path, with no steep climbs and varying views. The reserve competes with Seaton Wetlands as the best habitat for saltmarsh vegetation in Devon, and with the tidal mudflats this makes it an important place for over-wintering birds. There are hides, so if you're a birdwatcher bring binoculars. After about a mile walking north up the east side of the estuary, cross the bridge to the main part of the reserve.

To return to Otterton you can stay on the east side of the river, which is also a cycle route, or cross the bridge at South Farm Road (that leads to the nature reserve) and follow the west bank to the village. My preference is a compromise. Take the lane up the east side as far as the metal footbridge, then follow the lovely River Otter back to Otterton Mill for refreshments and then to your car. On a hot summer day there are plenty of accessible paddling places. Also keep an eye out for brown trout – surprisingly well camouflaged until they move.

being a prolific writer of articles in horticultural magazines. He was also no shrinking violet, having successfully sued Lady Louisa Rolle for libel because she accused him of leaving the gardens in a disorderly state when he retired.

Apart from the gardens, it's worth heading for the rustic Shell House, with its collection of shells and corals, some collected from

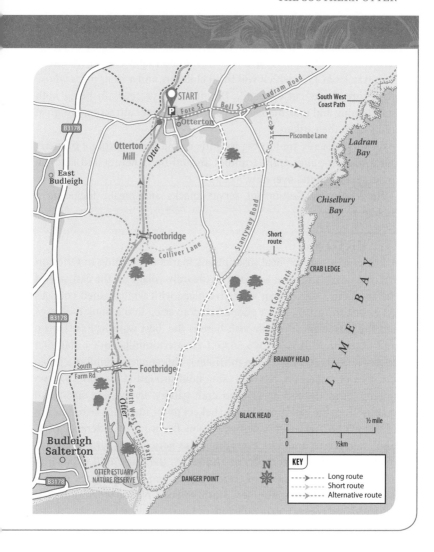

the Bahamas where Lord John Rolle had an estate, and the Hermitage where the old man took his ease during the later years of his life. Like the similar building in Killerton (page 77) the floor is paved with deer knuckle bones.

Finally there's the excellent **Countryside Museum** which has a little cinema to show archive film of farming and rural industry. When I was last there the museum had some delightful scarecrows scattered around to add humour to the exhibits. There are displays of all sorts of things relevant to rural history: farm machinery and implements, including a man trap from 1790 which will thrill children, and a cider press whose giant thread was cut by hand. The museum succeeds in being both entertaining and informative, and as an all-weather attraction is a great addition to the gardens.

Bicton's 63 acres are too big for little or old legs to explore properly, but a **narrow-gauge train** trundles around the pinetum and lakeside areas, giving a good overview.

The Orangery Restaurant serves snacks and meals, including a Sunday roast.

10 OTTERTON

A brick cross with biblical inscriptions marks the turning to Otterton, which enjoys its relative isolation as the only village on the east side of the southern Otter. It's an attractive place with whitewashed cottages set beside the green, and a phone box converted into a book exchange, but the reason most people visit here is the 'best walk in East Devon' and **Otterton Mill** (⊘ 01395 568521 ⊘ ottertonmill.com ⊙ Mar–Oct 10.00–17.00 daily, closed Mon in winter). This converted mill is a 'green' complex of restaurant, bakery (using flour ground at the mill), Devon organic produce, and an art and craft gallery. Everything smacks of quality, from the local produce and bakery to the meals in the restaurant (⊘ 01395 567041). The galleries exhibit the work of different artists and craftspeople and, like everything else here, this is seriously good-quality stuff. Twice monthly on Thursdays, the water mill is put into action for a demonstration of grinding flour, and regular events are also held including, in the summer, Music & Food Nights when dinner is followed by a concert, generally folk or blues.

11 EAST BUDLEIGH

This is both the prettiest – lots of whitewashed thatched cottages – and the most interesting village in this region, and one that has a flourishing community shop. A little stream runs between the road and the houses bordering the main street, and there are two pubs named after their famous past residents: The Rolle Arms and (of course) the Sir Walter Raleigh.

A free car park in Hayes Lane, opposite the Sir Walter Raleigh, gives access to the village and church, and there are a few spaces near the community shop.

In the 15th century ships could penetrate this far up the river, or so John Leland claimed in the mid 1500s: 'Lesse than an Hunderith Yeres sins Shippes usid this Haven, but it is now clene barrid.' These days the only connection East Budleigh has with the sea is as the birthplace of Sir Walter Raleigh. Note that although Raleigh's birthplace at Hayes Barton, about a mile west of the village, is signposted at the start of Hayes Lane, the house is not open to the public.

The village centre is to the west of the B3178; coming from the north, take the turn-off shortly after Otterton's Brick Cross into Vicarage Road. This accesses two places of exceptional interest, Salem Chapel and the church.

The Salem Chapel

This is a place of worship with a difference. It was built in 1719 on the edge of the village as a dissenters' chapel (a dissenter being anyone who didn't follow the Church of England). It has had a colourful history in which smuggling played a central part. The minister from 1768 to 1807 was Samuel Leat who is reputed to have been in the trade, a claim supported by the architecture of the chapel. Its roof is of particular interest, being of a unique construction which allowed the storage of smuggled goods in its massive attic and also gave the facility of a hidden vantage point where a lookout could be posted to forewarn of the coming of any revenue men.

Salem Chapel is on Vicarage Road. It was restored in 2006 and is now owned by the Historic Chapels Trust.

The church of All Saints

The church stands above the village (and the Hayes Lane car park) on a steep hill and has a Raleigh pew, with the family coat-of-arms and Sir Walter's dates, and even a Raleigh kneeler. He was born in Hayes Barton, about a mile to the west of the village, and his father was church warden here.

However, it is not Raleigh that makes this church a 'must-visit' but the wonderful carved bench ends. These are quite extraordinary, carved in the early 15th century, and deserve as much time as you can give them. While some other churches may have half a dozen or so, this has around 60. The old ones are thought to have been carved by local people and are all of secular subjects: a unicorn, dragons and monsters, an owl with a bearded human head, tradesmen's tools, a sailing ship with men climbing the rigging, and several very naturalistic portraits of ordinary folk, some smiling or laughing. The few religious carvings, at the back of the church, are from a later date, and are probably by the Victorian woodcarver Harry Hems, who created the pulpit.

Bring a torch so you can study the detail of this gallery of village art. Among the several carvings of heads is a bearded man wearing what seems to be a feathered headdress. This is on the shortest pew, next to the pulpit. It is popularly known as 'The Red Indian' but experts such as Todd Gray, who wrote *Devon's Ancient Bench Ends*, point out that the headdress is composed of leaves, and that the hook-nosed fellow is also sporting a leaf beard, 'a feature not common to early Americans'. Nevertheless, the charm of Devon's bench ends is that the subject matter can only be speculation; none of us has any idea what the carver had in mind. And this man's headdress does look rather like feathers which seem to be attached to a band round his head, rather than growing

SIR WALTER RALEIGH

Raleigh himself seldom spelt his name this way, but out of many variations it has become the best known. Facts about his early life are vague: he was born sometime between 1552 and 1554, in Hayes Barton near East Budleigh, and is thought to have studied law. Next he spent time as a soldier and landowner in Ireland, where he is credited with planting the first potato – but probably didn't. Nor was it he, as is often claimed, who first brought tobacco to England: Sir John Hawkins did. There's a story that one of Raleigh's servants doused him with water because the smoke from his pipe made her think he was on fire; it's said to have happened at his home in Ireland – or in Wiltshire – or in Dorset. Who knows!

Returning to England from Ireland, he quickly found favour with Queen Elizabeth. This is the Raleigh with whom we're more familiar: the dashing, gallant courtier beloved of the Queen. Whether or not he actually flung his cloak into a puddle so she could walk on it, he certainly charmed her. He also spied for her, and uncovered the Babington plot to replace her with Mary, Queen of Scots. She knighted him, and gave him lucrative positions and land but held back on his seafaring ambitions, refusing him two voyages that he had hoped to lead. At the time of the Spanish Armada he was Vice Admiral of Devon, in charge of its coastal defences, but did not go to sea.

organically from his face like other 'leaf heads'. And his beard is leafy rather than definitely leaves. Admittedly another fact against the Red Indian theory is that the indigenous people of the Americas don't have body hair but a sailor returning from the New World would have remembered the more flamboyant aspects and perhaps described them to the local craftsmen. Who knows.

There is also a carving which is described by J Stabb, in his book *Some Old Devon Churches* (1908), as 'a man's head with the mouth open, showing the teeth with something between them, whether his tongue or a substance he is supposed to be swallowing it is difficult to say'. Todd Gray sees it differently: 'A woman eating a chicken drumstick'. He or she is definitely eating something. The late Dr Michael Tisdall, the authority of the unusual in English churches, had his own theory:

> It is my idea that it is a banana. Bananas would have been known to Raleigh's crew. They sailed via the Azores where bananas were in production and some were taken across to these new West Indies and planted there. So either a banana or a drawing or other memory of a banana would be very likely in East Budleigh.

In 1592 he secretly married one of the Queen's ladies in waiting, for which 'offence' Elizabeth sent him briefly to the Tower. On his release, he gradually reintegrated and was elected to parliament, and also spent three years as Governor of Jersey. He also went to sea, first to seek (unsuccessfully) a fabled 'golden city' in Guiana, now Venezuela; his *Discoverie of the Large, Rich and Bewtiful Empyre of Guiana* became a best-seller. Embracing piracy, he was involved in the sack of Cadiz.

When James I succeeded Elizabeth he demoted Raleigh, eventually imprisoning him in the Tower under death sentence for alleged treason. In his 13 years there Raleigh started writing his mammoth *Historie of the World*. Released in 1616, he was sent off to seek gold again in Guiana, but the expedition failed and his death sentence was reinstated. He was executed in 1618. It's said that his wife had his head embalmed and carried it with her in a bag for the rest of her life.

Raleigh was undoubtedly a skilful soldier, seaman, explorer, administrator and painstaking recorder of current events, who played a leading role in Elizabethan history and society. But what has lasted until the present day is his poetry: straightforward, evocative, well shaped and often charming. The charismatic courtier and adventurer was also one of the foremost Elizabethan poets – and perhaps this is his greatest legacy.

There's a third carving which has inspired speculation. It's at the back of the church, up the aisle nearest the door, and is of a woman standing behind a counter or table with a dressed chicken or other fowl behind her. She is holding a dish in one hand and the tail of a dog in the other. So what's going on? Gray suggests that the dog is a 'turnspit dog' trained to turn the wheel of the kitchen spit. Maybe.

Wood carvings aren't the only things of interest in this church. Abutting the step up to the chancel is a very worn stone with a cross engraved on it. It's in memory of Raleigh's father's first wife, Joan Drake. What makes it particularly interesting is that the Latin inscription is engraved backwards, in mirror writing. No-one knows why. Perhaps the illiterate stonemason took an impression of the writing and accidentally reversed it.

¶¶ FOOD & DRINK

Otterton Mill Otterton EX9 7HG ✐ 01395 568521 ✆ ottertonmill.com. Excellent lunches and cream teas based on their famous bakery products. The menu is simple but wholesome, with natural organic juices or top-rate coffee to accompany the food. Indoor and outdoor seating. The bakery sells not only bread but a range of flour, cereals and hard-to-find grains.
Sir Walter Raleigh East Budleigh EX9 7ED ✐ 01395 442510. A busy 16th-century inn in the heart of the village offering a good range of home-cooked meals at reasonable prices, accompanied by a wide range of local ales.

AROUND THE RIVER SID

Although only about seven miles long, the Sid (whose name crops up in several places along its course, including Sidmouth) can get quite lively. During its short journey it flows over several weirs and in 2012, that winter of torrential rain, it burst its banks and flooded Sidmouth's popular Byes parkland.

12 SIDBURY

This attractive, unspoilt village on – you've guessed it! – the River Sid has some beautiful old cottages, although the number of cars either parked or driving through can be a drawback. Head for the side streets to enjoy its charm. It is said to be one of the earliest settlements in Devon and is mentioned in the Domesday Book as the Manor of Sideberia. An Iron Age fort above the village has views out to the sea and up the Sid towards

A short walk above Sidbury

❄ OS Explorer 115; start: near Higher Sweetcombe Farm ♀ SY157927; 2 miles; easy (on good path & quiet lane)

The East Devon Way (EDW) runs through Sidbury and on to Farway. It looks wonderful on the map but I'd reckoned without the almost vertical hill up from Sidbury village and the mud around Lower Mincombe Farm so decided not to include it here. However, there was a simply lovely footpath running through butterfly fluttering woods and wildflower meadows that I want to share. So do the sensible thing, drive up from Sidbury, park on the verge somewhere around Higher Sweetcombe Farm (but don't block a farm gate) and enjoy a fairly level and beautiful short walk. If you want to make it longer – and hillier – there are plenty of footpath choices.

Wherever you're parked, walk south down the lane, past the EDW where it joins the lane from the left, past Old Dairy House, and look out for the EDW signs on your right opposite Hatway Cottage (♀ SY151920). Take this path, which is a little over a mile long, and constantly interesting.

Sometimes you're walking through meadows full of wild flowers with clumpy hills rising to your right, sometimes you're brushing past bracken and then walking through ancient woodland. It shouldn't be muddy – and when it is, there's a boardwalk – and the path is clear and easy to follow. Just the last part is uphill.

When the path meets the lane, turn right and stroll back to your car.

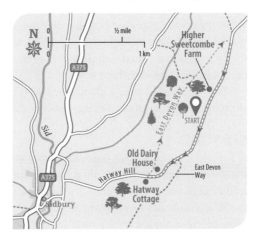

Honiton. The East Devon Way passes through and there are other good walks in the area if you don't mind climbing hills; the village lies in a deep valley.

There's a village store, a shop (J A Nice) selling decorative and interesting contemporary furnishings, and a pub, the **Red Lion** (✆ 01395 579313 ⊕ redlioninnsidbury.co.uk ⊙ closed Mon), which was rescued by the local community after the brewery had placed it on the open market. It also has four en-suite rooms. But Sidbury's great treasure is what's believed to be a **Saxon crypt** in the beautiful little church of St Giles & St Peter. One of only six known in England, it was discovered in 1898, and is open to the public only during the one-hour guided tours of it and the church that take place on Thursdays from June to September. The tour starts at 14.30 and costs £2.50, including tea and biscuits. For current details see the 'upcoming events' section of the village website, ⌀ sidbury.org.uk. I found the tiny, plain underground chamber unexpectedly moving; who knows what Saxon voices may have echoed there some 1,400 years ago, or what local preoccupations they may have discussed? The church itself, lovingly maintained, has Norman features (the tower is 12th century) but in fact is a mixture of styles, having been much altered over the years. It has some fragments of medieval wall painting, a painted gallery, some good Victorian stained glass and seven green-man carvings in the roof. Inside is a small model of how it may have looked in Saxon times. Rather surprisingly, gunpowder was stored above the porch during the Napoleonic Wars. The book *Sidbury's Church of a Thousand Years* by Barbara Softly (Westcountry Books, 2000) traces the lifetime of the church but links it to events taking place throughout the country; it's an absorbing read.

Before you leave, spare a glance for two very fine trees: a yew in the churchyard and an unusual evergreen cork oak just across the road.

13 SIDFORD

🏠 **The Salty Monk** (page 258) 🛖 **Oakdown Holiday Park**, Weston (page 258)

Many locals know Sidford only for its 20mph speed limit and double traffic lights, but as the community that grew up around the ford across the River Sid it has seen plenty of history. Porch House, built in 1574 (now the very attractive, thatched Porch Cottages), is reputed to have been a hiding place of Charles II when he was trying to escape to France (actually very unlikely since there is no record of the fugitive king travelling any further west than Charmouth). In medieval times the bridge at the eastern end of the village was an old packhorse bridge; and the **Salty Monk** nearby (page 148) was once named the Salt House, suggesting involvement in the coastal salt trade.

From Sidford a very pleasant seaward walk of about two miles takes you down the surfaced track known as The Byes into Sidmouth, crossing the Sid from time to time. Parts of the main track are shared with cyclists so you won't find long empty stretches. It's a lovely walk, enjoyable at any time of year, with a variety of paths through wildflower meadows, farmland, riverside and woodland. You're keeping roughly parallel to the main road between Sidmouth and Sidford, so if you don't want to do the full length you can always escape sideways to the road and catch a 9 or 9A bus either into Sidmouth or (via Sidford) towards Honiton, Exeter or Lyme Regis. Sidmouth's museum and tourist information centre have detailed leaflets showing this and other walks in and around Sidmouth and the Sid Valley.

14 THE DONKEY SANCTUARY

Dunscombe Ln, Weston EX19 0NU ✆ 01395 578222 ⌂ thedonkeysanctuary.org.uk/visit-us/ sidmouth ⊙ 09.00–17.00 daily

We British absolutely adore donkeys! The Donkey Sanctuary near Sidmouth is one of the most popular free attractions in England, and at the time of writing had just celebrated its 50th anniversary with a royal visit (the Duchess of Cornwall dropped in on her own birthday in 2019) and a new reception area containing an informative display of *Donkeys Through the Ages*, starting with the first evidence of domestication 6,000 years ago. The sanctuary was the life's work of Dr Elisabeth Svendsen who died in 2011. She just loved donkeys, began keeping them in 1969 with the arrival of Naughty Face, and was catapulted into starting the sanctuary in 1974 when bequeathed 204 donkeys which would otherwise be put down. Since then it has given a lifelong home to over 16,000 donkeys and mules.

The animals here must be some of the most pampered in the country, but the sanctuary is far more than just giving a forever home to these animals. Generous donations and bequests have allowed it to do valuable work abroad, particularly in Ethiopia. If a donkey gets sick or lame in Africa it can spell disaster for the family that depends on it for transport. The Sanctuary works with these owners, helping them keep their donkeys fit and healthy. Excellent work is also done closer to home with children with special needs, who benefit from donkey-assisted therapy.

The sanctuary is open year round, there's no charge for visiting and it is blessedly free of commercial trappings apart from the large shop. You can admire donkeys of all sizes and colours with their stories told through labels on the enclosures, browse the shop that has such donkey-themed items as their own version of Monopoly, and there's a very good and spacious new restaurant, **The Kitchen**. It's easy to get to with plenty of parking and the Sidmouth Hopper bus comes here, as does the number 9A bus (stopping at the top of the road). It's also the start of some good walks down to sea. No wonder it's so popular.

FROM SID TO SEATON

Once past the Donkey Sanctuary most motorists' sights are set on the seaside towns and villages described in the next chapter, but there is plenty of interest north of the A3052 if you know where to look, as well as a charming monument and intriguing sign by the road itself.

15 BLACKBURY CAMP

Colyton EX24 6JF ♀ SY1874092363; English Heritage

An Iron Age hillfort surrounded and overgrown by tall woodland, Blackbury Camp, sometimes called Blackbury Castle, gazes out – as it has done for almost 2,500 years – over valleys formed by tributaries of the River Coly. Its massive defences consist of a bank and outer ditch, enclosing a flat oval area of about 6.5 acres or two hectares. Unusual among hillforts is the triangular earthwork extension protecting its main entrance; little is identifiable to the casual visitor, but it would have had an outer entrance at its apex and ramparts that channelled people along a narrow track between the outer and inner gates. The central part of the triangle would have formed an enclosure for livestock. A timber walkway above the inner gate allowed people to pass along the top of the bank without dropping down into the entrance. The site was excavated in the 1950s but the small finds were not particularly illuminating: plentiful Iron Age pottery sherds, worked flints, four whetstones, two spindle whorls, fragments of bronze – and over 1,000 beach pebbles used as sling-stones, some of which are in Exeter Museum. The age of the pottery indicates that the fort was used from the early 3rd century BC onward, probably by a pastoral community rather than defensively, but otherwise there's little conclusive information. Interpretation boards at the site clarify the layout for visitors.

"The age of the pottery indicates that the fort was used from the early 3rd century BC onward."

Archaeology apart, what is magical about Blackbury Camp is its display of bluebells in spring. The whole of the vast interior is a haze of soft purple, spotlit by sunbeams filtering down through the canopy of branches. It's extraordinarily peaceful – visitors liken it to a cathedral and talk about 'unbelievable beauty' – and man (or woman) suddenly seems infinitely small. Its mood changes with the weather and seasons: bright, sunless, thick with vegetation, bare in winter, trees agitated by wind, frosty crispness underfoot . . . a fascinating and atmospheric place.

It's well signposted down a winding lane off the A3052, a short distance east of the Branscombe turning, and there's ample parking. At weekends you can also visit the nearby Blackbury Honey Farm.

16 BLACKBURY HONEY FARM

$\mathscr{D}$ 01404 871600 $\mathring{\mathscr{D}}$ blackburyfarm.co.uk $\odot$ Mar–Dec 10.00–17.00 Thu–Sun (dates on website). Don't try to find this by sat nav & postcode; head for Blackbury Camp & you'll see it signposted nearby.

This farm is owned and run by the Basterfield family, who began beekeeping in 1972 as a hobby but it gradually took them over. They settled here a few years ago and now welcome visitors to their café, shop and gardens as well as running beekeeping courses and other bee-linked events. 'You need to meet my husband Ken,' we heard Maureen Basterfield say to a customer who'd asked her a question. 'He's been talking about bees and honey for more than 40 years!' In the entry lobby there's a video and other sources of bee-based information, while honey and wax from the bees are used in items (fudge, flapjack, preserves, chutney, candles, lip balm ...) for the shop. A range

"Visitors can stroll in a wildflower meadow where skylarks nest or along a path around the site."

of honeys is also on sale. Visitors can stroll in a wildflower meadow where skylarks nest or along a path around the site, sit peacefully in the garden or climb up to enjoy the view from the 'lookout point' that Ken has built. The very informative website is kept up to date, so check for any current events.

The **café** serves snacks and light meals (sometimes using their home-grown vegetables and fruit) and has tables both inside and outside in the garden, a bee-friendly place with a mass of flowers. Indoors, for muddy days when outdoor boots need removing, there is even underfloor heating to cosset chilly toes! We love it.

17 DR THOMAS GILBERT-SMITH MEMORIAL & A 'HANGMAN'S STONE'

Sharp-eyed drivers approaching Seaton from the west may be curious about two memorials beside the road. The first is more visible than the other: for years as I've driven by I've been catching a glimpse of some sort of stone structure almost hidden in the long grass just before the Branscombe turn-off. I've wondered idly what it was but never stopped to look. Now I have, and it's delightful! It's a three-sided marble slab – perhaps originally a seat – with wording on each of its sides. On the left side it says:

> At this spot at half past nine o'clock after watching the glorious sunset of August Third, 1904, Thomas Gilbert-Smith, M.D., F.R.C.S. fell dead from his bicycle. Thunder and lightning immediately followed.

The other side continues:

> Thus closed a noble life spent in the service of his fellow men. He never turned his back on duty, but faithful to his motto "Dare and do" remained undaunted to the end.

Then the date, 1904. At the back is a sad plaque explaining that there used to be a portrait of Dr Gilbert-Smith in profile, but all the plaques were stolen in 1981.

Who erected the memorial we'll never know and now you take your life in your hands to see it – at least in the summer when the grass is high, necessitating walking on the edge of the road. If you want to give it a go approach from the east and park in the lay-by just after the Branscombe turn-off. It's about 20 yards before the monument.

You'll see the name of the second on the signpost where the B3174 to Beer forks off the A3052: the **Hangman's Stone**. The 'stone' or chunk of granite will have been put there (or thereabouts: it has probably been shifted a few times) long ago, when roadways were less distinct, to mark the Beer turning, and the 'hangman' legend grew up around it. Supposedly a local man had stolen a sheep, tied a rope round its neck and was trying to lead it home, when he sat down beside the stone for a rest and fell asleep. Somehow or other the sheep then got its rope tangled round his neck, gave a good tug and strangled him. Rough justice. The sheep's subsequent fate is not recorded. But since a similar tale is attributed to at least a dozen other 'hangman's stones' in various parts of England, you should take it with a hearty pinch of seaside salt!

18 HOLYFORD WOODS

This lovely woodland reserve is the closest one to Seaton and much loved by walkers and nature enthusiasts for its display of bluebells in the spring and, later, wood anemones, while birds can be heard year round including the drumming of woodpeckers. A little stream runs through the central part of the reserve and interpretation boards show you the circular trails and explain the policy of letting dead wood rot to provide habitat for a variety of wildlife. There is no parking adjacent to the reserve; leave your car in the lay-by before the Tower service station, cross the main road, and take the signed footpath down a meadow and into the woods.

FOOD & DRINK ALONG THE A3052

There's absolutely no reason to go hungry when driving or cycling the 22 miles between the Clyst St Mary roundabout and Lyme Regis. The road abounds with some of the best restaurants, farm shops and cafés in the region.

To start you off and described on page 116 is Clyst St Mary's **Half Moon Inn**. Then about a mile after the roundabout, on the right, you'll come to The Kitchen 1925 at **St Bridget Nursery** (EX5 1AE ✆ 01392 531277 ⚭ stbridgetnurseries.co.uk). You wouldn't go here just for the food, but as a garden centre and plant nursery it's excellent, winning an award in 2019 for the Best Family Business of the Year, and with a huge selection of plants. The nursery has been run by the same family for four generations so clearly they know their stuff. Some of their plants are unique to them. Go for a snack but expect to come out with enough plants to start a rival to Kew Gardens.

If it's a pub you're looking for, your first option is the **Cat & Fiddle** (EX5 1DP ✆ 01392 873317 ⚭ catandfiddleinn.co.uk ⊙ 11.00–22.30) about a mile further on. Newly refurbished with a spacious dining area, it is particularly family friendly, serving traditional pub food all day.

'Please don't feed the ostrich' is not a sign you'd expect to see in Devon, but nothing surprises me at the **Greendale Farm Shop** (EX5 2JU ✆ 01392 232836 ⚭ greendalefarmshop.co.uk ⊙ 08.00–20.00 Mon–

Sat, 09.00–18.00 Sun). This exceptional place, on the right soon after Crealy Adventure Park, is perhaps the best of its kind in the region and – who knows – beyond. First, there's its pedigree. As if it wasn't enough to farm 1,500 acres, the family also have their own fishing fleet. That's the secret of fish that was described to me as 'the freshest I've ever tasted'. They do eat-in or take-out fish and chips, and have a range of other seafood dishes. The fish counter is a marvel: you can see how fresh it is and there's a huge variety to choose from including local lobsters (alive in a tank) and crabs. Did you know that male and female crabs are cocks and hens? I didn't. The farm raises cattle and sheep and has its own butcher, so again you know that the meat is not only as local as you can get, but outdoor reared in the best possible conditions. I'm sure the fruit and vegetables, also grown on the farm, are happy too and I wouldn't be surprised if the bees that provide the local honey had smiles on their faces. This place defines 'locally sourced food' and I defy you to come out empty handed. It's child-friendly too, with two tractors for kids to play on, free-range chickens scuffling around and some contented-looking geese – and the ostrich.

"I wouldn't be surprised if the bees that provide the local honey had smiles on their faces."

Next stop, just before the turn-off to Exeter Airport, is the popular, family-friendly **White Horse Inn** (✆ 01395 232244 🖥 whitehorsewoodburysalterton.co.uk ⊙ 11.30–14.30 & 17.30–22.30), which prides itself on its local food and does a good Sunday roast from 12.00 onwards. A large children's play area keeps the kids entertained.

Halfway Inn (✆ 01395 232273 🖥 thehalfwayinnexeter.co.uk ⊙ 11.30–15.00 & 17.00–23.00 Tue–Sun) is on the left, a mile further on. The name could refer to it being halfway between Sidmouth and Exeter, or halfway between Penzance and London on the old roads. It won the Silver award from Taste of the West, and serves traditional pub food at lunch time with a more elaborate menu in the evening, including such local delicacies as Exmouth mussels. The excellent Sunday carvery is served from 12.00 to 19.00.

You now pass through Newton Poppleford (page 120) which has lost three restaurants since the last edition of this book – hopefully the situation will be rectified soon. Meanwhile you can enjoy a great lunch or cream tea at the **Southern Cross Tea Rooms** (✆ 01395 568439), either inside or in the lovely garden.

After crossing the River Otter you'll see the sign for **Four Elms Fruit Farm** (📞 01395 568286 🌐 fourelmsfruitfarm.co.uk) on your left. Their six varieties of award-winning apple juice are sold throughout the county, and they have recently added a range of ciders. Their own outlet, **The Apple Shed**, is normally only open weekdays, October to February (best to check by phone), when they sell their fresh apples, juice and cider, as well as their own honey.

The road now climbs steeply uphill before the next place, **East Hill Pride Farm Shop** (EX10 0ND 📞 07969 024749 🌐 easthillpridefarmshop. co.uk ⊙ Easter–Sep & Dec 09.00–17.00 Mon–Sat, 10.00–16.00 Sun, Jan–Easter, Oct & Nov 09.00–16.00 Mon–Sat). John and Cynthia Coles are licensed slaughterers, which means that their free-range animals have the best possible life before appearing on our dinner tables. Thus their Sunday roasts (Easter to Sep) stand out as the most animal-friendly in the area; served at one of the outdoor tables overlooking the spacious Otter Valley, they are hard to beat. Indeed, they are our choice for the best roast dinner in East Devon, with the vegetables equally fresh and perfectly cooked. There's usually a good selection of cakes and an indoor eating area for year-round snacks. Fruit and vegetables are grown in poly tunnels – the strawberries ripen early and are particularly delicious – and pick-your-own fruit is also available.

Continue for a mile and you'll come to **The Bowd Inn** (📞 01395 513328 🌐 thebowdinn.co.uk ⊙ 12.00–midnight Mon–Sat; food 12.00–15.00 & 17.00–21.00, 12.00–20.00 Sun), on the left at the turn-off to Ottery St Mary. This classic thatched Devon pub is deservedly very popular; its meals are reasonably priced and well cooked, and it has an every-day carvery to satisfy the most ardent carnivore. A further mile and there's **Kings Garden Centre** (📞 01395 516142) bought in 2018 by the Kings who also own a similar garden centre in Exmouth. It has now regained its happy ambience of a few years back, with friendly and helpful staff. The café/restaurant is very good, with an outside terrace overlooking the gardens and indoor seating by the picture windows. The homemade food includes a good range of cakes, scones and desserts, and the cafeteria-style service ensures that you get your meal quickly. The region's only **Waitrose** comes up next on the right, and then traffic slows down (this is a 20mph zone) as you pass through Sidford. **Bloaters fish & chips** is an option here, or a Chinese restaurant if you are experiencing a craving. Serious eating is done at the Salty Monk and Blue Ball pubs.

The Salty Monk (☏ 01395 513174 ⌂ saltymonk.co.uk) gets its charming name from the fact that it was once the salt house for Benedictine monks, and is becoming known for gourmet meals and its boutique guest rooms, providing a complete treat for a special occasion, including a seven-course taster menu. The food is very good

PAST TIMES

Did you spot the vintage petrol pumps at the side of the A3052 in Colyford as you drove by? Their history spans over 90 years.

A local farmer named W H Davey started the ball rolling in 1927. At a time when petrol was often sold from pumps outside a barn or shed, he saw the potential of a purpose-built petrol station and called on Axminster architect Frederick S Kett, who based his design on a wooden station at Countess Wear but built it in brick and blocks. It opened in 1928, dispensing Shell, BP, National Benzole and Redline petrol from four hand-operated pumps.

Aircraftman Thomas Edward Shaw, better remembered as Lawrence of Arabia, was a frequent visitor, stopping to fill up his Brough Superior Motorcycle (he described it as 'a skittish motorcycle with a touch of blood in it') when roaring it between his home near Wareham in Dorset and his Royal Airforce posting in Plymouth. We can imagine that he got to know Mr Davey, and that they chatted while the pump gurgled out its fuel. Apparently it was on one of these trips that he had his fatal accident in Dorset in 1935.

In the 1930s Devon Council demanded that local petrol stations be smartened up, and Colyford's was quoted as the best example to follow. Meanwhile, relevantly or not, Frederick Kett was entrusted (in 1937) with the installation of public conveniences in

Charmouth. Then during World War II petrol was rationed and petrol coupons were issued, to ensure that enough remained available for the vital services, so sales slumped. The post-war end of rationing boosted them again, leading the main petrol companies to persuade garages to switch exclusively to their brand. Mr Davey, who continued running the Colyford station until the 1970s, ditched his other suppliers in favour of Shell.

Petrol was dispensed there until 2001. In 2003 the then owner built an extension at one end to house his large collection of motoring memorabilia, and opened it in 2004 as a motoring museum. By 2011 it had become too much and he closed it down. In 2012 the original station (minus his extension) was designated a Grade II-listed monument, interesting for its pumps and as 'a rare surviving example of a 1920s architect-designed filling station, intended to be sympathetic to its rural location'. And the pumps (the original ones were replaced in 1950 and the early 1980s) remain at their posts.

Today you can buy equipment for your cycle – or even an e-bike – in Colyford Cycles behind them, and pause for a snack in the Filling Station Café as you drive by. Perhaps Aircraftman Thomas Edward Shaw would have approved?

indeed, the service attentive but not overbearing, and the décor done with a flair. Prices are in the upper range, with side dishes extra, so if you are just looking for pub grub the **Blue Ball** (✆ 01395 514062 🖥 blueballsidford.co.uk) is a better bet. Originally 14th-century and skilfully rebuilt after a devastating fire in 2007, it has been in the same family for five generations and serves reasonably priced meals including a Sunday carvery.

There is now quite a gap in places to eat until you get to Colyford. If you just want to pick up a quick bite there, the village shop, **Pritchards**, sells lunch-time snacks and picnic supplies. Continuing down the hill, behind a row of antique petrol pumps (no, they don't work! see box, opposite) on the right there's **The Filling Station Café & Colyford Cycles** (good coffee, irresistible cakes and hot or cold snacks), on the left the **Wheelwright Inn** (a welcoming 17th-century pub with a changing menu) and at the bottom by the tramway station (you may need to pause for trams crossing the road) the popular **White Hart Inn**. The above four are covered on page 209.

Since it opened in 2015 the **Rousdon Village Bakery** (✆ 01297 442342 ☉ 08.30–14.00 daily), run along similar lines to its counterpart in Lyme (Town Mill Bakery; page 240), has had a Marmite response from its diners: you either love it or hate it (read the TripAdvisor reports before going). Its brunches are definitely good but by lunchtime the food has often run out. The ordering process is confusing to newcomers: you help yourself to home-baked bread (sourdough a speciality) and anything else that's available, sit at a long table with other eaters, and just tell the staff what you've eaten when it's time to pay. It's very casual, but the formula works and the bakery part is very good.

Continue a few miles beyond Rousdon and you'll get your first sight of the sea. Dorset and Lyme Regis, with its gastronomic delights, are below you.

EAST DEVON & THE JURASSIC COAST ONLINE

For additional online content, articles, photos and more on East Devon and the Jurassic Coast, why not visit 🖥 bradtguides.com/edevon?

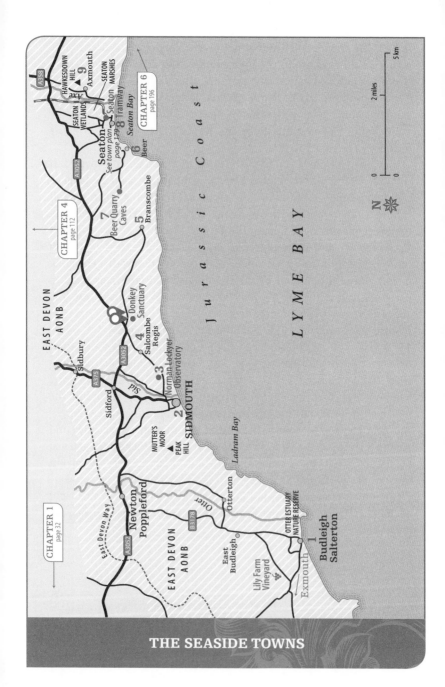

THE SEASIDE TOWNS

5

THE SEASIDE TOWNS

> The grand rocks sink at intervals to give place to magnificent bays which sweep gracefully from cliff's point to cliff's point, and help to fling all over the coast scenery of this most beautiful of English counties the same aspect of variety which is its most charming characteristic.

Francis George Heath, *The Fern Paradise*, 1875

Seaside towns as such started to develop in Heath's 'magnificent bays' in the Regency period; 1750 saw the first record of claims that sea bathing was beneficial, and by the end of that century the familiar attractions of seaside towns were well established. Originally bathing took place in the winter, whether a quick spartan dip in the ocean or in heated sea water. To reap the full benefits, immersion before 10am was recommended, as was drinking four quarts of sea water. Then, as that new-fangled monster the railway began to reach the coast, previously sleepy towns saw an increasing influx of visitors and a consequent spread of bathing paraphernalia (tents, machines, attendants …) to preserve their modesty.

It's a very different scene today, although the seaside towns and villages in this chapter have all retained traces of Victorian sedateness. Their beaches are still fringed by small colonies of much-loved, cheerily painted beach huts, where families and retired couples set out their deckchairs and brew up tea on camping stoves; visitors stroll along the promenade admiring the view, or sit, often bravely windswept, on strategically placed wooden benches. Children build castles or patterns out of stones for want of sand (although some stretches are sandy), or play in rock pools, or catch crabs; and seagulls are poised to grab at that last chip or sandwich crust.

But meanwhile a new buzz has been creeping into our old traditional seasides, like the tide creeping up a beach. Watersports have taken hold in a big way, with kayakers and stand-up paddleboarders now enlivening the bays. Today's visitors show greater interest in the history and culture of the towns they visit, so local museums have improved and the work of local artists and craftspeople has become more visible. Food has increased in importance, and even small places compete to serve the freshest and highest-quality local produce. Music and literary festivals such as those in Budleigh Salterton and Sidmouth attract top-range speakers and visitors from far afield. The fiendish cross-country Grizzly race in Seaton has international participants, and the Donkey Sanctuary near Sidmouth receives visitors from every part of the UK and beyond.

But alongside the new animation we still have the tranquil and perfectly curved bays along this stretch of coast, the extensive views and fresh, fresh air on the cliffs, and the peaceful lanes and side-roads that link the villages together. Moreover, these same cliffs are a part of UNESCO's Jurassic Coast with its multi-million-year history (see the Jurassic Coast boxes on pages 26 and 154), and the paths beneath your feet lie on land where dinosaurs roamed. This exciting heritage is celebrated in Seaton Jurassic, which opened in early 2016; and these Jurassic links and their uniqueness rank high among reasons to visit this very special part of Britain.

 WET-WEATHER ACTIVITIES

Budleigh Salterton Fairlynch Museum (page 157)
Sidmouth Museum (page 162)
Seaton Jurassic Centre (page 185)
Seaton Museum (page 181)

GETTING THERE & AROUND

Writing in 1922 and advocating exploring the area on foot, Eric Holmes (*Wanderings in Wessex*) makes some rather grumpy comparisons.

> To go from one Dorset or East Devon town to another by rail involves an amount of thought and consultation of timetables that would not be required for a journey from London to Aberystwyth ... From Lyme to Seaton by the Landslip is barely seven miles; by rail it is 15, involving two changes. From Seaton to Sidmouth is nine miles by road and 24 by rail, with two changes and a possible third.

Perhaps it's just as well that Sidmouth and Seaton lost their railway links in the Beeching cuts of the 1960s! Both now have good bus links to the Exeter–Waterloo line via Honiton and Axminster respectively and there are other bus services throughout this area, some taking the 'scenic routes' (beautiful!) and others more direct.

Driving is mostly easy; there are a few single-track stretches, but not too fearsome. For motorised travel the map you need is ✱ OS Landranger 192, *Exeter & Sidmouth*. Walkers and cyclists will want the more detailed Croydecycle maps: ✱ *East Devon Exeter* (which stretches to Lyme Regis and beyond) or ✱ *Exmouth & Sidmouth Cycle Map*. Also see the *Sidmouth Hopper* box below.

SELF-POWERED TRAVEL

The busier roads make cycling more challenging near the popular resorts, but there are two dedicated cycle ways. NCN Route 2 runs from Exmouth to Budleigh Salterton along a disused railway line, and through Sidmouth and Seaton to Axminster and beyond, while The Buzzard Route (NCN52) follows the NCN2 from Exmouth to Knowle on the outskirts of Budleigh Salterton, then along lanes to Sidmouth and up the Byes to Sidford. Seaton and northward to Kilmington are on the Stop Line Way (page 21). For cycle hire and service see page 183.

Walkers can enjoy the very best of East Devon: its South West Coast Path and a plethora of footpaths inland. Some are described in this chapter and *Chapter 4*, but with Croydecycle's maps ✱ *Sidmouth*, and ✱ *Beer, Branscombe & Seaton* you don't need written directions. OS Explorer Map 115, ✱ *Exmouth & Sidmouth*, will fill in any gaps.

SIDMOUTH HOPPER

This terrific summer service (late May to early September), run by Sidmouth Town Council, provides an almost hourly shuttle around Sidmouth taking in the main places of interest: Sidmouth centre, Mutter's Moor, Kings Garden Centre, the Lockyer Observatory and the Donkey Sanctuary. This allows you to leave your car in Sidmouth and still get to a variety of local walks. The bus will, if it's safe to stop, pick you up or drop you anywhere on its route. One note of warning: it carries only 16 passengers so on school holidays not everyone who is waiting may be able to get on at the most popular visitor attraction, the Donkey Sanctuary. A family of six were turned away when I was there. Buses 899 and 9A are alternatives, or you could just pat some more donkeys and wait for the next Hopper. To help finance the service there's a flat-rate single fare of £1 for adults, 50p for children and 50p for dogs, and bus passes aren't valid, but honestly it's worth it!

When planning walks along the coastal path, bear in mind that the stretch just east of Sidmouth is very tough, with a lot of steep hills. It is also very beautiful with terrific views. Bus-assisted walks are easy to organise as the seaside towns are well served by public transport. Take binoculars on all cliff walks; you stand a chance of seeing dolphins, seals, basking sharks or even (if you're really lucky) whales, as well as a large variety of seabirds, including cormorants and shags basking in the sun on the cliffs at Beer.

The annual **Sidmouth Walking Festival** in late September offers a week of free local walks in Sidmouth and beyond, run in groups with knowledgeable leaders and ranging from four to ten miles. They must be booked in advance through the Sidmouth TIC (✆ 01395 516441 ✉ ticinfo@sidmouth.gov.uk). There are also longer ones taking in parts

THE GEOLOGY & HISTORY OF DEVON'S JURASSIC COASTAL TOWNS

Mike Green

There's no escaping geology. It affects architecture, flora and fauna, industry, farming and history, all of which constantly change as you travel along the Jurassic Coast.

Your Jurassic journey began in **Exmouth** (page 68) at the geoneedle on Orcombe Point. The rocks there have recently been reassessed as Permian (the previous period), but soon you enter the Triassic period. In **Budleigh Salterton**, the outstanding geological feature is the pebbles on the beach. These are characteristically flat and originate from the pebble beds, observed in the cliffs to the west of Steamers Steps. They are much older (probably Silurian from Brittany) and were washed into the Triassic desert by a huge river running north as far as Bristol. Another feature is the calcareous concretions (calcified ancient roots) on the seafront. The cliffs to the other side of the estuary are Otter sandstones. This sandstone, along with cobbles, buns and local clay bricks, can be viewed in local buildings. Note that the eastward drift of the pebbles has created a shingle bar, closing the river mouth and pushing it eastwards.

Ladram Bay's outstanding feature is its sea stacks, left behind when arches created by the sea eventually gave way. The Otter sandstone at the bottom of the stacks resists erosion better than the mudstones above.

Sidmouth is ideal to view the gentle tilt in the rocks and faulting near Jacob's Ladder. The Otter sandstones disappear below the surface here, but are visible again, due to this faulting, on the other side of town at Pennington Point. A rare rhynchosaur fossil was found here. With a keen eye one can spot an ancient burrow in the cliffs on the Millennium Walk. The brick kilns of Sidmouth, like the others, are now long gone.

To the west of **Branscombe** on the beach can be seen layers of gypsum salts (calcium sulphate – plaster of Paris), the result of of the East Devon Way, which include coach transport (paying) to and from the starting point. Also see ⊘ visitsidmouth.co.uk.

WATERSPORTS & ACTIVITIES

The popularity of sports such as kayaking, kitesurfing, windsurfing and stand-up paddleboarding is increasing rapidly, and the wide but sheltered bays along this coast are ideal sites. Equipment is more readily available for hire, and once-sedate beaches are now attracting a new wave of more energetic visitors. Even if Slower travellers don't want to 'take the plunge', the activities are still fun – and sometimes quite breathtaking – to watch.

temporary *playa* lakes evaporating after flash flooding in the Triassic desert. As you progress eastwards the clifftops become more and more capped with Cretaceous upper greensand and eventually chalk, all laid down under the sea. Many of the buildings here are built with chert, a flint-like stone from the upper greensands. In the cliff to the west of Branscombe Mouth the Cretaceous sits directly on the Triassic; the Jurassic is missing. It is a classic *unconformity*, highlighted by the break of slope and a change in vegetation. The greensand is porous and absorbs the rain which, when it reaches the impervious Triassic clays below, is forced out and causes a spring line. At **Beer** the geology becomes entirely Cretaceous forming impressive white chalk cliffs; these shelter the bay from the prevailing sou'westerly gales, creating a haven for fishing and, at one time, smuggling. The geology provides Beer freestone, a good carving stone discovered

by the Romans and used for building along with chert and flint. The flint was first used by Neolithic settlers for tool-making. The sea erodes caves in the limestone and fossils can be found on the beaches.

Between Beer and **Seaton** at Seaton Hole is a fault line where the cliffs turn red again. Used for making the famous 'SEATOИ' brick, these soft mudstones are constantly eroding, causing cliff falls and destruction. A long shingle beach pushes the river mouth eastwards at **Axmouth**.

Beyond Axmouth Harbour and Culverhole Point (near a fine spread of ammonites on the shore), the Jurassic makes its first brief appearance, eventually dominating at Pinhay Bay. Further on, just before the Dorset border, lies another magnificent ammonite pavement. Finally, over the border in Dorset is **Lyme Regis**, birthplace of the 19th-century fossil collector Mary Anning and arguably also of palaeontology.

BUDLEIGH SALTERTON & AREA

Tourist information: Fore St, Budleigh Salterton EX9 6NG ✆ 01395 445275 🖥 visitbudleigh. com ⏰ 10.00–16.30 Mon–Sat (check for seasonal changes)

Walkers, cyclists and particularly birdwatchers are catered for here: the South West Coast Path runs through, to either Ladram Bay or Exmouth, as does part of the Buzzard Cycle Route, and the Otter Estuary (page 159) is a haven for birds.

1 BUDLEIGH SALTERTON

🏠 **Long Range Hotel** (page 259), **Pebbles B&B** (page 259), 🏠 **Pebbles the Apartment** (page 259)

> This village is caullid Salterne, and hath beene in tymes past a thing of sum Estimation.
>
> John Leland, 1540

Towns have different specialities. One may have a historic church, another some picturesque cottages, a third particularly fine gardens. Budleigh Salterton has – pebbles. It's attractive in other ways too, of course, but the stones on its beach are remarkable: smooth, multi-hued and rather smug, as they gleam up at you with an air of 'yes we *know* we are beautiful'. In fact they're probably saying 'nous sommes beaux' because, as the box on page 154 explains, they're foreigners, probably French. 'Budleigh Buns', they're sometimes called, and indeed some are plump and bun-like, but no bun has such subtle colouring. And no, you must not collect them! A local woman told me with horror in her eyes of someone who had been spotted going to the beach with – gasp – a *wheelbarrow*. Just not done. Another resident remembered hearing of a freak storm that stripped them away in the night, leaving just grey silt. In the morning the townspeople were appalled. Where was their beach? Fortunately Neptune was on their side and the sea threw back the pebbles (or possibly washed away silt that had been hiding them) on the next rising tide.

"The stones on its beach are remarkable: smooth, multi-hued and rather smug, as they gleam up at you."

Walking along Fore Street with its thriving independent shops and businesses, you'd never guess that two miles of curving beach were just a stone's throw (sorry) away. Residents use it extensively: walking, exercising dogs, flying kites, swimming – it's a beautiful bay, and the town's biggest natural asset. The town's previous name of Salterne or Salterton refers to salt pans in the area, back in the days when panning sea-salt was an important coastal industry.

The beach plays a starring role in the 1870 painting by Sir John Millais, *The Boyhood of Raleigh*, now in Tate Britain. A young Walter Raleigh (who was born nearby; see box, page 136) and his brother are sitting by the shore, listening raptly to tales of 'wonders on sea and land' told by a 'sunburnt, stalwart Genoese sailor'. And there are Budleigh Buns (although not particularly fine ones) at their feet. Millais painted part of it in Budleigh Salterton, in the Octagon in Fore Street, and some of the rough stone wall shown in the background is still *in situ*. There's plenty of other history here too, and some fine old houses. For instance the **Fairlynch Museum** (Fore St ✆ 01395 442666 ⊘ devonmuseums.net/fairlynch ⊙ Apr–Oct 14.00–16.30), dating from 1811, is one of very few thatched museums in the UK (the building is Grade II-listed), and a typical example of a marine *cottage orné*: really one of the prettiest museums in the South West and with a beautiful, colourful garden. It has an extensive collection of period costume, including some rare clothing from the early 18th century, as well as displays covering the geology and archaeology of the area, a lace room, early seafaring explorers, period toys, railway memorabilia, important works by local artists, a smugglers' den, a Walter Raleigh room (the 400th anniversary of his execution was in 2018), a local history room with information on all aspects of Budleigh Salterton life throughout the ages, and changing temporary displays. Its staff and helpers between them have a huge fund of knowledge, enterprise and enthusiasm; do note its rather limited opening hours, and try to fit in a visit.

"Its staff and helpers between them have a huge fund of knowledge, enterprise and enthusiasm."

This is an artistically minded town: there are some good galleries, for example the **Brook Gallery** in Fore Street (✆ 01395 443003 ⊘ brookgallery.co.uk) with its striking range of work by mainly established artists. An important week-long classic **Music Festival** is held annually in July (box office ✆ 01395 445275 ⊘ budleighmusicfestival.co.uk) with an impressive programme of established and emerging talent; and there's always an outstanding line-up of authors at the annual **Literary Festival** in September (box office as above budlitfest.org.uk), whose Honorary President is Dame Hilary Mantel. For current details of the **Jazz and Blues Festival**, **Food Festival** and other upcoming events, check visitbudleigh.com or contact the tourist office (page 156).

Lily Farm Vineyard

Knowle EX9 7AH 01395 443877, 07977 057864 lilyfarmvineyard.com
 10.00–16.00 Thu–Sat, tours Apr–Sep 14.00.

At Knowle, which is just a couple of miles west of Budleigh and signposted from the town centre, this small, family-run vineyard (the owner describes it as 'boutique') produces award-winning, world-class wines that are unique to Budleigh Salterton. One of England's smallest commercial vineyards it may be, but I counted more than 50 awards that it has received in the past ten years.

The wine is made exclusively from grapes grown and picked at Lily Farm, and each batch has its own distinctive character. Some finds its way to local restaurants or retailers, but most is sold via mail order and direct from the vineyard.

Also – the vineyard is beautiful! The vines stretching neatly up the hillside, and their particular shade of green, seem to belong there; to be a part of the countryside. We know the Romans planted vines in Devon, and I found myself wondering whether any had made their way down the estuary from Isca Dumnoniorum and discovered this little corner.

Guided tours of the vineyard cost £10 per person. They cover the life cycle of a vine from planting and how it is cared for, a brief outline of English wine, a tasting of three wines, and of course the chance to buy some to take home. It's a Slow, peaceful, fascinating place and well worth a visit. There's parking, and bus 357 (Exmouth to Budleigh) stops a two-minute walk away in Knowle.

¶| FOOD & DRINK

Granny Gothards Ice Cream & Desserts 53 High St 07895 345033 grannygothards. co.uk 10.30–17.30 daily (17.00 Sat & Sun). Exactly what the name suggests, plus homemade cakes, toasties and very good waffles.

Marco's Italian Restaurant 7 High St 01395 442676 approx 11.00–15.00 Tue, 11.00–16.00 & 18.00–23.00 Wed–Mon. A new and cheery arrival in Budleigh, serving authentic Italian food. Times, etc, may change as it settles in.

A Slice of Lyme 1–2 Rolle Rd ☎ 01395 442628 ⌂ sliceoflyme.co.uk ⌚ 10.00–14.30 Mon–Fri, 10.00–16.00 Sat, 12.00–16.00 Sun, plus 18.00–21.00 Fri. Its Daily specials always include a fresh fish catch, with international bistro food in the evenings. Good all-day breakfasts.

Tea & Tittle Tattle 4 Fore St ☎ 01395 443203 ⌂ www.teaandtittletattle.co.uk ⌚ from 10.00 Tue–Sat, from 12.00 Sun. Award-winning licensed café for lunches and vintage afternoon teas. Good, unpretentious home cooking and pleasant staff. Popular Sunday lunches.

OTTER ESTUARY

As is also the case elsewhere along this pebbly coast, the mouth of the estuary was once much wider and deeper and could accommodate shipping, but over the centuries the tides and silt and shingle have closed it in. Back in 1901 it was – surprisingly – host to an invasion of several thousand octopuses, which raided the crab and lobster pots offshore and devoured the contents. (It's to be hoped that the townspeople then devoured the invaders.)

It has a year-round bird population and there are hides on both banks; on the west bank is the Otter Estuary Nature Reserve. You may see egrets and the occasional glossy ibis, together with shelduck which breed in small numbers. The meadows adjoining the river's lower reaches provide nesting sites for lapwings, while sand martins are found on both the lower and the middle reaches. Grey wagtails, dippers and herons are also numerous, as are overflying buzzards – and the Otter is particularly important for kingfishers, with breeding recorded along its whole length. On the cliffs you may spot peregrine falcons. The most rewarding way to see the reserve is to combine it with the beautiful cliff-top walk from Otterton (see box, page 132). Don't forget your binoculars.

SIDMOUTH & AREA

Sidmouth is not a staring jerry-built town. Its streets are fringed with shops of sober appearance and houses not of yesterday's build, many of them gay with flowers in the summer months; it bears an air of quiet, decent prosperity, and is essentially restful and comfortable.

From a 1930 guidebook

Today's Sidmouth has strayed somewhat from that description. It's such a popular resort that it's not particularly Slow; at busy tourist times the beach and promenade are buzzing. But indeed it is still a pleasant place. Its curving, shingly bay is beautifully positioned between red cliffs (a striking contrast to nearby Beer's chalky white ones), it blazes with flowers and floral displays in spring and summer, and there are some charming, dignified old buildings.

John Betjeman loved it, as shown in *Still Sidmouth*, the poetic commentary he wrote to Jonathan Stedall's 1962 television film on Sidmouth, and the town is rich in commemorative 'blue plaques' (the museum and TIC have informative leaflets about these).

2 THE TOWN

⛪ **Elizabeth Hotel** (page 257), **The Old Farmhouse** (page 259)

Tourist information: Ham Ln (near the lifeboat station) ✎ 01395 516441 ✎ visitsidmouth. co.uk ☉ May–Sep 10.00–17.00 Mon–Sat, 10.00–16.00 Sun, Oct–Apr times vary.

Sidmouth is such a mix of styles. Only a block or two from the beach you're in the narrow streets of the old town, where historic buildings rub shoulders cosily with new arrivals; while Peak Hill stretches up the west side of town with gracious houses and the neatly tended Cliff Fields, a mass of daffodils in spring.

There's some worthwhile architecture (see the *Sidmouth Orné* box, page 164); much of it in the early 20th century was the work of little-known architect R W Sampson (1866–1950). He was responsible for the massive Victoria Hotel, which (as described beforehand in 1903) was to be:

> An hotel of a very substantial and excellent description, and of a distinctly high-class order, fitted with all the best and most modern requirements, including the installation of electric light. The prices too would be high class – not less than four guineas – and there was no intention of having anything in the shape of a bar.

The last phrase was a sop to the Temperance Society, which had been raising objections. The hotel opened in 1904; today, skilfully restored to its original grandeur, equipped with a bar and costing rather more than four guineas, it has become a Sidmouth institution.

Other architectural delights include the 'strawberry Gothic' houses in Coburg Terrace, the Royal Glen Hotel in Glen Road, and the *cottage orné* Woodlands Hotel in Station Road with its wonderfully ornate eaves (currently blushing prettily after a coat of pale pink paint!). The music room at the Sidholme Hotel (Elysian Fields *℘* 01395 515104 *♂* christianguild. co.uk/sidholme), with its cut-glass chandeliers, marble fireplaces and superb hand-painted ceiling, dates from 1848 and is said to be the finest in Devon; regular musical events are held there. In Coburg Terrace, the privately owned Old Chancel looks historic but in fact was built in the 1860s from reclaimed church materials by historian, antiquarian, author and watercolourist Peter Orlando Hutchinson (1810–1897).

The TIC and museum have leaflets for a Sampson Trail around the town, devised by the active Sampson Society (*♂* rwsampson.com). There are also leaflets for self-guided walks round Sidmouth, particularly to see the variety of its architecture; and guided walks (Tue & Thu) leave from the museum, as does a fossil walk on Wednesdays.

There's a traditional indoor food market in – yes – Market Place, and small independent shops of all kinds, several of them tucked away from the two main shopping streets in attractive side lanes and courtyards. In Church Street the excellent butcher, Hayman's (*♂* haymansbutchers. co.uk), run by the Hayman family since 1907, has an impressive range of good local meats, including unusual items like goat-leg steaks or beef-and-seaweed burgers. Next door is The Dairy Shop, 'home of Sidmouth Gin' (was it mother's milk to them...?), where you can also take your own bottle or container to fill up with milk. The gin is indeed made locally, in the centre of town in their own still, which is named Verity, and it has enticing flavours: sea truffle, honey and orange, pink gooseberry, seashore and rhubarb (see *♂* sidmouthgin.co.uk). More soberly, two good bookshops, Paragon Books (*♂* paragonbooks.wordpress.com) and Winstones (*♂* winstonebooks.co.uk/sidmouth), are within a stone's throw of each other at numbers 10 and 38 in the High Street. Modernisation hasn't quite caught up with Sidmouth: a sign on the wall of the happily old-fashioned Fields Department Store proclaims 'For Service as it used to be'; the Radway Cinema, while presenting modern films and streamed productions, maintains its charming 1930s décor and often a friendly greeting at the door from the manager; and the traditional Manor Pavilion Theatre's summer season of weekly repertory includes – to the evident pleasure of its audiences – plays that were already rep stalwarts

"The gin is indeed made locally, in the centre of town in their own still, which is named Verity."

DAME PARTINGTON & HER MOP

In November 1824, a terrible storm hit Sidmouth. Gale-force winds coincided with a high tide, and waves lashed up from the shore into the streets. One lone soul struggled vainly to protect her cottage. The Rev Sydney Smith, likening it to the Lords' attempted rejection of the Reform Bill in 1831, recalled the story:

> In the midst of this sublime and terrible storm,
> Dame Partington, who lived upon the beach,
> was seen at the door of her house with mop and pattens,
> trundling her mop, squeezing out the sea-water,
> and vigorously pushing away the Atlantic Ocean.
> The Atlantic was roused: Mrs Partington's spirit was up.
> But I need not tell you that the contest was unequal;
> the Atlantic Ocean beat Mrs Partington.
> She was excellent at slop or puddle, but should
> never have meddled with a tempest.

Never mind that Sidmouth is actually on the English Channel rather than the Atlantic – the Reverend made his parliamentary point.

50 years ago and more. (The theatre is open year-round, with a variety of productions from one-man shows to musicals.)

However, the annual week-long **Sidmouth Folk Festival** in early August (box office ☏ 01395 577952 ⌕ sidmouthfolkweek.co.uk) is strictly 21st-century and is one of England's best folk festivals, with a miscellany of established and emerging performers, as well as storytelling, workshops, dance and much more. It's huge: it fills the town, blocks the traffic, defies the weather, caters for every age group, attracts a mass of national and international visitors and is a thoroughly enjoyable jamboree. If such things appeal (Betjeman might not have liked it …) and you are in the area at the beginning of August, don't miss it, but ideally come by bus (the 9A between Exeter and Lyme stops right in the heart of town) rather than trying to drive in and park.

Sidmouth Museum

Church St ☏ 01395 516139 ⌕ sidvaleassociation.org.uk/museum ⌚ Mar–Oct 10.00–16.00 Mon–Sat

The museum in this attractive large Regency cottage, by the lych gate of the parish church, illustrates the development of the town from its start as a fishing village through its growth in Regency and Victorian times and to the present day. Many famous residents and visitors are commemorated, and changing exhibitions celebrate local and national events. It's a fascinating place, really a case of 'cramming a quart into a pint pot', and worth a Slow visit. Exhibits include antique dolls, lacemaking, railway memorabilia, and of course the geology, archaeology and history of the area. One treasure is a replica of a Roman hand mirror, found during excavations in Upper Holcombe (Uplyme); also, rather gruesomely but fun for children, a model (not to scale!) of the recently demolished 'Sidmouth fatberg'. Author R L Delderfield has a section, as do Norman Lockyer

"One treasure is a replica of a Roman hand mirror, found during excavations in Upper Holcombe."

(page 166) and the artist Lawson Wood, whose cartoons and comic art remain so collectable. In the geology section on the top floor are fossil footprints from the nearby cliffs, showing that animals (possibly large reptiles) roamed the area 240 million years ago. Among the displays there are some delightful stories, for example the kidnapping in 1860 of five lapdogs from the Emperor's Summer Palace in Peking (one was presented to Queen Victoria and named Looty). Guided walks leave from here, and lace-making demonstrations are held.

The old town stocks have been placed outside, just in case …

Next door to the museum is Kennaway House (⏚ kennawayhouse.org. uk), a handsome and gracious Regency mansion built in 1805, where a variety of functions and events are held. It also houses the offices of the East Devon AONB.

Flowers

Sidmouth's floral displays are another attraction: you'll see them throughout the town, in various forms. They've been impressive for as long as I can remember, but then a few years ago a Canadian investment banker, Keith Owen, with fond memories of Sidmouth, left the Sid Vale Association (⏚ sidvaleassociation.org.uk) £2.3 million in his will, with instructions that some should be used to plant a million bulbs. Planting began energetically in 2013 and is still continuing. Some are on Peak Hill and in The Byes, a pleasant stretch of open National Trust land beside the River Sid; others are in a variety of gardens, verges, lawns and flowerbeds.

In 2010 the Sid Valley to the east of the town was turned into a 'civic arboretum' (⊘ sidmoutharboretum.org.uk); it's attractively laid out, the trees have grown well, tree trail leaflets are available, and walks and talks are held.

THE BEACH

In summer, the promenade and the beach below it are traditional seaside, with ice creams, deck-chairs and a good supply of cafés and restaurants, set inside the sheltering bay. Shops here have the usual displays of plastic buckets and spades, sunglasses and unflattering sunhats. Kayaks, bodyboards, surfboards and stand-up paddleboards are for hire in season from Jurassic Paddle Sports (✆ 07580 161367 ⊘ jurassicpaddlesports. co.uk ☉ Jun–Aug daily, May & Sep w/ends; weather permitting they're on the beach around 09.00–18.00 but best phone to check). Saltrock (50 Fore St ✆ 01395 519085 ⊘ saltrock.com ☉ long hours in summer, phone to check) have surf gear and clothing. More sedately, Connaught Gardens (above the seafront at the western side of town and around 70 years old) is a popular place for sitting. Within it is **The Clocktower Café** (⊘ clocktowersidmouth.com ☉ from 09.00 or 10.00 daily), for breakfasts,

SIDMOUTH ORNÉ

Philip Knowling

Sidmouth may be the little cousin of Torquay and Exmouth, but it has benefited from the way in which development largely passed it by. It was nearly fashionable in the late 18th century but never quite made it. The harbour was never expanded, the railway came late. The 20th century failed to ruin the town.

Thanks to this, Sidmouth is truly Picturesque. The *Picturesque* was an early 19th-century fad for the rural, the rose-tinted and the rustic. To some the style is fey and sentimental; to others it is painterly and gloriously indulgent.

This is the best place in Devon to spot *cottages orné*. The *cottage orné* of the Picturesque period is an organic, asymmetric blend of genteel Gothic and tidied-up rustic. The style blends simple thatch-cottage charm with pointed windows, ornamental gables, Regency balconies and crenellations. You'll see them, for example, in Coburg Terrace. On occasion the *cottage orné* bears little resemblance to a cottage; Knowle, built in 1810 and recently home to East Devon District Council, has 40 rooms.

Thanks to fashion, Sidmouth acquired a mix of Picturesque mock cottages, Regency terraces and crescents, and Arts and Crafts villas. Also thanks to fashion, this is one resort that has kept its period character.

lunches, teas (including cream teas and good cakes) and snacks. There are fine displays of flowers and plants in its attractive surrounding garden, from which the dramatic wooden **Jacob's Ladder** zig-zags straight down to the mile-long Jacob's Ladder Beach below, as it has done for more than a century. Red cliffs tower impressively above the beach and you may find a few shells along the tideline.

For an original 'taste of the sea', walk eastward along the promenade towards the harbour and into Sidmouth Trawlers ($\mathcal{O}$ sidmouthtrawlers. co.uk), tucked away on the left at the end, where the assorted catch of the day is scattered all glisteningly fresh on the slab, and you can indulge in a fish bap or some freshly made fish soup. It's a small, simple, family-run place with a big reputation. I asked for a fish bap; son Ryan picked a plaice fillet from the slab and went off to fry it. He explained that customers come from far away – even the home counties – to stock up their freezers.

"It's a small, simple, family-run place with a big reputation."

While I was enjoying my bap, a woman from Salisbury came in; she had brought her elderly mother for a day at the seaside, and wanted some fish to take home for supper. And friends of mine swear by the fish soup, just in a take-away mug but hot and flavoursome.

PEAK HILL & MUTTER'S MOOR

Peak Hill is the steep hill at the far side of Sidmouth and is famous for its displays of bluebells and daffodils in spring. Park in the town and use the Sidmouth Hopper (see box, page 153) to climb the hill (it drops you off at the car park for Mutter's Moor) then you have a wide range of footpaths, downhill, to take you back to Sidmouth or on to Otterton or Budleigh Salterton to link up with the walk described in the box on page 132.

The fragment of pebblebed heath that is Mutter's Moor is named after a 10th-century smuggler, Abraham Mutter, who used his trade as wood- and turf-cutter to smuggle contraband. Bottles could successfully be hidden under logs or lumps of peat. The arrival of the railway and cheap coal ended the demand for logs and he was put out of business. The moor is not accessible by road, giving it additional appeal to walkers, and is networked by wide level tracks. In August there is plenty of heather to brighten the otherwise fairly austere landscape.

The Croydecycle ✻ *Sidmouth* map will give you lots of ideas for walks in the area.

3 NORMAN LOCKYER OBSERVATORY

Salcombe Hill, Sidmouth EX10 0NY ✆ 01395 579941 🖉 normanlockyer.com ⊙ evenings for special events & some afternoons

Built by Sir Norman Lockyer in 1912 and now manned entirely by volunteers (fortunately it appears that plenty of people of astronomical bent retire to Sidmouth), this is such an inspiring little place. Lockyer started with virtually nothing – he was actually a linguist and a clerk in the War Office – except a lively interest in the heavens. Quite by chance he used to commute to London with one George Pollock who, it turned out, had a 3¼-inch telescope. He lent this to Lockyer, thus fuelling his interest. Then in 1862, aged 26, Lockyer met Thomas Cooke, a telescope manufacturer – who promised Lockyer a 6¼-inch lens if he could build his own tube to house it. This Lockyer did, in papier maché, using a telegraph pole as a mould! He constructed the stand from various pieces of scrap metal. And this telescope, almost 150 years old, is in the Norman Lockyer Observatory today, working perfectly and being used by visitors.

Lockyer is remembered for having discovered the gas helium, an achievement for which he shared credit with the French scientist Pierre Jules Janssen. In 1868 he identified a previously unknown element in the sun's atmosphere and named it helium after the Greek god of the sun, Helios. He was also the founder and first editor of the influential journal *Nature*.

The observatory now has several telescopes, including a donated 20-inch Newtonian telescope, as well as a lecture theatre and planetarium, and is open to the public at least twice a month, for talks, one-day astronomy courses and various sky-related evening events. These include a spring moon watch, meteor watch, observing the Milky Way and so on. All dates are on the website. There are also a couple of 'open afternoons' a month, depending on the season, when you can look around and find out more about the place; a small library here has relevant reference books and documents. There's a spot outside where you can turn yourself into a sundial: position your feet correctly, and the sun will cast your shadow on to the current time.

It's a steepish (but green and leafy) walk up from Sidmouth – start on Salcombe Road, which branches off Vicarage Road almost opposite the Radway Cinema, and then turn up Salcombe Hill Road – but in summer the Sidmouth Hopper (see box, page 153) will stop in the lane outside.

From the Donkey Sanctuary to the Norman Lockyer Observatory or Sidmouth via Salcombe Regis

❋ OS Explorer 115 or Croydecycle *Sidmouth*; start: Donkey Sanctuary; 2 or 3 miles; moderate. Or, as a circular walk: 5 miles, steep hills, quite strenuous.

This is a lovely, varied walk, mostly downhill, which makes use of the hourly Sidmouth Hopper (see box, page 153). It takes you through the attractive village of Salcombe Regis and through woodland to Salcombe Hill, a National Trust area with spectacular views. You can end your walk here by catching the bus at the Observatory or continue along the coast path to Sidmouth.

From the car park walk due west, past lots of grazing donkeys, to a T-junction where you turn left and immediately right. This footpath takes you to Salcombe Regis (page 168); pause to look at the church, which you pass on your left, before continuing to the end of the lane and a choice of paths. Take the right-hand bridle path. A path soon leads off to the right, passing through woods. This has the least incline, but you can continue straight ahead and take the next right fork; there is not much difference between the two – both bring you out to the edge of Salcombe Hill and some terrific views. If you turn left you follow the cliff edge to the SWCP at Frog Stone which really does look like a frog. Turn right and you're in National Trust land with splendid views over Sidmouth. When you reach a tarmac lane, if you've timed it right, you can finish the walk at Salcombe Hill Road and take the Hopper back to your car. It is scheduled to stop at the Norman Lockyer Observatory, a bit up the road, but you can hail it anywhere on that road where it's safe to stop. Make sure you can be seen and hail it vigorously.

To continue to Sidmouth carry on down to the SWCP and turn right along a lovely stretch of cliff path until you come to a T-junction; turn right and when you reach the lane follow it to the bridge across the Sid and the town's Esplanade.

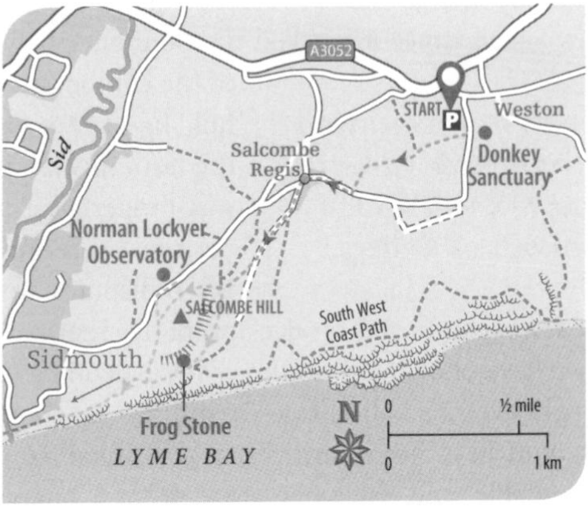

This can easily be made into a **circular walk** if you don't want to rely on buses, although there are some steep hills. At Frog Stone turn left and follow the coast path east to one of the several footpaths that lead back to the Donkey Sanctuary.

¶¶ FOOD & DRINK

In Sidmouth you're never far from food; cafés offering cream teas and home baking abound! For evening meals, particularly in summer, a number of places along the promenade have their menus outside for passers-by to browse.

Neil's Restaurant Radway Pl ✎ 01395 519494 ♦ neilsrestaurant.com ☉ from 18.30 Tue–Sat. Next to the Radway Cinema, away from the bustle of the seafront. Fish is a speciality – the menu depends on the catch of the day. Quality dining, casual or smart casual. Friendly, attentive staff. Booking always recommended: we went on a Tuesday and only one table was left.

Pea Green Boat The Esplanade ✎ 01395 514152 ♦ www.thepeagreenboat.com ☉ 11.00–15.00 daily & 17.00–21.00 Mon–Fri, 10.00–21.00 Sat & Sun. Overlooking the bay; good food with a local and/or Mediterranean bias. Strong on fish. Booking advised on summer evenings.

Selley's Coffee Shop & Restaurant Libra Court (off Fore St) ✎ 07770 251360 ☉ 09.00–15.00 daily. Very busy and popular little café/restaurant tucked away in a courtyard setting; good fresh food (snacks and light meals with imaginative recipes) and home baking. Pleasant staff.

4 SALCOMBE REGIS

⚑ Salcombe Regis Camping & Caravan Park & Campsite (page 259)

Driving into Salcombe Regis today, you will pass a thorn tree and plaque on a corner site. There was a thorn on the site at least as early as 1149. Legend tells that if it prospers the village will prosper, but if it doesn't then it must be replaced or else the villagers will come to harm. In Saxon times it marked the boundary between the cultivated fields of the combe and the open common of the hill. In 1149 a Canon was sent to live at the farm; his job was to see that the manor was properly farmed and that agricultural customs were followed, to decide the law when disputes arose, and to make sure the

"If you start counting the many tree varieties you see, you'll soon run out of fingers."

parson conducted services properly. That record was the first mention we have of a church in the valley. Salcombe (the Regis came later) was only ever a small village (it still has no shop or pub) and the church would have been hard for its few inhabitants to build. Masons were available, and Salcombe stone from a quarry at nearby Dunscombe; considerable amounts were also used in Exeter Cathedral. Once quarried, it was either taken down the cliff to the sea and shipped to Topsham, or carried laboriously by road.

The church of St Mary, probably at that stage small and with a thatched roof, was most likely built in around 1120–30; only two pillars and some remnants survive from that period. Like so many Devon churches it then endured various changes and renovations. After those completed in 1450 the restored and enlarged church was rededicated and became the church of St Peter and St Mary, in much the form that it is today. The triptych behind the altar is a great treasure, designed by Sir Lawrence Whistler and engraved by his son, Simon Whistler, who also engraved a window in Seaton's church. The 15th-century lectern, carved from a single piece of timber, is thought to be either a chough or an eagle. Visit the church today and you'll be in no doubt that it's part of the community; vegetables and plants are on sale inside and out to raise funds, sometimes with helpful notes on how to use them. There's no vehicle access from Salcombe Regis to the beach – you'll need to walk, and it's extremely steep – but there's a handy car park just beyond the church where you can leave a donation. Salcombe Regis today is a peaceful, green, leafy little place; if you start counting the many tree varieties you see, you'll soon run out of fingers.

BRANSCOMBE & BEER

These two extremely pretty villages are separated by a pleasant walk, some beautiful clifftop views and scenic but sparse journeys on the 899 bus, which links them four times a day in each direction on its route between Seaton and Sidmouth.

5 BRANSCOMBE

🏠 **Baldash Cottage B&B** (page 258) 🏠 **Baldash Lodge** (page 259), **Forge Cottage** (page 259), **Margells** (page 259) ⛺ **Coombe View Farm** (page 259)

Branscombe is not so much a village as a haphazard line of blossomy cottages folded into a combe. There's nowhere to go but along, so the 'village street' is a mile-long curve between steep hills with a pub at each end, and the church, a cluster of National Trust properties and the only parking area (apart from down at the beach) roughly halfway along, by the village hall and the forge. It is picture-postcard pretty, with a spacious pebble beach and its inviting café, so is one of the most visited villages in East Devon.

The National Trust owns the outrageously photogenic thatched tea room, The Old Bakery, the Manor Mill down the hill towards Branscombe Mouth, and Branscombe Forge, thought to be the last thatched forge in the country. Blacksmiths have been hammering their wares here for at least 200 years and it is now managed by the Hall family. Andrew Hall and his brother Gary and son Simon together create some classy forged metalwork – not cheap but beautifully made and very varied – which you can also find at the Powderham Forge in Kenton. See ⚭ wroughtirondevon.co.uk.

The **Old Bakery** (☉ summer 10.00–17.00 daily) is a wonderfully peaceful place, with comfort foods like homemade cake, soup, cream teas, local apple juice, homemade cordial and a range of other snacks. It also sells local wines from Sidbury and Pebblebed vineyards, and ale, cider and gin from Branscombe Vale Brewery. Sit out in the sun in the blossomy garden; when I visited, there was a stand of local bee-friendly plants for sale. Nearby are a couple of small rooms in an old barn with National Trust displays of local life.

"It is decorated with a skull and four bizarre heads, which look like hybrids between lion and man."

The historic **Manor Mill** is still in working order; it's open 14.00 to 16.00 on Sundays from mid-April to late September, plus Wednesdays in August. See National Trust website for more information.

The church of St Winifred squats menacing and low on the side of a hill, looking more like a Norman castle than a place of worship; you quite expect arrows to rain down on the approaching congregation. An enclosed spiral staircase giving access to the Elizabethan gallery is stuck on the side of the squat tower.

St Winifred was one of those saints who were rather casually beheaded, but barely inconvenienced by the fact, simply replacing her head and going on to do good works. She was the niece of St Beuno, a Welshman, and one story goes that he restored her head to its rightful place, leaving only a thin red line to show its misadventure, and allowing its owner to live on to become an abbess; another version has it that her head remained on the ground, from whence a sacred spring gushed to become the Holy Well.

The original church was probably Saxon, and the plaster has been removed on a section of wall inside to show the contrast between early

English stonework and Norman stonework. The church has a feeling of colour and light, partly through the kneelers, hung high in the pews, displaying the coats of arms of all (or most) of the monarchs of England and partly due to the light flooding through the plain glass windows. The wagon roof is lovely, largely constructed from the original, worm-eaten timber. The rarest feature is a triple-decked pulpit, allowing different levels for the lesson, for prayers, and for the sermon, but there is also a strange monument, carved in Beer stone, to the Cornish woman Anne Bartlett, who died in 1606. It is decorated with a skull and four bizarre heads, which look like hybrids between lion and man.

The church has had some colourful vicars, including John Cardemaker who was burned at the stake, and Thomas Puddicombe who supplied a dunce's hat for any member of the congregation who, in his view, was acting inappropriately during the service.

Above the church is a row of cottages, one of which, in the spring and summer, is almost completely covered in flowers. It must be one of the most photographed private houses in Devon, and deservedly so.

This delightful, peaceful village has a surprisingly disreputable history – of smuggling. Its men were heavily involved in the illicit trade, even up until the mid 19th century, and hid their contraband in a way that is apparently unique in Britain: they dug a sloping tunnel leading to the centre of a field, and at its end hollowed out a circular pit, some 12ft underground. The entrance to this chamber was then concealed with earth and turf. These storage places have repeatedly been uncovered during farming: a 1953 estate map showed the locations of six of them, found between 1909 and 1939.

If ever the advice not to travel by car into a village was pertinent, it's here. There is one small car park near the National Trust places, but that's it, unless you park by the Sea Shanty down at Branscombe Mouth and toil up the long, steep hill. The most enjoyable way of seeing Branscombe is to amble down its full length (a bit over a mile).

FOOD & DRINK

The Fountainhead EX12 3BG ✆ 01297 680359 ⌂ fountainheadinn.com. At the Sidmouth end of Branscombe, this 500-year-old pub is popular with walkers and their dogs, and has extensive outdoor seating so no need to muddy the carpet. On cold days it has a log fire. As their website says, 'this is a place to enjoy some good conversation, to sup some ale, to relax. There are no juke boxes, pool tables or wide screen televisions.' The food is excellent:

Walking from the Donkey Sanctuary to Branscombe or Beer

❋ OS Explorer 115 or, better, Croydecycle *Beer*, *Branscombe*, *Seaton* plus *Sidmouth*; start: Donkey Sanctuary car park; between 4 & 7 miles; moderate (some steep hills)

This walk is packed full of pleasures. You start with donkeys (and who doesn't love donkeys?), there's a choice of path down to the coast, steep or gentle, but both through varied scenery and some woodland, and it culminates along one of my very favourite sections of the South West Coast Path. At Branscombe you can choose between strolling the length of the village (two pubs and a tea room), then catching a bus back to your car or continuing to Beer along another lovely bit of coast path and getting the bus from there.

Make the most of the free car park at the **Donkey Sanctuary**, and use a map to guide you down to **Weston Mouth**. If you go straight down, through the evocatively named Field of Dreams, you'll have a steep descent to the beach and up again to the continuation of the coast path. If you take Slade Lane to Weston and then the footpath to Weston Cliff, you avoid this and stay high above the sea. The section of coastal path east from here is gorgeous – I think my favourite in all East Devon – passing close to the edge of high cliffs. You have a **choice of footpaths to Branscombe**, the first being the reasonably level one to **Berry Barton** which puts you on the lane that dives steeply to **The Fountainhead** pub. Or, if it's not yet lunchtime, continue along the coast path to the short but steep path that takes you to **Branscombe church**. The **Mason's Arms** is further down the road towards Beer.

If you've been clever with your timings, you can take the 899 bus back to the Donkey Sanctuary from The Fountainhead or Village Hall (the last one of the day is currently 16.30). Or, if you want to continue to Beer – a further two miles – walk down to **Branscombe Mouth**

traditional pub fare and a good selection of sandwiches, along with specials such as bacon-wrapped scallops. In the summer they do a spit-roast and BBQ evenings with live music. Beer is from the local Branscombe brewery, including Branoc which is ideal if you have a long walk ahead of you – you'll stay upright.

The Mason's Arms EX12 3DJ ✆ 01297 680300 ✆ masonsarms.co.uk. At the lower end of town, this very picturesque 14th-century building became a pub to slake the thirst of the workers in nearby Beer quarry; it is now owned by St Austell's Brewery. A good though somewhat pricey menu, with an emphasis on fish. There's plenty of outdoor seating and in the winter a huge log fire; displays of historic photos decorate the walls. Also has 28 B&B rooms.

The Sea Shanty Branscombe Mouth EX12 3DP ✆ 01297 680577 ✆ theseashanty.co.uk ☺ summer 09.00–17.00 daily; winter 10.00–16.00 Fri–Mon (may be closed in bad weather

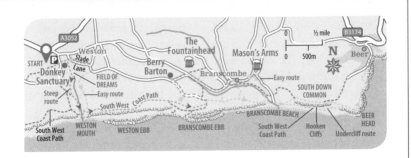

(the village beach) along the gentle surfaced track, where you can pick up the coast path again. You'll be offered the choice of the high route over the top of **Hooken Cliffs**, which is shorter and more level, or the longer, more undulating **Undercliff**. This is perhaps more interesting if you're still full of boundless energy, but I'm very happy with the high path and its gorgeous views, and watching the hang-gliders from Beer Head in the summer. From Beer it's the same 899 bus or you can continue to Seaton (page 179) for the more regular 9A back towards Sidmouth and ask to get off at the road to the Donkey Sanctuary.

Shorter, circular walks around Branscombe are shown on the Croydecycle map, or you can also head west on the coast path from Weston to walk the three miles into Sidmouth, high on the cliffs with superb views. Be warned, however: this stretch is rated as 'severe' – the toughest – by the South West Path Association. If you do end up in Sidmouth you can hop on the free Sidmouth Hopper (see box, page 153) and get taken right to the Donkey Sanctuary.

so phone before arrival). This is a charming café right on Branscombe's beach and the South West Coast Path, so it's used to hosting walkers. It has tables outside facing the beach and in a secluded garden as well as inside. The menu is limited but good, with fish dishes predominating. Food is served pretty much all day which is a great bonus. There's also a small shop selling beachy things.

6 BEER

It has nothing to do with drink! *Beer* derives from the Old English *bearu*, meaning either 'peninsula' or 'grove', which crops up in one form or another in many Devon names. John Leyland, in 1540, called it Berewood and describes how it once had a pier 'for Socour of

Shippelettes … but ther cam such a Tempest a 3 Yeres sins as never in mynd of men had before beene sene in that shore, and tare the Pere in Peaces'. It was never rebuilt, but the fishing and tourism trade have managed perfectly well without it.

More ambitiously, in 1825 a bill was passed in parliament proposing the building of a 44-mile ship canal between Beer and Stolford, on the Bristol Channel. The canal was to have 60 locks, accommodate vessels up to 200 tons, and have a substantial harbour at either end. It was also to cost £1,750,000. The money could not be raised, and Beer lost its potential place in maritime history.

When Honiton lacemaking was at its height, Beer was an important source of outworkers, and much 'Honiton' lace (including the trimmings for Queen Victoria's wedding dress) was actually made here.

Beer today is utterly delightful – and that's its problem. We first saw it on a sunny March day and were enchanted by the curved bay, enclosed by great chalk cliffs; the fishing boats drawn up on the pebble beach; the fishermen's cottages stacked up the hill; and the shack selling fresh fish at the shore's edge: it was everything a fishing village should be. Running up from the beach is the main street, where a little channelled stream gurgles next to the pavement, and visitors browse in the galleries and small shops. My next visit was in August when its charms had a tough time trying to survive the onslaught of cars and tourists.

The 'official' attraction in the village is **Pecorama** (page 176), with its model railway exhibition and passenger-carrying miniature railway, and **Beer Caves** give an intriguing glimpse into the history of local stone quarrying. In Fore Street are two high-quality art galleries both under the same management: **Marine House** at Beer (✆ 01297 625257) and **Steam Art Gallery** (✆ 01297 625144). For both galleries see ⊘ marinehouseatbeer.co.uk. Selections of work by over 100 local and national artists and craftspeople are always available or on display, and several times a year the galleries host major solo shows from leading artists.

"Selections of work by over 100 local and national artists and craftspeople are always available."

The **Dolphin Antiques and Collectables Centre** (✆ 01297 24362 ⊙ 10.00–17.00 Wed–Mon), situated behind the Dolphin Hotel and close to the central Clapps Lane car park, is an Aladdin's cave of affordable antique, vintage and collectable items and well worth

JACK RATTENBURY: THE 'ROB ROY OF THE WEST'

This colourful seafaring smuggler was born in Beer in 1778. His father was lost at sea before Jack's birth, and his mother sold fish for a living. From the age of nine Jack worked on his uncle's fishing boat; but then, aged about 14, seeking adventure, he joined the crew of a privateer, was captured by the French and thrown in jail, escaped, and spent a year or so voyaging (New York, Copenhagen …) before making his way home. More privateering and other voyages followed, Rattenbury's escapes becoming increasingly daring – from the French, customs men, the navy, press gangs, soldiers – as he hid in caves, bushes, chimneys, cellars and no doubt the occasional lady's chamber too. He headed a gang of smugglers based in Beer; they stashed their loot in caves along the coast, including those of Beer quarry, Beer cliffs and Ladram Bay. He traded in boats, which he used for smuggling, and amassed considerable wealth. A foray into 'respectability' – he bought a pub and ran it for a while – ended when it proved unprofitable. In 1837, with the improbable help of a local clergyman, he wrote his autobiography, *Memoirs of a Smuggler*, in which his heroism and daring were perhaps somewhat over-coloured. Rattenbury died in 1844 and was buried in an unmarked spot in Seaton churchyard, but his name lives on – not only in history and fiction, but also in Lyme Bay Winery's Jack Ratt scrumpy and cider. Not a bad memorial!

a browse. St Michael's Church in Fore Street has a good selection of secondhand **books**. The **village store** by the bus stop is a good source of supplies, with friendly and helpful owners, and down by the beach in a small shed beside the jetty is a **fish shop** selling whatever fish has come in on the boat, so it's extremely fresh. The small building tucked away behind Jimmy Green's in Fore Street and named **Bomb Shelter** (it doesn't shelter you *from* bombs, it shelters a bomb!) displays the wartime bomb that missed Beer, along with an appealing story showing the humanity of the English and German people despite the horrors of war. It also has information about the Devon Greater Horseshoe Bat Project (⌀ devonbatproject.org) and bats in general. With changing displays, it's always a fascinating little place to pop into for a browse.

Beer Heritage Centre

Also down by the jetty you'll find the Beer Heritage Centre, a small wooden building run by Beer Village Heritage. It has a good stock of information, plus seawater tanks containing marine species, and is the place to find out more about Beer's beach and marine environment –

but its website ($\oslash$ beervillageheritage.org.uk) offers far more. It's buzzing with events and information – rockpooling, walks, history, geology, hillforts, fossils, talks, bats, self-guided – endless! The 'Beer history' button in particular reveals some treasures. Something you can find in the Beer Heritage Centre but nowhere else on earth is a tiny, pea-sized piece of Beer rock, millions of years old, which was sent into space in 2008 to determine how bacteria within it would survive conditions beyond the Earth's atmosphere. They did well! Back home again, after its spell in the International Space Station's Columbus Laboratory, it can be visited. There's also an invitation to visitors to do their own ten-minute litter-pickup on the beach – and some recycled plastic bags (from loaves of bread, vegetables, etc) are thoughtfully provided for this.

Walking to Seaton or Branscombe

Walking to Seaton at low tide is easy and rewarding, taking only about half an hour. The surfaced coastal path climbs up the cliffside opposite the Anchor Inn, and takes you via some lovely views to Seaton Hole where you descend some steps to walk the final stretch along the beach. When the tide is up you may need to walk inland which, since a landslip closed the Old Beer Road, is longer and less interesting. When you arrive at the road you have to turn left, counterintuitively away from Seaton, and look out for the permissive path, the Clinton Way, which goes steeply uphill through the woods on the right, to meet Beer Road. Turn right here to walk to Seaton along the road (there is a pavement).

Whether or not you can walk from Seaton Hole to Seaton depends as much on the beach configuration as the tide. Sometimes it is passable at all but high tide, but at other times the shingle has been sucked into the sea making the boulders too high. We don't recommend trying to teeter along the top of them.

See the box on page 189 for the thrilling walk through the chalk arch to the west of Beer and on to Branscombe.

Pecorama

Beer EX12 3NA $\mathscr{D}$ 01297 21542 $\oslash$ pecorama.co.uk $\odot$ 10.00–17.00 daily (check website for low-season hours)

Peco is the leading British manufacturer of model railways, so Beer's leading 'official' attraction evolved from its model railway display and now encompasses extensive gardens and a delightful passenger-

SAVOUR THE TASTE

Sustainability and animal welfare are a focus of food production in East Devon, with farmers' markets and farm shops selling a wide range of produce.

1 A variety of apple products are made at Four Elms Fruit Farm, from seven types of apple juice to craft ciders. 2 Mussels and muscles. The Exmouth Mussel Company harvests 2,000 tonnes of the shellfish a year. 3 Wine production is the fastest-growing agricultural sector in England and Devon, with its mild climate, is at the forefront. The small region of East Devon boasts six vineyards, including Lily Farm shown here, with sparkling wine a speciality in many of them. 4 No stay in the region is complete without a cream tea; in Devon the clotted cream is spread first, then the jam.

TONY HOWELL

SS

WALK ON THE WILD SIDE

East Devon's unique pebblebed heaths are wildlife hotspots, with the region's ancient woodlands and gardens providing floral displays in the spring.

1 Devon's heathland is carefully managed, with grazing stock such as ponies introduced to keep the vegetation in check. 2 Heathland is the best place to see the rare Dartford warbler. 3 Badgers are common in East Devon but, being nocturnal, are rarely seen. 4 Sidmouth's million colourful bulbs include this display of daffodils on Peak Hill. 5 Bluebells carpet the beech woods at Blackbury Camp.

SS

ADRIAN BAKER/D

Discover Seaton

Whatever your interest, you'll discover a wealth of activities on offer!

▶ **Enjoy Cycling**
There are endless opportunities to explore lanes and cycle paths in Seaton, and don't forget the annual Cyclefest which will be returning to Seaton in July.
www.axevalleypedallers.org.uk

▶ **Year-Round Entertainment**
From poetry and kids' activities to theatre, music and ballet.
www.seatongateway.co.uk

▶ **Canoe Along the Estuary**
Our beautiful River Axe is navigable all year round.
For details on local conditions check
www.axevalecc.co.uk

▶ **Walk the Coastal Path**
With its outstanding views over cliff tops the South West Coast Path is one of Britain's favourites.
www.southwestcoastpath.com

Pick up your copy of the Seaton Town Guide from the Tourist Information Centre.

Seaton, new experiences await you on your doorstep...
Keep in touch /VisitSeatonDevon @VisitSeatonUK visitseato

Run Wild
Join the coastal town's weekly Park Runs along the seafront on a Saturday at 9am. If you love running, you also can't miss Seaton's Grizzly running event in March. A demanding run with 3,000 ascents in its 20 miles.

Lovely Parks & Open Spaces
Jurassic-themed playpark at the Underfleet, open-air gym equipment, tennis court and Jurassic-themed adventure golf course at Seafield Gardens, and lovely ocean views at Jubilee Gardens and Cliff Field Gardens.

A Beautiful Beach
Seaton's beach is the perfect spot to relax, recognised by environmental charity Keep Britain Tidy with a 2019 Seaside Award for its quality.

Explore the Seaton Wetlands
Explore Seaton Wetlands and its 4km of level trails and enjoy beautiful marshland and reedbeds alongside the River Axe. Runner up in the Best Nature Reserve category in *BBC Countryfile* Magazine's 2019 Awards.
www.eastdevon.gov.uk/countryside

Seaton
DEVON

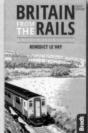
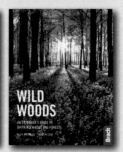

carrying miniature railway. Model-railway enthusiasts still make this their first port of call in Devon – after Buffers, at Colston Cross, north of Axminster ($\oslash$ buffersmodelrailways.com) – but it is the Beer Heights Light Railway that catches the general public's attention. An assortment of little steam locomotives take passengers on a mile-long, 7¼in-gauge track including a long tunnel, tooting as they go. It's a delightful trip for all ages and deservedly very popular. In 2018, musical legend Jools Holland launched a new steam engine here – named *Jools*. There are 'refreshment stops' along the line including pizza at **The Junction**, and the **Garden Room Restaurant** for more substantial meals.

Attention has been given to the family area, where the children's covered play station, provides comprehensive play ideas (and a soft-play area) for little kids, as well as a challenging adventure playground for their older siblings.

Pecorama gardens are, in contrast, very peaceful, with the focus on themed planting. **The Millennium Garden**, for instance, follows a celestial theme. The Sun area shines in warm yellows, oranges and reds, whilst the Moon hosts cool blues and silvers. The Rainbow is, naturally enough, an arc of brilliant colours. These are set off with stone mosaics and a grotto, and are on different levels so new surprises are discovered

"The Rainbow is, naturally enough, an arc of brilliant colours."

around each corner. Indeed, Pecorama is built on a steep hillside (something to be aware of if you're short of puff) and the views across Lyme Bay to its eastern end at Portland Bill are the best in East Devon.

Various weekend events are also held during the summer season.

7 Beer Quarry Caves

Quarry Ln, EX12 3AS $\mathscr{D}$ 01297 680282 $\oslash$ beerquarrycaves.co.uk $\odot$ Apr–Oct 10.00–16.30 (last tour 15.30) daily (but may change, so phone to check). Not wheelchair-friendly.

These vast, manmade caves are about a mile due west of Beer (a pleasant walk along Quarry Lane but there is also an adjacent car park), with a short steep lane leading up to the check-in area. This has a ticket desk, a small shop/café selling souvenirs and light snacks, and some information (much of it bat-related) pinned up around the walls.

Hoskins called this underground stone quarry 'one of the most exciting things in Devon … a deeply impressive place when one calls to mind what strength and what sunlit beauty have come from its heart over so many centuries'. More recently Sir Tim Smit, founder of the Eden Project, commented that the cave complex 'inspired awe at the labour and skills of man throughout 2,000 years, and is particularly moving because of its testament to the injustice of a system which allowed such labours to be valued so lightly'.

The qualities of Beer stone were discovered by the Romans and the quarry has been worked since then for the white, easily carved limestone which is a feature of great buildings throughout the land, including 24 cathedrals. It closed in 1920.

Tours take place every hour on the half hour in summer (the café is handy if you need to wait), but less frequently in spring and autumn. The full hour in the caves may be a bit much for some people – it certainly was for the wailing child in a pushchair when I was there – but the quality of the guide's narrative makes it well worthwhile. We learnt little nuggets of information, such as that the expression 'stone deaf' comes from the quarry-men's loss of hearing resulting from being exposed to the relentless echoing bangs of pickaxe on stone. And that the quarrymen had to buy their candles, but were only paid for perfect stone, so some blocks were 'not worth the candle'. We also saw greater horseshoe bats hanging from the electricity wires – no candles these days – and were told that if we'd done a tour in the early spring there would have been scores of them. We learned that, behind an enormous pile of rubble, the 400-year-old remains of a quarryman's lunch (rabbit and cider) had been found, and that the caves have been used for growing mushrooms and rhubarb as well as storing ammunition during World War II. There is also a secret chapel which was used for centuries by Catholics practising their forbidden religion.

Recently performances of *Macbeth* were held in the caves, also a candlelit tour and music by candlelight. It's an atmospheric place.

ᵱ FOOD & DRINK

Dolphin Hotel Restaurant Fore St, Beer ✆ 01297 20068 ⊘ dolphinhotelbeer.co.uk. A cheery place (pub plus restaurant) with generous portions and a popular Sunday carvery. Tea and coffee available all day in lounge bar.

Steamers New Cut, Beer EX12 3DU ✆ 01297 22922 ⊘ steamersrestaurant.co.uk ⊙ 10.00– 13.45 & 18.45–21.00 Tue–Sat. Family-run, with high-quality food in pleasant surroundings. Very experienced chef Andy uses the best local food, with fish and seafood often straight from the waters around Beer. The building was once a steam bakery, hence its name.

8 SEATON & AREA

🏠 **Gatcombe Farm** (page 259)

In 2010 when we wrote the Bradt Guide to *Slow Devon & Exmoor*, we said that while Sidmouth and Lyme Regis could be described as 'seaside towns', Seaton was 'a town by the sea', plainer and less geared for tourism. Not any more! Since the opening of Seaton Jurassic in 2016 there has been a new buzz about the town, as it gently adapts to its enhanced status as an informative, enjoyable and innovative 'gateway' to the Jurassic Coast.

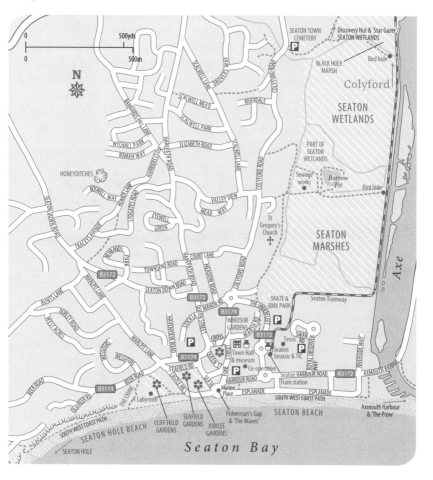

THE TOWN

🏠 **Fring House B&B** (page 259), **Mariners B&B & Apartments** (page 259)
Tourist information: Seaton Jurassic, The Underfleet ✆ 01297 300390
🖱 seatontouristinformation.co.uk ☉ 10.00–16.00 daily, closed Tue during Devon school
terms & 22 Dec–31 Jan; see ad, XX colour section.

Seaton is a pleasant and welcoming town in its own right, with a variety
of activities for all ages.

The three main shopping streets have some good and original
independent shops, including a butcher with 'happy' local meat, a baker
(Paul's in Marine Place) still using old family recipes, fishmongers selling
fish caught from their own boat, a traditional ironmonger, and two
good bookshops: The End in Queen Street (secondhand) and the Owl &
Pyramid in Fore Street (mainly children's). Part of the shopping area has
named itself the 'Cultural Quarter' and contains various small galleries,
craft shops, boutiques, antiques and collectable items. There's plenty of
scope for browsing. The Coastal Craft Collective shop (10 Marine Pl
🖱 coastalcraftcollective.co.uk) holds a range of interesting one-day craft
courses, including some for children during the school holidays, while

THE GRIZZLY

An almost-marathon run may not seem the ideal 'Slow' activity, but the Grizzly is different. No-one is trying to beat a world record here, just survive. It is described on the Axe Valley Runners' website as '20 muddy, hilly, boggy, beachy miles of the multiest terrain running experience you will find this side of the end of time.' The first factor to help pile on the misery is that the Grizzly is held in March, ensuring the worst possible weather conditions and the most mud; second the course is along shingle beaches, narrow tracks and stretches of the hilly cliff path so you can't go fast, even if you want to; and third, it includes the Black Bog, a sticky morass which, in some years, encases runners' legs from shoes – if they can keep them on their feet – to crotch with glutinous mud. There's a river to wade down (remember, this is March) and the run generally finishes over a long stretch of Seaton's pebble beach which most of us find hard work just to walk along. For some reason the runners come back year after year, and for us, the spectators, it provides a very jolly picture of suffering. And it's definitely different. As one blogger put it: 'Around the course, there were lots of nice children handing sweets to disreputable-looking men, which is a good bit of role-reversal.' Amazingly, it's so popular that entry is by ballot: details from 🖱 axevalleyrunners.org.uk.

Imagine Design Create (Queen St) also holds some courses, keeps a big stock of everything craftmakers need and has a small gallery at the back.

Seaton Museum (Fore St ✎ 01297 24227 ⌨ seatonmuseum.co.uk ⊙ late May–Oct 10.30–12.30 & 14.15–17.00 Mon–Fri) covers all aspects of the Axe Valley and Seaton's past, from prehistoric times to the present day: history, archaeology, geology, natural history, fossils, the great landslip, local life, World War II and much more: a fascinating collection. Other displays feature Victorian costume, Honiton lace (see box, page 89), tradesmen's tools, and old documents and photographs for anyone researching their family tree. Various books on the history of the area are for sale. A warning: it's on the second floor and the stairs are steep, but there are seats on the first landing if you need them.

History & heritage

The town hit the national headlines in 2014 with the discovery of the **Seaton Down Hoard**: 22,888 Roman coins, dating from around AD260 to 348, were found on Seaton Down by a metal-detecting enthusiast. It was one of the largest hoards ever unearthed in Britain, and is now safely housed in Exeter's Royal Albert Memorial Museum (page 47). It weighs 150lb, according to the Assistant Curator, so whoever buried the coins (probably in around AD380) went to considerable trouble. (And why were they never retrieved …?) The Romans were already known to have been in Seaton at the time, as substantial traces had been discovered of a Roman settlement on the west side of town. Fragments of fine mosaic found there were at first thought to be from a villa, but now opinion has veered towards a *mansio* or guesthouse. Considerable remains of a bath house have also been found – on land where there was earlier Neolithic, Bronze Age and Iron Age occupation. Seaton's Roman remains were only partially excavated and are now covered again, so who knows what treasures may still lie hidden. Harepath Road, nearby, may derive from the Saxon 'herepaeth', meaning an ancient route or a track followed by a Saxon army; and Axmouth across the estuary is believed to have been on a side road from the Fosse Way, the Roman road leading from Exeter to Lincoln.

Seaton's oldest building, and the only one that is Grade I-listed, **St Gregory's Church** was gazing across the estuary when trading vessels sailed to and from Axmouth Harbour; in the old stone wall there were once iron rings where boats could be moored when their occupants came to a service, like some medieval cycle park. Started in the 13th century to replace an earlier Saxon building, the church has been altered or added to in most centuries since then, so it's a mixture of styles; however, its mostly plain leaded windows, golden wood and whitewashed walls give a sense of simplicity and cohesion. One window has a beautiful and delicate engraving done in 2001 by Devon-born Simon Whistler, as part of a millennium project called *The Waters of Life*.

In Fore Street there are two Grade-II listed buildings, the charming Jasmine Cottage (originally from around the 16th century but remodelled in the 18th) and the (probably) 18th-century Manor House, the original rear part of which survives. The Town Hall in the same street dates from 1904.

During World War II, Seaton had considerable coastal defences. Apart from extensive barbed wire, there was a searchlight emplacement just up from what is now West Walk on the esplanade and, above it, a quick-firing 6-pounder Hotchkiss gun on a hexagonal slab, disguised as a small ruined building. The slab and searchlight housing are still in place, with an interpretation board on the esplanade below. Near the gun, in the back garden of one of the houses on Castle Hill, was an ammunition store; the house at the time belonged to the Bishop of Birmingham, and after the war his wife had to chivvy the MOD to remove their weaponry. Across the bay, the Axmouth gun emplacement near the harbour was at the English Channel end of the 50-mile anti-tank Stop Line, which stretched from East Devon and Somerset to the Bristol Channel. In the run-up to D-Day in 1944 hundreds of young American soldiers were stationed in Seaton; to commemorate their bravery and the kindness they received from Seaton people a memorial was unveiled in July 2014, in Windsor Gardens opposite the Town Hall.

Activities

Summer pitch-and-putt and tennis courts are available in **Seafield Gardens**, as are a café (in season), a children's playground and an adult 'outdoor gym', with apparatus to stretch every muscle as gently or as energetically as you wish. Just beyond Seaton Jurassic is a more extensive and dinosaur-themed playground.

In **Cliff Field Gardens** you'll find a boules pitch (bring your own boules), a labyrinth and, winding through the gardens, a fascinating **Geological Timeline**: a series of 21 small metal plaques or tiles are set into the path, each illustrating a different stage in the Earth's development from its beginning to the advent of humans. There are interpretation boards throughout and the images on the tiles are raised for 'brass rubbing': rubbing sheets can be downloaded from *⊘* seaton.gov.uk (search for *Timeline*), or obtained from the TIC for a small donation.

The **labyrinth** was designed by Axmouth's Spiral Sanctuary group (page 193) and opened in 2005, celebrating the 1,000 years since the town received its first charter. The pathways are grass and the divides are made from different stones of the Jurassic Coast. Labyrinths date back more than 4,000 years; they are symbols of life's journey and can be used for relaxation or meditation. The walk to the centre of this one and back is about half a mile. There are regular full-moon labyrinth walks (check with the Spiral Sanctuary group for times/dates). Beside it is a finger labyrinth (traceable with your finger rather than on foot), replicating the main one and carved by sculptor Michael Fairfax, who is also responsible for the Jurassic geoneedle in Exmouth (page 68) and the Riddle Statue in Exeter (page 40).

On the first Saturday morning of each month in summer there's a colourful **Artisans' Market** down by the tramway station, with a big variety of crafts from local craftspeople: pottery, cards, prints, weaving, wood carving, stitchery, soaps and perfumes, jewellery, engraved glass – and much more. Cyclelife (*⊘* cyclelifeeastdevon.co.uk), next to the Co-op, sells and repairs bikes of all kinds, as well as biking accessories and clothing.

The Tourist Information Centre (page 180) has leaflets about local walks, orienteering trails and current activities, as well as Devon bus timetables.

Entertainments

The entertainment hub in the Town Hall, known as the Gateway Theatre Company (*✆* 01297 625699 *⊘* thegatewayseaton.co.uk, thelittleboxoffice. com/seatongateway), provides this small seaside town with a huge range of top-class entertainment. Apart from live music and theatre events, it offers cinema and the live streaming of international productions: ballet, opera, Shakespeare and other plays from the National Theatre and Stratford-upon-Avon, and exhibitions from the British Museum and elsewhere.

THE BEACH

Bathing is safe and uncrowded on Seaton's long pebbly **beach**, with occasional sand at low tides. Dogs are allowed on the western end all

STAND-UP PADDLEBOARDING: IF I CAN, ANYONE CAN

You know the feeling? You see someone achieve something and think 'I could do that!' For two years I've watched the graceful, bikinied women standing effortlessly on their stand-up paddleboards in Lyme Bay and been quite sure I couldn't do it. After all, I can barely stand on level ground without falling over. Then, last week, I watched a man fall off and scramble back on to his board about a dozen times and thought, well yes, I could do that. So I booked a SUP lesson the following morning.

When I told Lisa about my wobbly balance she reassured me that some people prefer just to kneel, which is the prelude to standing, but I reckon only Catholics have had a lot of practice at that. I gave it a go in my sitting room. It hurt, but I could do it for a short while. The morning was windless and calm, perfect for SUP. After learning about the structure of the paddleboard (it has a nice set of shark fins underneath to keep it straight) and how to hold the paddle, I waded in, clambered on top, got into a kneeling position and started paddling. It was OK. I could go forwards and make turns. But of course after about ten minutes my knees hurt and I told Lisa I wanted to try standing. And I did. And I could do it! I know I shouted at Lisa 'Look at me, I'm standing!' which is rather pathetic, but the feeling of achievement was huge. And the trick of it, I decided, is the same as when you boulder hop. You know how you have to keep a forward momentum and eyes ahead, and then you can do it, but as soon as you try consciously to keep your balance you wobble and fall off. So with the paddling, as long as I thought about moving forward I was fine, and it was wonderful.

Now I have to practise falling off and getting on again.

year and on the eastern end in winter. The promenade is the site of a parkrun every Saturday morning, and is well stocked with cafés and ice-cream kiosks. The sea can lash dramatically during winter storms, but on a clear day the view stretches from the cliffs of South Devon in one direction to Portland Bill in the other.

In the past few years the beach has burst into new life with the arrival of stand-up paddleboarding, which originated in Hawaii and is now one of the country's fastest-growing watersports. Kayaking is also increasing in popularity. The family-run Seaton Bay Watersports ($\mathscr{O}$ 07850 695200 $\mathring{\partial}$ sbwatersports.co.uk) can provide paddleboards, kayaks, buoyancy aids, wetsuits and tuition; the staff are mostly on the beach (weather permitting) from late July to September but also work in the estuary, so phone or check their website for current information. Kayaks are also for sale from the Seaton Angling/Kayak Centre at Axmouth Harbour (page 191).

SEATON JURASSIC

The Underfleet, EX12 2LX 🕾 01392 279244 ⬧ seatonjurassic.org ⊙ 09.00–17.00 daily

One thing to make clear: this isn't Jurassic Park. *Tyrannosaurus rex* doesn't stalk the corridors nor does a *velociraptor* terrify visitors in the toilets. It is as much about survival as it is about extinction as it takes you on a journey through time, over land and underwater, celebrating the fact that Seaton is unique on the Jurassic Coast in that you can see in one place all three components of the Mesozoic period: the Triassic, Jurassic and Cretaceous eras. And it celebrates the great landslide of 1839, which exposed these rocks and so excited the Victorian geologists of the time.

Operated by the Devon Wildlife Trust and aimed at inquisitive children – isn't that all of them? – and adults who want a better understanding of our natural world, it sets out to explain the evolution of life on earth in as dynamic a way as possible, using modern technology to inspire and enthral. 'Everything's changed but nothing's changed' is, perhaps, the enduring theme as we look at the story of Lyme Bay through its 250-million-year history.

So what's it like? Seaton Jurassic consists of three buildings, 'pods', each coloured outside according to a Mesozoic period: terracotta red (Triassic), grey (Jurassic) and white (Cretaceous). You step into a welcoming shop and café with a bird evolution theme – because Seaton's dinosaur is the *archaeopteryx* – where you wait to join enough of a group to be summoned into the next room to be initiated into what the centre is all about. It's about touching, children are told. Touch everything, pull out drawers, turn handles, try on costumes.

You then meet TT, aka Time Traveller, who will be your guide. What's she like? You'll see. You find yourself inside a Victorian study with period furniture and rows of books, but the books are coloured to match the Jurassic Coast and some of them open, to reveal – surprises. They take you back through those millions of years, and the five mass extinctions that played such a major part in evolution are shown in ways that will imprint themselves on your memory.

TT guides you into her Timeship and encourages you to row yourself backwards or forwards in time as the underwater world changes through the portholes; look up to see recent images of storm surges in and around Seaton, getting us thinking about climate change and our uncertain future. There is so much to learn. Children benefit hugely from being accompanied by an adult who will take the time to point out things of special interest – such as how exactly tides work, and the Seaton Orrery, a mechanised solar system. Clever cartoon marine creatures explain ecology in entertaining as well as informative ways, making learning fun for adults as well as children.

Time to move on to the outdoor Infinity Pool, to explore life beneath the waves of Lyme Bay and learn why some of our beaches are pebble and some are sand, before strolling through the wildlife garden. Then go back inside for a coffee, snack or light meal at the very good **Taste of the West** café and a browse in the gift shop.

Seaton Jurassic is not cheap – nor should it be for such an immersive experience – but for a small additional payment you can make your entry ticket into a season ticket, allowing you to revisit it again and again within a year.

SEATON TRAMWAY
Harbour Rd ✆ 01297 20375 ⏍ tram.co.uk ⏲ Apr–Oct 10.00–16.00 daily or later; check website for winter opening

Such a popular attraction: colourful traditional trams (from a fleet of 14, built between 1904 and 2007) rattle up and down the Axe Valley between Seaton, Colyford and Colyton, with beautiful views out over the river and marshes. For bird enthusiasts there's an absolute feast of waterbirds and every so often a special birdwatching trip with guidance from experts. Other wildlife that you may spot includes otters, deer, foxes, badgers, water voles and distinctive Devon ruby red cattle (although they're placid rather than wild!).

"For real tram enthusiasts there are also tram-driving lessons and a 'driver's eye experience'."

There are also themed trips for families (including Guy Fawkes, pirates, dinosaurs, Hallowe'en and Santa), as well as trips linked to special dining or music events in the Tramstop restaurant at Colyton station (page 206). The whole trip, there and back, takes around an hour, but the tickets are 'hop on/off' so you can explore Colyford and Colyton too, or do the tram-assisted walk on page 208, and travel as many times that day as you want for just one fare. In peak season the trams run every 20 minutes, so you have no worry about catching one. For real tram enthusiasts there are also tram-driving lessons and a 'driver's eye experience'. In Seaton's newly built tram station there's a small café and

A BIRD HIDE ON WHEELS

I did Seaton Tramway's special birdwatching trip – the 'bird hide on wheels', they call it – in April. Diehard birders immediately informed me that April wasn't the best time: 'The widgeons have gone. And if you'd been here in September or October you might have seen the osprey.' Nevertheless in the spring warmth and slanting evening sun it seemed a wonderful way of looking at birds. I left the competitiveness to my fellow passengers who always needed to identify something before the guides. There was plenty of 'No there. Can't you see? 3 o'clock. Yes, a wheatear.' I was happy with the pair of roe deer that no-one paid much attention to (no feathers) and with the explanation that the dapper female shelduck can afford to be sartorially equal to the males since they nest in old rabbit burrows so don't need the camouflage. And I learned how to differentiate between a greater black-backed gull and a lesser, and to pick out the redshank (well, yes, the red legs are rather a giveaway) and the ringed plover which was invisible against the shingle until it moved.

Altogether we identified about 40 species which wasn't bad in two hours. And we also saw spring blossom, green fields, and Axmouth church from a new angle.

Be there at least half an hour before departure to make sure of getting a seat near the front, where the guide sits.

gift shop; also one or two of the trams are sometimes parked inside, so you can admire their detail from close up.

¶¶ FOOD & DRINK

Seaton has so many tea places! Just a few that we like are **Seventeen Coffee Shop** (17 Fore St, with an attractive courtyard garden), **Pebbles Coffee House & Bistro** (4 Marine Pl, a cheery hardworking place near the beach), **The Terrace Arts Café** (Marine Pl, tasty and imaginative vegetarian food in a pleasantly arty atmosphere), and **The Hideaway** (West Walk, Esplanade ⊙ Mar–Oct), with hot & cold snacks, delicious home baking and outside tables directly above the beach. Most are closed by 16.00 or 16.30. For evening meals **The Wild Caper** (Fore St ⊙ generally 18.00–23.00 Wed–Sat) is a good tapas restaurant. **Frydays** (Harbour Rd ⊙ daily) has excellent fish and chips, both take-away and eat-in; and a popular newcomer in town is **The Hat** (34 Queen St ⊙ 17.00–23.00), a micro-pub with a changing range of good beers, gins, ciders, etc, where mobiles must be turned off or to silent so customers can chat, play games and enjoy the friendly atmosphere.

'Seaton Eats Boutique', a pop-up, outdoor evening food festival, brings international street food to Jubilee Gardens on the first Friday of the month in summer; and finally, we (authors) couldn't manage without the traditional pasties and diet-busting Eccles cakes provided by **Paul's Bakery** in Marine Place.

SEATON WETLANDS

Colyford Rd (for the Wetlands car park go through Seaton cemetery entrance, EX12 2SP)
♀ SY248914, ☎ 01395 517557 ⟨ wildeastdevon.co.uk

Seaton Wetlands began in the 1980s as part of the flood protection for the town, and has since been developed by the East Devon District Council (EDDC) and the Environment Agency to create a mosaic of different wildlife habitats while retaining its value as a flood defence. A tidal valve controls the salinity of the incoming water to create a salt marsh; as such it is one of the best wetlands in England and both a delight and an education for anyone with the remotest interest in natural history. That this haven for wildlife has been almost entirely manmade is a credit to the EDDC Countryside team who manage the site, and an active group of volunteers. Over three miles of level tarred paths and boardwalks connect the hides and viewing platforms, making it both wheelchair- and stroller-friendly, and cyclists are also welcome. You can also rent an off-road mobility scooter. Dogs are not allowed.

The main wetlands, accessed through the cemetery, is made up of three areas: Black Hole Marsh, Safford Marsh and Colyford Common. Black Hole Marsh, perhaps the most interesting, is an intertidal saline lagoon with several islands. The Island Hide sits in the middle of the lagoon and Tower Hide is, as the name implies, tall enough for wonderful views over the estuary as well as wildlife spotting.

"At high tide the ditches flood with saline water bringing a wealth of salt-loving invertebrates."

Oyster catchers are one of the success stories at Black Hole Marsh. Care was taken to create the perfect habitat, and now they breed here – one of only two places in mainland Devon. Their favourite breeding place is shingle beaches, but these are favourites with people too so there is too much disturbance. At Black Hole Marsh an oyster-catcher-friendly island was created. And they came. Another success story is the Devon Water Vole Recovery Project. This endearing mammal (Ratty in *Wind in the Willows*) was declining because of predation by mink, now being controlled, and steps have been taken to make the habitat more water vole-friendly. Although you'd still be lucky to see one, they are increasing in numbers.

There are two **information centres**: the Lookout, unmanned, nearest the entrance, and the **Discovery Hut** (⊙ 10.00–16.00), at Stafford Marsh, which is the main hub, with refreshments, toilets, and volunteer wardens on hand to answer questions. Adjacent to the hut is the sand martin cliff, built a few years ago to provide luxury accommodation for these rare birds. But – like many humans – they seem reluctant to move from the old and familiar.

Nearby is the **Star Gazer**, a circle of carved log seats angled upwards, around a carved wooden wing. The perfect place to observe a meteor shower.

A lively programme of **events** are run throughout the year: check the noticeboards at the entrance or the website. Kids can revel in pond-dipping (and what child doesn't love pond life?) while birders have five **hides** to choose from, each overlooking a different type of habitat: river, pond, lagoon or marsh. Each has a whiteboard or log book with the latest sightings, and pictures of the birds you are likely to see.

The most northerly hide is on Colyford Common, a salt marsh accessed via a boardwalk. (Although there is an entrance on Colyford Road, this is only safe for cyclists. There is no car park and no sidewalk beside this road of fast-moving traffic.) At high tide the ditches flood with saline water bringing a wealth of salt-loving invertebrates.

Reeds flourish here; children love the circular reedbed walk (which may be flooded, so inaccessible, at high tide). One of the great discoveries here was of the very rare grey long-eared bat. They have enormous, almost rabbit-like ears; and because their favourite food, moths, also

WALKING BETWEEN SEATON & BEER – & BEYOND

In 2012, after heavy rain, a chunk of Old Beer Road fell down the cliff taking with it one of the most popular local walks. The SWCP from Seaton to Beer used to be a 20-minute stroll along the clifftops. Now, with the road permanently closed, walkers need to use Beer Road to access the new Clinton Way which takes you back to the top of Old Beer Road (see map, page 179) from where you walk down to the cliff path. At low tide you can avoid this diversion by walking along the beach to Seaton Hole and up the steps, so check your tide table and the varying level of the pebbles on the beach.

At extreme low tides, once or twice a year, the chalk arch beyond Beer is exposed. It's quite a thrill to crunch through a natural arch and on to the pristine beach beyond. It's quite a slog over the pebbles, but keep going and you'll get to Branscombe. The tide does need to be to be really low if you are to walk round the headland beyond the arch. Otherwise you'll have to scramble. Don't risk wading – there are deep bits.

have very good hearing, their ultra-sound is muted to avoid frightening their prey. So they are known as 'whispering bats'.

Seaton Marshes, the marshland nearest to Seaton, is not connected to the larger area to its north. Private farmland intervenes. Access from the town is via Cycle Route 2 from The Underfleet, which runs beside the grazing land. The sheep keep the grass short, which is just how the birds like it so you can often spot flocks of waterfowl such as widgeon here. There's also limited parking on Hillymead, past the football club off Colyford Road, which brings you to the path/boardwalk running around the deep freshwater pond, the Borrow Pit, with benches for gazing and reflection. A fenced path leads to the hide overlooking the Axe, making this a great place for watching waders. Ospreys are regularly spotted from here in the spring and autumn, and it's a favourite place for seeing herons and the snazzily dressed shelduck. The large bird feeder is always busy with garden birds and, if you're really lucky, you may spot a water vole.

Other special events include canoe safaris and the birding tram ride (see box, page 187).

9 AXMOUTH

> Ther hath beene a very notable Haven at Seton, but now ther lyith between the 2 Pointes of the old Haven a mighty Rigg and Barre of pible Stones in the very Mouth of it, and the Ryver of Ax is driven to the very Est Point of the Haven, callid Whit Clif.
>
> John Leland, 1540

Indeed, two thousand years ago the River Axe was broader and much deeper, and the Romans built a harbour at what is now Axmouth (they called it Uxelis), directly across the river from Seaton; the Saxons expanded it, and by medieval times Axmouth was a busy and important port with apparently as many as 14 inns. Leland described it as 'an old and bigge Fischar Toune'. But then changing tides began to form his 'barre of pible stones' at the Axe's mouth and a great storm in the 15th century caused more damage; the villagers did what they could to prevent it, but the river gradually silted up, shipping dwindled and the harbour crumbled. In the early 19th century, local people tried to dig out and repair its ruins; a pier was built in about 1803, enabling 100-ton vessels to unload, and for the next 50-odd years two vessels traded regularly between Axmouth and London. However, the coming of the railway in 1868 caused the death of this shipping trade, the harbour again crumbled into disuse, and a severe storm in January 1869 swept away much of the pier.

The first bridge across the estuary was built in 1877, replacing an overhead cable ferry whose ferryman charged 1d per person per trip. This old bridge, now a footbridge and a scheduled ancient monument, is the oldest concrete bridge still standing in Britain. The little toll house opposite the bridge, built in the same year and also from concrete, was one of the first concrete houses to be built in Britain and is now the oldest one surviving. The tolls collected there were one penny per person, fourpence for a horse and cart, one penny per leg for a harnessed animal and a halfpenny a leg for loose animals. Locals were known to try to avoid these by going piggy-back, unharnessing their horses, and pulling their carts across by hand! In 1907 the tolls were abolished and the villagers, in great delight, burned the tollgates. In 2014 the toll house was given a blue plaque.

"In 1907 the tolls were abolished and the villagers, in great delight, burned the tollgates."

Across the bridge, past the marina and on the quay at the tip of the estuary, there's a conglomeration of fishing nets and lobster pots and a small group of houses. That's **Axmouth Harbour**. Jean's Tea Caddy sells hot and cold snacks and meals including great fish and chips and fresh crab sandwiches, while next door is the Seaton Angling/Kayak Centre (✆ 01297 625511 ⌂ seatonanglingcentre.uk ◷ summer 07.00–18.00, winter 07.30–17.30), whose stock stretches from kayaks through wet-weather gear and professional angling equipment to shrimping nets and plastic buckets for crabbing. During school holidays you'll often see children on the quayside here, crabbing away competitively. Continue past the houses to the narrow harbour mouth (look for blackberries to your left, in season) and you'll come to Seaton Jurassic's dramatic 'The Prow' Discovery Point – and a further shingle beach, stretching eastward. For a strenuous walk along this as far as Lyme Regis, see *Walking along the Shore* on page 193.

Jean's Tea Caddy is a popular meeting place for local fishermen; if you want to be taken out on a fishing trip, ask around here or contact John Wallington of Devon Bass Pro Charters (✆ 01297 21986 ⌂ devonbassprocharters.co.uk) who skippers a fast deep-sea angling boat from the harbour (licensed to carry seven passengers, and with light line 'sports' tackle provided) and specialises in catching bass. You may see his sign, or his boat, beside the quay.

Parking is very restricted in the harbour area, limited to 30 minutes and then only for visitors going to the café or shop. Drivers would do better to park in Seaton and walk over the bridge – which in any case offers a beautiful view up the river, with the occasional chance of spotting a kingfisher.

AXMOUTH VILLAGE

It is hard to believe that Axmouth village was once a full-scale port that could welcome sizeable trading vessels; now it lies three-quarters of a

THE GREAT BINDON LANDSLIDE & UNDERCLIFF

On Christmas Day in 1839, after a period of heavy rain, a great chasm opened up in the cliffs just east of the Axe River. The ground had been showing signs of movement for some weeks, and finally around eight million tonnes of earth and rock slid forward and fell to the beach below. It was described thus in the *Bath Journal*:

One of the Coast Guard men, whilst on duty near the Undercliff, observed the sea to be in an extraordinary state of agitation. The beach on which he stood rose and fell. Amidst the breakers near the shore, something vast and dark appeared to be rising from the bottom of the sea amidst the noise of crashing rocks, flashing lights, attended with an intolerable stench... In the morning, immediately in front of the Undercliff, which though still much rent and shaken, still retains its former position, there appeared a stupendous ridge of broken strata of blue lias, together with rocks of immense size immovable by human power, covered with sea weed, shell fish and other marine productions.

The geologist William Buckland (an Axminster man) was quickly on the scene, along with his wife who made careful drawings. They were joined by William Daniel Conybeare, and together they published a book about the landslide, the first such detailed scientific study ever made.

The event utterly changed the nature of this stretch of coast, pitching agricultural land into the abyss and returning it to nature. Over the years the fallen land has been colonised by scrub, ash and hazel, taking their place beside some pre-landslip field maples. The whole area is now a National Nature Reserve and a true wilderness since no land management is possible here.

mile upriver from today's harbour, the only reminder of its maritime past being the passing canoes and kayaks enjoying a waterside view of the Wetlands. It has two traditional **pubs**, The Harbour and The Ship (page 195), both dating back many centuries, some beautiful old cottages, and a much-loved 12th-century **church**, St Michael's, whose most notable feature is its medieval wall paintings. They were discovered in 1889, protected by limewash, and have since deteriorated, but are still impressive. There is a saint, probably St Michael, and the resurrected Christ showing the nail wounds on his hands. The stained-glass windows showing sentimentalised country scenes date from 1922. One shows a hen feeding a worm to her chicks, blackbird fashion; the windows were made in Bristol so perhaps the maker was ignorant of the rural scenes he depicted.

The village is East Devon's centre for the **Resurgence** movement. The Spiral Sanctuary (01297 23822 tinabows@hotmail. com thespiralcentre.wordpress.com/spiral-sanctuary) is a non-denominational organisation created to encourage and promote healing on all levels. There's a library and a programme of events throughout the year, such as crafts, discussion, walks, meditation and healing, as well as outdoor seasonal celebrations and work parties.

Looming steeply behind Axmouth is Hawkesdown (or Hawksdown) Hill; the remains of the fort at the top probably date from the late pre-Roman Iron Age (no public access). It's the last in a chain of forts stretching along the summits of the Blackdown Hills.

WALKING ALONG THE SHORE

From Axmouth Harbour you can continue along the shore as far as you want – even to Lyme Regis if your legs are strong.

However, this is *not* to be undertaken lightly, and if you plan to do the whole stretch you need to pick an extremely low tide – a spring tide – and start from Lyme, since the part where the sea is most likely to block you is less than an hour from there. Wear boots or strong trainers, and remember that the shoreline is changing constantly, as differently angled tides and currents build up new banks of shingle or strip away old ones. You may need to do some boulder-hopping. If you do find your way blocked then just turn back to Lyme. Don't try to climb the cliffs – they are unstable. Walking the full distance is a commitment you must take seriously, as there's no public access to the high path if you change your mind; the way up from the beach roughly below Rousdon is private. Make a day of it and plan a barbecue: there's masses of driftwood to burn.

Also plan your expedition well in advance with your tide table. The best low tides are about 1½ to two days after the full and new moon and tend to be a couple of hours after 12.00; so starting from Lyme at about midday gives you plenty of time to be past the tricky bit before it starts to rise. Thereafter it's simply a slog along the pebbles for about six miles (if you're lucky there may be some stretches of sand), but a slog with plenty of interest. Piles of sea-scoured and twisted driftwood, great for flower-arrangers and sculptors, compete for attention with coloured pebbles and small fossils (though this is too far west for really rich

BOTANICAL SECRETS OF THE UNDERCLIFF

Donald Campbell

Even before the landslide closed the South West Coast Path in 2014, the walk to Lyme Regis could be a disappointing experience as increasing tree cover obscures the views.

Goat Island never disappoints, however, now it is more easily accessible. The orchids continue to do well, with over a thousand common spotted, more than a hundred twayblade, and a good number of greater butterfly, bee and pyramidal orchids. Wet and unstable Culverhole, between Goat Island and the sea, is a typical site for marsh helleborine. The recent decline of this species, and of southern marsh and fragrant orchids at the site, is causing concern but changes of management will hopefully restore the habitat.

Some of the tiny chalk-loving plants are particularly splendid when examined through a hand lens. These include squinancywort, eye-bright, fairy flax and autumn ladies' tresses. In some years, thousands of autumn gentians flower. To give an idea of the richness of this flora, 258 flowering plants were identified in one day in 2012; they were in the company of 1,125 animal species. The charity Buglife has found the Undercliff particularly rich in invertebrates. Butterflies include green hairstreak, marbled white , silver washed fritillary and the wood white which is only rarely seen.

The cliffs are home to many birds, notably peregrines and ravens which nest there. Unusually fulmars nest on the inland cliff not directly above the sea, and along the path you may see or hear blackcaps, bullfinches and marsh tits.

In addition to the guided nature walks, the conservation agencies run work parties. These help to maintain the secret places on one of the most dynamic landslide sites in Europe. Come and join us!

pickings). Shortly after leaving Lyme you'll come to the huge ammonites embedded in flat blue lias rocks known as 'the ammonite graveyard', and there's another group, The Slabs (though we call them 'the dinner plates'), 2½ miles from Axmouth Harbour. They're worth walking to from Seaton. A bit further towards Seaton (if they're not covered by shingle) are the remains of the Brixham trawler, the *Fairway*, wrecked here in 1978, along with those of the digger that tried to salvage her. Another shipwreck visible at low tide is the *Berar*, which ran aground in 1896. She and the Gusher, a freshwater stream, are just east of the *Fairway*, near The Slabs, and mark the sensible stopping point if you are walking from Seaton and intend to return the same way.

The walk is a serious undertaking and, with the risk of slips and trips, should not be done alone. Also, do not walk close to the cliffs, as the rocks are friable and falls can occur at any time.

Pamela and David Morling, who did the walk in March 2019, started from Lyme Regis an hour before low tide, and took 3½ hours to walk to Seaton. 'Tiring but rewarding and a great lesson in geology,' they commented. 'The rock strata are easy to see as you go along, as are the colours on the cliffs denoting various types of material. It is interesting to see the way different rocks start to be shaped once they have fallen into the shore line.'

The cliffs continue to fall and the coastal path often needs to be diverted, sometimes for a less interesting inland route. But thanks to the site manager Tom Sunderland a new path now crosses Goat Island and then goes down a series of steps to join the original coast path.

FOOD & DRINK

The Harbour Inn Axmouth EX12 4AF (opposite the church) ✆ 01297 20371 ◌ theharbour-axmouth.co.uk ⊙ 11.30–23.00 daily (to 22.30 Sun), food 12.00–21.00, roast on Sun from 12.00 until it's finished. Thatched Grade II-listed building, with outdoor patio and garden. Dog friendly. 'Burning of the Ashen Faggot' ceremony (see website) on Christmas Eve.

The Ship Inn Axmouth EX12 4AF ✆ 01297 21838 ◌ shipinnaxmouth.com ⊙ 12.00–23.00 daily (to 21.30 Wed), lunch 12.00–14.30, dinner from 17.30 summer & 18.00 winter. A traditional free house with good food, especially seafood and pizzas, and a large beer garden overlooking the river. Various events (including the annual Axmouth Beer Festival) and live music.

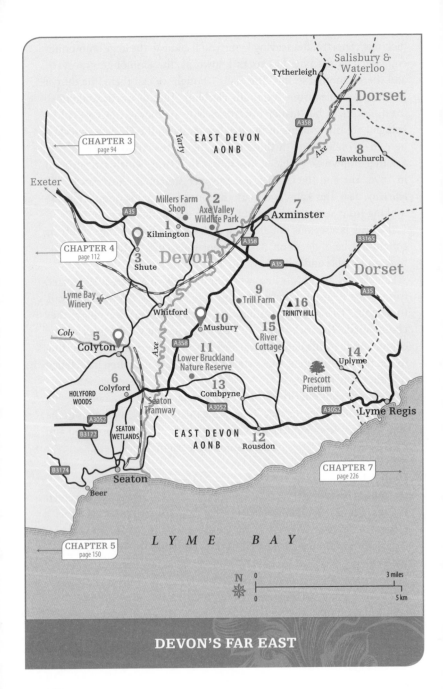

CHAPTER 3
page 94

CHAPTER 4
page 112

CHAPTER 5
page 150

CHAPTER 7
page 226

Salisbury &
Waterloo

Tytherleigh

Dorset

A358

Axe

Yarty

EAST DEVON
AONB

Exeter

Millers Farm
Shop

2
Axe Valley
Wildlife Park

7

Axminster

1
Kilmington

A35

A358

3
Shute

Devon

A35

B3165

Dorset

4
Lyme Bay
Winery

Whitford

9
Trill Farm

▲ 16
TRINITY HILL

A35

Coly

5
Colyton

Axe

A358

10
Musbury

15
River
Cottage

14
Uplyme

11
Lower Bruckland
Nature Reserve

6
Colyford

HOLYFORD
WOODS

13
Combpyne

Prescott
Pinetum

A3052

Lyme Regis

A3052

Seaton
Tramway

A3052

A3052

SEATON
WETLANDS

A3052

EAST DEVON
AONB

12
Rousdon

B3172

B3174

Seaton

Beer

LYME   BAY

N

0   3 miles

0   5 km

DEVON'S FAR EAST

6

DEVON'S FAR EAST

As one approaches by train down the green-clothed valley of the Axe – that like a knife seems to cut in twain the counties of Devon and Dorset, and in cutting blesses each with a watered valley that is the pride and joy of both – one needs to have faith in one's fellows: it looks as if the train that has so sedately travelled by the riverside from the junction with the London and South-Western Railway were going to rush – no, the train does not really rush – into the sea. It stops just short of the pebble ridge that borders the sea and chokes the outlet of the river.

Ward Lock 1925 guidebook

The Beeching railway closures in the 1960s shortened the train's coastward 'rush' somewhat, although the little tram between Colyton and Seaton now travels on part of its old route, but the 'watered valley' that borders this area is still beautiful. The Axe still cuts like a knife through the region, carving its valleys and whittling its hills, along with its sister river the Coly. Both give their names to several places here.

In 1805, Axminster and Kilmington were both on the 'Trafalgar Way', the 271-mile route from Falmouth to London up which news of the victory at Trafalgar was rushed by post-chaise. The four horses were changed 21 times during the journey, which took a breathless and bone-shaking 38 hours; the ninth change was in Axminster, at a recorded cost of £1/11/7d. Other East Devon towns along the route included Exeter and Honiton (see page 88 and ⊘ thetrafalgarway.org). For this chapter we have taken the Far East as extending from the Somerset border in the north, Dorset in the east and in the west the little Umborne Brook, a tributary of the River Coly, and the A30.

 WET-WEATHER ACTIVITIES

Colyton Heritage Centre (page 205)
Axminster Heritage Centre (page 211)

GETTING THERE & AROUND

The public transport hub for this area is Axminster, with its hourly train services to and from Exeter and Waterloo; many of these connect at the railway station with buses for Taunton, Lyme Regis, Dorchester, Honiton and Seaton. The First X53 bus runs a two-hourly service eastward between Axminster and Weymouth via Bridport and Lyme Regis, and Stagecoach bus number 4 runs hourly westward between Axminster and Exeter via Honiton and Ottery St Mary. Stagecoach 9A and 9 between them cover routes from Lyme Regis and Honiton to Exeter via Seaton and Sidmouth, and there are various smaller village services. See also the *Public Transport* information on page 20.

Exeter Airport with flights to/from other parts of Britain and the continent is only about 20 miles away; it has the usual car-hire companies and a regular bus service into Exeter. Roads in this area are adequate although the remoter ones may be narrow or twisty, and some have the high hedges typical of Devon.

SELF-POWERED TRAVEL

The single-track lanes that network this region through open countryside and farmland are a nightmare for drivers but perfect for cyclists. Many have grass growing down the centre. Every few miles there's something of interest, as well as the ever-changing views. For details of East Devon's cycle routes see page 20.

The final stretch of the **East Devon Way**, from Musbury to Lyme Regis, passes through many of the highlights described here. The Axe itself meanders 24 miles from tip to toe; much of its upper stretch is in Somerset and Dorset. With the large-scale Croydecycle maps (⊘ croydecycle.co.uk) you can easily devise your own walks; the ones of this area are *Musbury & Axminster*, and *Lyme Regis*.

WEST OF THE AXE

The A35 forms the northern limit to this region. Above the main road are the farms and small villages of the Blackdown Hills (*Chapter 3*). Nearer the sea and the larger towns the countryside is more popular and populous.

1 KILMINGTON & AREA

> The village . . . was originally called Kilmenton; it is said to have got that name, signifying 'the place of slain men', from a great slaughter of Danes at it in the time of Athelstan.
>
> John Marius Wilson's *Imperial Gazetteer of England and Wales*, 1870–72

Athelstan was the grandson of Alfred the Great and became king in 925; this battle seems to have taken place in 937, and another 18th-century historian mentions it as 'the most bloody conflict which had ever been known in England'. Athelstan fought (and won) against 'the kings of England and Scotland confederated with the Danes' but in fact the location isn't certain. Athelstan is said to have instructed priests in Axminster to 'pray for the souls of seven knights and many Saxon soldiers who were slain near the town in a great battle with the Danes'. Kilmington today is rather better known for one of East Devon's largest farm shops, enthusiastically used by local residents, but turn off the A35 into the village and you're immediately into a quiet Devon community, complete with church with gargoyles around the tower, shop (Hurfords Store), a huge weeping willow overlooking a small stream and a sign announcing its success in the Best Kept Village competition.

In front of the village hall is the **Kilmington Boulder**. A plaque tells us that it was found in the quarry and is probably a hundred million years old. A detailed description hangs by the village hall; the boulder dates from the Cretaceous period, and probably rolled into its position through the force of water, which also gave it its rounded shape. It's a nice bit of geology to have on display.

Millers Farm Shop

EX13 7RA ✆ 01297 35290 ⌨ millersfarmshop.com ◷ 07.00–18.00 Mon–Fri, 08.00–18.00 Sat, 08.00–12.00 Sun

Millers is just off the A35 at Gammons Hill; the entrance is off a side road almost opposite the service station (easily missed if you don't know). In fact it is more like a supermarket than a traditional farm shop, with packaged health foods such as pulses and seeds accompanying the fresh produce (meat, greengrocery, cheeses and other dairy products, baking, wines and so on) from a number of nearby farms and businesses – and France, since the owners visit the continent weekly in search of special foods.

The Teapot coffee shop serves tasty cakes and light snacks.

2 AXE VALLEY WILDLIFE PARK

Kilmington EX13 7RA (off the slip road to Axminster from the A35) ✆ 01297 34472
🖰 axevalleypark.co.uk ⏰ 10.00–17.00 Tue–Sun

'Amazing to see so many animals we didn't even know existed!' This comment in the visitors' book sums up this lovely little zoo. Andrew and Jayne Collier sensibly specialise in small mammals and a wide range of birds, although there are grazing animals such as zebra and deer, and domestic pigs and goats. Among the unusual creatures are Patagonian mara, which look like a cross between a hare and a deer, a potoroo and bustling racoon dogs. That's not to say the ever-popular staples of wildlife parks, such as meerkats and lemurs, are missing – they're here too. Birds include several species of owl including a beautiful dignified great grey owl, and cranes from all over the world. And lots of friendly ducks. A recent addition is the 'warm room' which houses heat-loving reptiles and amphibians.

"Birds include several species of owl including a beautiful dignified great grey owl."

It's such a surprising place to find tucked away off the A35. I asked Andrew how it all began. 'Madness!' he said with fervour. A pretty truthful response given that the Colliers are really dairy farmers, and have been for generations. It helps that he is an expert at building animal enclosures, having worked at other West Country zoos, but even so it's quite a jump from milking cows to keeping an armadillo happy. Education plays an important part, with visits to schools and animal 'experiences' for children who, for an hour, can learn about and look after a choice of animals: meerkats, lemurs, wallabies, 'creepy crawlies', 'small furries' or reptiles.

3 SHUTE

🏰 **Shute Barton Gatehouse** (page 260), **Shute Barton House** (page 260)

An easy three-mile drive from Colyton, at Shute, is the medieval house of Shute Barton (EX13 7PT), managed by the National Trust; it's the gatehouse and remaining wing of what was a much larger dwelling dating back to the 14th century. Also known nowadays as Old Shute House, it's said to be haunted by an unsociable 'grey lady', who glares and vanishes into thin air if she encounters a human. The legends aren't too clear about who she is, but it's unlikely that she's Lady Jane Grey; although that 'grey lady' does also feature in the house's history. Primarily now let by the National Trust and the Landmark Trust as accommodation, it's open to the public on just four weekends a year, when a 45-minute guided tour of the interior brings its intriguing history to life. The 22ft-long fireplace in the great kitchen is thought to be the largest remaining medieval fireplace in England; two full-sized oxen could have been roasted there together, and several people can comfortably stand inside.

Shute acquired its name because the first owners, in the 13th century, were Sir Lucas and Sir Robert de Schete. Its attractive little 13th-century **church of St Michael** was first built as a chapel, and is thought possibly to be on the site of an earlier Saxon place of worship. It has been much refashioned over the years but retains some attractive decoration (much of it in Beer stone), roof bosses, effigies and panels. There's a touching memorial to Sophia Anna, wife of Sir William Templer Pole, who died in 1808 aged 20:

> Her disconsolate husband, who no less tenderly loved her person than adored her virtues, unfeignedly lamenting his irreparable loss here consecrated this monument to her memory.

St Michael's is a busy, active church with a strong sense of community. We have visited it for two flower festivals, which include a great many cream teas and homemade cakes as well as a blaze of flowers, and always people have come up wanting to tell us proudly about *their* church. The iron ring in the centre of the south door may be an old sanctuary ring or handle. The Millennium Plaque in the church, commissioned in 2003, is the work of Moussa Al Korda of Exeter University, a Muslim, whose design was unanimously considered the best of all those submitted. Exeter Diocesan Council objected to Muslim involvement so Shute Parochial Council confirmed their choice (again unanimously) at a special meeting. Exeter Diocesan Council then took three years to approve the plaque, and only did so when told that it would otherwise be installed in St Mary's Chapel, Whitford, over which they had no control.

The historic Shute Estate contains the impressive 800-year-old 'King John's Oak', still going strong (or strongish – it's feeling its age a bit, as well it might) after so many years of history. It has been 'adopted' by Shute Primary School and is looked after locally.

Shute Festival (⊘ shutefest.org.uk; Sep) describes itself as a boutique literary festival' but I'm not sure about the 'boutique' bit, because it attracts big names and big ideas that physically larger festivals might

A walk to Shute Beacon House

❋ Croydecycle *Musbury & Axminster*; start: Haddon Rd, Shute; less then half a mile but can be extended; ⚲ SY258973; easy woodland walking.

Shute Beacon House or hut really does have a claim as the region's best kept secret: it took me two excursions to find it, hidden as it is in Shute Woods, to the south of Shute Hill, with no signage to indicate its presence. Shute Woods are privately owned but are networked with permissive paths. The wood is small enough that you won't get lost but large enough to have an enjoyable walk of a couple of miles with occasional far-reaching views.

The beacon can be reached on a longer walk by parking at Shute and walking up a track, Ashes Road, which gives you access to the woods (see map). For the short walk, drive up Haddon Road, past the church and primary school to the parking area on your left at the lower end of the woods. Take the path to the extreme right (there is an overgrown link to it from the car park) and walk uphill, through conifers, turning left when the path forks. This level path soon opens out, running between dense bracken in the summer. Pass two benches on your right, the first decorated with Permissive Path green arrows, and keep your eyes peeled just after the second bench for a narrow path leading up to the right and a glimpse of your destination, the Beacon House.

The little beehive-shaped hut is an appealing remnant of local history. It was probably built in 1567. In the 1990s it was deteriorating and in danger of being condemned. It was rebuilt with the help of local school children, and a sign nearby explains the duty of the watchman – which doesn't sound much fun, even for Elizabethan times. He was expected to keep watch 'day and night from March to October, he should not even be allowed a dog for company, sheltered by a hut without seates or ease less he should fall asleape'. What happened if the Armada invaded during the winter months is not explained.

Look south from the hut and you can indeed see the Axe Estuary up which the Armada would have sailed.

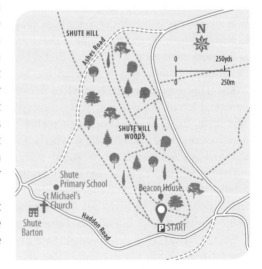

envy. Beautiful St Michael's Church is the main venue, and in recent years speakers have, among many others, included Esther and Annie Freud, Sophie Hannah, Anne Swithinbank, Christina Lamb, Laurence Anholt and Diana Darke.

Shute Hill & Beacon

To the east of the church is one of the region's beacon hills, complete with its beehive-shaped **Beacon House** (see box, opposite), one of the few surviving. The best example of an Elizabethan beacon house is near Culmstock (page 98). Shute's is particularly significant since from there the Elizabethan watchman could see Axmouth and spot the Spanish Armada attempting to invade. If this happened he would light a fire, probably in a purpose-made fire basket on a pole, which would be picked up by the other watchmen on beacon hills and the region warned of the imminent danger.

4 LYME BAY WINERY

Shute Rd, EX13 7PW ℘ 01297 551355 ⌂ lymebaywinery.co.uk ⊙ 09.30–17.00 Mon–Fri, 10.00–16.00 Sat, 11.00–16.00 Sun; see ad, 2nd colour section.

A mile or so from Shute on the way to Musbury (follow the brown signs) you'll find the extremely tempting Lyme Bay Winery. Step inside the rather anonymous-looking 'warehouse' and you're greeted by row upon row of shining jars and bottles in a miscellany of shapes and colours: specialist country wines, liqueurs, draught and bottled ciders, preserves and much more.

It's not just about the shop, however. Since launching their own still and sparkling wines on to the market in 2015, Lyme Bay Winery has won an astonishing 70 awards, 33 of them in 2018. And in July 2019 they achieved the important BRC (British Retail Consortium) Global Standard with an A rating – the only English wine producer currently to have reached this level.

Wine apart, they take great care crafting traditional recipes into award-winning drinks, tailored to the 21st-century palette and using secret local ingredients. Each of these is fermented, blended and aged, as appropriate, at the winery itself. A current favourite is mead, using their own secret blends of honey. Arguably the world's first alcoholic drink (traces of something very similar have been found dating back to 6500BC), it's created by fermenting honey with water and sometimes adding fruit, spices, grains or hops. Its wide range of flavours depend on the source of the honey, the additives used (including fruit and spices), the yeast employed during fermentation and the ageing procedure.

"Wine apart, they take great care crafting traditional recipes into award-winning drinks."

Predictably, Lyme Bay Winery's has won many awards, as has their Jack Ratt range of cider and scrumpy, made from the freshly pressed juice of locally grown traditional cider apples and named after the notorious West Country smuggler Jack Rattenbury (see box, page 175). Then there's fruit cider, apple juice, cider vinegar cream liqueurs – and in 2019 they launched Devon's first spiced rum, Lugger! The shop also sells quality items from other local producers, and there's a mail order service.

The spacious parking area also contains a small branch of **The Coffee Factory** (✐ 01297 551259 ☉ hours currently variable), where you can drink and/or buy a range of specialist coffees. The aroma inside is wonderful.

THE COLYS & AREA

Colyton and Colyford are (unsurprisingly) located on the River Coly, whose valley offers some beautiful walks. There are also good – though hilly – cycle rides in the area. Bus 885 (Seaton–Axminster) runs through both Colyton and Colyford, as does the Seaton Tramway (page 186).

5 COLYTON

🏠 **The Old Bakehouse** (page 260)

The little town of Colyton, with its steep, twisty streets and beautiful old cottages, oozes history from every brick and cobble. Prehistoric man used its veins of hard flint to fashion axes and arrowheads, then the Romans settled nearby and linked it by road to Exeter, Sidmouth and Lyme Regis. The present layout of its streets harks back to Saxon times; in AD827 it had a Saxon parliament, and it appears in the Domesday Book.

Wealthy families who came over with William the Conqueror settled and became lords of the manor. By the 15th century Colyton was Devon's third richest wool town. In 1549 its Chamber of Feoffees (local government) was established and still meets regularly today. Colyton was involved in the Civil War of 1643 (it supported parliament), and at the time of the Monmouth Rebellion earned the reputation of being 'the most rebellious town in Devon' (see box, page 207). One-hour guided history walks set off from the central car park at 14.00 on Thursdays from April to September, tracing Colyton's picturesque past (⌀ colytonhistory.co.uk).

Colyton today is a town with the soul of a village: warm, friendly, active and community minded. Its old houses (some dating from the 16th and 17th centuries) cluster confidentially together in the narrow lanes. The unusual octagonal tower of 12th-century St Andrew's Church (one of only three in the UK) looks down on a patchwork of little rooftops, some still thatched. Inside the light, spacious interior of the church is a beautifully carved Saxon cross; it was found, built into the west face of the tower, when the church was being repaired after a serious fire in 1933. There are some interesting memorials and monuments, particularly in the Pole Chapel, and two fine brass chandeliers that were purchased in 1796 for £82. Its west window is one of the largest in Devon; the original frame was carved from Beer stone some 600 years ago, but in the early 20th century it was returned to Beer quarry when new tracery was fitted. An oak display case contains various ancient religious books, including a 1717 'vinegar Bible'. These got their name from the misprinted heading in Luke 20: 'The parable of the vinegar' rather than 'vineyard'.

"Colyton today is a town with the soul of a village: warm, friendly, active and community minded."

Back in the mid 19th century, Colyton had butchers, bakers, a candlemaker and just about every other shop or business a small town could possibly need, including hairdressers and bookstores. The list is somewhat less exhaustive today, but still the several small, independent shops provide a service gloriously far removed from that of supermarkets and chain stores. The town has three royal market charters, granted by King John, Edward III and Henry VIII.

The **Colyton Heritage Centre** (Market Pl, EX24 6JR ⌀ colytonheritagecentre.org ☉ Apr–Oct 10.00–16.00 Mon, Tue, Thu & Fri, 10.00–13.00 Wed & Sat) is located in a 15th-century building, the Merchant's House, in the heart of Colyton; it was once the home of a wealthy cloth merchant. The many fine features include an elegant decorative ceiling, a Tudor fireplace, half-timber walls and a medieval wall mural. Staffed by volunteers from the Colyton Parish History

Society, the centre has exhibitions of local interest, and a Family History Service Point with a large selection of books, local records and maps.

Next door, still in the Merchant's House, with heavy timber ceiling beams and the remains of a once-handsome fireplace, is the **Merchant's Tea Room and Tea Garden** (∂ merchantstearooms.co.uk $\odot$ year-round from 10.00 Mon–Sat but times vary seasonally; check website), a traditional tea room offering cream teas, light lunches and snacks with daily specials (good baking!).

Art galleries include the **Dolphin House Gallery** (∂ www. dolphinhousegallery.co.uk) in picturesque old Dolphin Street, with the paintings and detailed, distinctive etchings of Roger St Barbe, and the **Bellflower Gallery** in Market Place (∂ millhousefineart.com) with Anne Cotterill's attractive flower prints, fine-art cards and notelets. It's opposite **Chandos Books**, which has a browsable collection of antiquarian and secondhand books. In a turning off King Street, The Garden Shop (EX24 6PD ∂ gardenshopcolyton.co.uk $\odot$ 09.00–17.00 Mon–Sat, 10.00–16.00 Sun) is a peaceful little haven with ample parking space. Apart from its miscellany of healthy, well-watered plants (most of them raised in the South West) and many other garden needs from tubs and tools (and a tool-sharpening service) to fertiliser, the gift section has a colourful range of imaginative and unusual items, many made by local craftspeople. Changing displays of arts, crafts and other items are also housed in an adjacent barn. Owner Sue told me that – one day – she hopes to add a 'rescue' repair service to save old tools and other items from being wastefully thrown out. Finally, there's also a pleasant café ($\odot$ 10.00–16.00 daily) providing drinks, snacks, light meals and home baking, where I succumbed to buttered crumpets. The place is full of ideas, so check the website for up-to-date news.

"Changing displays of arts, crafts and other items are also housed in an adjacent barn."

Cyclists will like to know about **Soanes Cycles** in Queen Square ($\mathscr{J}$ 01297 552308), a friendly and helpful shop offering new and used sales, cycle repairs and hire.

The **Tramway Station** (for more details of the trams, see page 186) has a well-stocked shop with some original rail-based gifts and a café/restaurant, the Tramstop. I stopped for tea there, and the counter assistant apologised that my scone might crumble when I tried to cut it open. 'It's just fresh out of the oven this minute,' she warned me, 'So don't burn yourself'. Indeed,

THE MOST REBELLIOUS TOWN IN DEVON

During the 16th and 17th centuries, religious dissent and persecution were rife in England, seesawing according to which religion (broadly, Catholicism or Protestantism) was uppermost. When James II came to the throne on the death of Charles II in 1685, there were general fears that he would give more weight to Catholicism. The (Protestant) Duke of Monmouth, illegitimate son of Charles II, hoping to overthrow James, landed at Lyme Regis and tried to raise a rebellion. He had stayed briefly in Colyton five years before on a visit to gauge public support, so the (Protestant) people of Colyton felt involved, and 105 marched off to join him in the fight for religious freedom. This was a larger number than from any other parish in Devon, hence 'the most rebellious town …'. None had military experience, but this was not a 'rabble

army'; several were skilled craftsmen and one a doctor. But the duke's army was routed at Sedgemoor, and 71 Colyton men were sent to face trial by the notorious Judge Jeffreys. He sentenced 14 to be hanged (two were hanged, drawn and quartered in Colyton itself), and 22 to be transported to the West Indies as slaves. Two of the slaves eventually escaped captivity, pirates and numerous other hardships and made it back to Colyton – and how welcome the return to their quiet rural life must have been! The duke fled from Sedgemoor but got only about 20 miles before his horse sank beneath him. He was captured by the king's men lying in a ditch, disguised as a peasant, worn out by hunger and fatigue; subsequently he was beheaded, an incompetent executioner taking five blows of the axe to complete the deed. Gruesome times.

it was the freshest scone I've ever tasted; I ate it sitting on the platform in the sun, looking out across the track at Colyton and its impressive church and chatting (improbably) to a group of weavers complete with spinning wheel. They'd decided it was too nice a day to stay indoors so were having a little outing. On another visit I enjoyed local crab cakes in a crunchy coating, with salad and sweet chilli dressing.

6 COLYFORD

Colyford is equally rooted in history. Back in 1341, it was granted a charter to hold a Goose Fair – which it does now, annually, generally on the last Saturday in September. This medieval-inspired romp features mummers, morris dancers, strolling players, displays of traditional crafts such as felting, weaving and thatching, a ram roast, lots of people in medieval costume and a ceremonial opening by the mayor and his lady. The surroundings are beautiful and, weather permitting, it's a fun afternoon, with all profits going to help the community.

Tram-assisted walk: Colyton to Colyford

✤ Croydecycle: *Beer, Branscombe, Seaton*; Start: Colyton; 1½ miles; easy

Most people taking the tram ride to Colyton have a snack in the café, and then ride back to Seaton. But Slow travellers can do better than that. If it's a fine day you can stroll for 1½ miles next to the River Coly and catch a later tram from Colyford; they run every 20 minutes in summer.

From the tram station take the road into Colyton (signposted), cross the Umborne Bridge, and then turn left through some workshops to pick up the footpath to Colyford. On the first stretch, when the river is on your right, there are some good paddling places for children (stony, bring footgear) but once you cross the wooden footbridge there are deeper places where swimming is possible. So if it's a fine summer day bring a picnic and make the most of this lovely river. When you reach the main road at the White Hart pub in Colyford you'll see the tram station across the road to your right.

A few old buildings survive in the short main street (it's the A3052, so watch out for fast traffic) including a row of obviously vintage petrol pumps. No petrol has passed their lips since 2001 but they do remember Lawrence of Arabia (see box, page 148). Behind them, surprisingly, sits **The Filling Station Café & Colyford Cycles** (✆ 01297 553013 ☉ 09.30–16.30 Mon–Sat, 10.00–14.00 Sun) where, beyond the stands of cycles, you'll find an efficient café with good coffee, irresistible cakes (from a talented local baker; 'yes, they're to die for!' agreed Amy behind the counter when I commented) and a range of hot and cold snacks. At the tramway station at the bottom of the hill is a Victorian urinal – unused now but rather beautiful as urinals go, with frilly wrought ironwork. The little St Michael's Church, built as a private chapel in Arts and Crafts style in 1889, still has many of its original features.

It's worth knowing, as you pass through Colyford, that the village shop, Pritchards, sells lunch-time snacks and picnic supplies, as well as housing the excellent Colyford Butchers.

¶¶ FOOD & DRINK

The various cafés mentioned in the Colyton section (page 206) are fine for lunch or tea but shut at around 17.00. These are open later.

The Kingfisher Inn Dolphin St, Colyton ✆ 01297 552476 ⊙ from 11.00 Mon–Sat, from 11.30 Sun; food 18.00–20.00 Sun & Mon, 18.00–20.30 Tue–Thu, 18.00–21.00 Fri & Sat. Friendly pub in a 16th-century building, with a wide range of ales and ciders. The landlord and his wife have their own fishing boat, so expect very fresh local seafood. May be crowded at busy times.

The Wheelwright Inn Swan Hill Rd, Colyford ✆ 01297 598228 ⌂ thewheelwrightinn.co.uk ⊙ 11.00–23.00 daily; food 12.00–14.30 & 18.00–21.00 daily. On the left of the A3052 as you follow it downhill. A 17th-century thatched pub, only just reopened under new management: check progress on the website. The vibe when I went in was immediately warm and welcoming. The menu is a mix of traditional pub grub and some original additions. It's now a free house, so they can – and do – pick and choose the best local brews. Very promising!

The White Hart Swan Hill Rd, Colyford ✆ 01297 553201 ⌂ whitehartcolyford.co.uk ⊙ 11.00–15.00 & 17.00–23.00 Mon–Thu, all day Fri–Sun. Good-value pub food, Sunday carvery (12.00–14.30). A cheery place by the Colyford tram station, so you could stop off here for lunch or coffee on the tram ride between Colyton and Seaton. Dog friendly & wheelchair accessible.

EAST OF THE AXE

Until the 19th century much of the area north of Axminster was part of Dorset, with the churches belonging to the Diocese of Salisbury rather than Exeter. Not that anyone would notice, but it's still nice to have them back.

7 AXMINSTER

⌂ **The George Hotel** (page 259) ⛺ **Lower Keats Glamping**, Tytherleigh (page 260)
Tourist information: Axminster Heritage Centre, Thomas Whitty House, Silver St ✆ 01297 639884 ⌂ axminsterheritage.org ⊙ Easter–Oct 10.00–16.00 Mon–Fri, 10.00–13.00 Sat, Nov–Easter 10.00–16.00 Tue & Thu

Long ago, the Axminster area was a hub for less mechanised transport than today: it's at the crossing of two ancient roads, adopted by Romans as the Fosse Way to Aquae Sulis (the modern Bath in Somerset) and Isca Dumnoniorum (Exeter). Romans, Saxons, Normans, Danes and prehistoric peoples have all left their mark here.

Journeying round the country in 1788, the Rev Stebbing Shaw commented of Axminster: 'The manufacture of this place is chiefly carpets, and esteemed superior to the Wilton, being worked by the pliant fingers of small children, from patterns and colours laid before them.' (Alas, child labour on our own home ground!) Shaw was right; for it was in 1755 that Thomas Whitty, a local weaver, wove his first carpet, and thus laid the foundations for a product that gained renown worldwide. Axminster carpets quickly became the furnishing of choice for wealthy homes in England, as well as many countries overseas. King

"Quietly bustling in the peaceful beauty of the Axe Valley, this market town has some attractive old buildings."

George III visited the factory in 1789, with his whole family, and the Prince Regent ordered huge carpets for Brighton's Royal Pavilion. Axminster was on the itinerary of anyone visiting the South West. An American visitor wrote, in 1864, 'Passed through Axminster, famous for giving an everlasting name to the carpets of royal palaces and mansions of nobility and gentry'. For the full carpet history, see *♂* axminster-carpets.co.uk, or visit the excellent Axminster Heritage Centre. Even today, the carpets are as durable and attractive as ever, and its shop (on the Musbury Road, near the junction with the A35) offers some good bargains.

Quietly bustling in the peaceful beauty of the Axe Valley, this market town has some attractive old buildings (but some bland modern stuff too), lovely walks out into the countryside and down the Axe, and a strong feeling of community. A **market** fills the central square with trade and chatter every Thursday, and small traditional independent shops (including a baker, butcher, jeweller) are holding their own. The **Archway Bookshop** (*♪* 01297 33744 *♂* archwaybookshop.co.uk) has a good stock of books, cards, maps and other browsable items. Its atmospheric 13th-century premises are next to the historic Old Courthouse in Church Street, which now houses the **Arts Café** for light meals and snacks including cream teas. There are tables inside and outside in its peaceful and attractive 'secret garden', where in summer there's a Saturday programme of live music from local performers. The site for the courthouse was bought by the Devon police in 1855, and on it they erected the first purpose-built police station in Devon. Two of the old cells are still *in situ* and are now used (redecorated!) as part of the café where customers can sit. (Just don't order porridge …)

The compact town centre is wrapped protectively around the church, as it has been for many centuries: a minster (monastic convent) is recorded as having been here in 786, and the tower of the present **Minster Church of St Mary the Virgin** dates from the 13th century.

As happened to so many churches in the area, every century has left some traces of alteration or acquisition. The interior today is peaceful, beautiful and well used; short lunchtime concerts followed by a light lunch have been held here on summer Thursdays for more than three decades, and evening concerts and other events take place throughout the year. In the lane bordering Church Green you'll spot seven reliefs: they depict different scenes from Axminster's history, including George III's visit there in 1789.

The centre is likely to undergo quite a change in the next year or so, as a result of the closure in 2019 of Fields Department Store with its long street frontage. What will fill the site isn't yet known, as a department store is hard to replace; at the time of writing a possible buyer was rumoured, but with mystery surrounding any future plans. We'll see.

The recently opened **Axminster Heritage Centre** ($\mathcal{O}$ axminsterheritage. org), housed in the historic Thomas Whitty House in Silver Street (yes, *the* Thomas Whitty who wove the first Axminster carpet), is Axminster's star attraction and very well worth a visit. As well as illustrating the history and heritage of Axminster through the ages, with memorabilia and displays linked to the town and its people, it has models, artefacts, photos and documents showing the development of carpet-making, not only in Axminster but throughout England. After all, when you talk of 'buying an Axminster', people countrywide know immediately that you mean a carpet, and not so many other English towns have similar claims to fame.

Rather surprisingly Axminster also has a **feather factory**, Jaffé et Fils Ltd ($\mathcal{O}$ jaffefeathers.co.uk). Feathers for the late Queen Mother's hats were prepared there, along with, more recently, colourful feathered creations for countless film and theatre productions, from *Paddington 2* and *Downton Abbey* to *Game of Thrones* and *Les Misérables*. It's in the 'Old Brushworks' or former brush factory at the bottom of Castle Hill, an imposing building dating from the 18th century (sadly, not open to the public). Brush- making was also an important industry in Axminster, with a

"The compact town centre is wrapped protectively around the church, as it has been for many centuries."

directory dated 1883 recording two brush factories in the town; one of which, Bidwells, was shipping out up to 14,000 toothbrushes weekly by 1910. For more details of this, search the Axminster Heritage Centre website (⌀ axminsterheritage.org) for their painstakingly researched survey of brush-making in Axminster.

It's lovely to see the old **George Hotel** in George Street back in business after several years of closure. Its doors had just reopened at the time of writing and it's sparkling. Refurbishment of the beautiful old building has been thorough but sympathetic, retaining its character. Opened in 1760 on the site of an earlier inn, the Cross Keys, which was destroyed by fire the previous year, it was the town's historic heart for centuries. The Earl of Monmouth and his supporters are said to have sought refreshment there, and it provided headquarters for Oliver Cromwell and his troops. Lord Nelson slept at the hotel, as allegedly did Judge Jeffreys, and King George III wined and dined there before visiting (and no doubt discussing royal carpets with) Thomas Whitty. In its heyday, as a post house on the route between Exeter and London, more than 16 coaches a day would stop there; passengers trooped out for refreshments while the horses were changed. More recently the splendid Adam Room, with its unique minstrel's gallery, was used in World War II by army commanders planning D-Day tactics. In 1950 it was declared a Grade II-listed building. And now you too can wine, dine and sleep in this historic place! It's still getting settled in, but the menu is generous and reasonably priced, the rooms are comfortable and very clean, and the staff are friendly and attentive. (Also see *Food & Drink*)

Among this century's arrivals in the Axminster area is the multi-talented Hugh Fearnley-Whittingstall and his **River Cottage** activities (⌀ rivercottage.net). His canteen and deli settled very quickly into Axminster and are used steadily, while activities out at the headquarters (page 223) have been increasing in scope and attracting big crowds. He has been – and is – a great benefit to the area.

A much newer arrival in town is the **Community Waffle House** (⌀ waffle.org.uk), a truly communal undertaking opened in 2019 with help from crowdfunding. Aside from its very good waffles and other sweet delights (good coffee too), Waffle has a social purpose: to help tackle loneliness and exclusion by helping people of all ages, particularly the lonely or isolated, to meet and possibly form friendships. Waffle's customers don't have to rush off after eating; some may well linger to chat or just enjoy the friendly atmosphere, and it's a safe (alcohol-free) meeting place for young people in the evenings. The café also has a 'pay-it-forward' scheme, where for £5 customers can buy a card that entitles the holder to a free waffle and drink. The card can then be left with Waffle, who will pass it on to someone within the community who they know would benefit from an act of kindness.

Axminster's **Axe Vale Festival** (⟨⟩ axevaleshow.com), held annually in June, is an extensive and very popular showcase of local crafts, trades, activities and products: in particular, don't miss the food marquee, packed with tempting West-Country goodies.

¶¶ FOOD & DRINK

Arts Café Bar Church St ⟨⟩ 01297 631455 ⊙ 09.00–16.00 Mon–Fri, 09.00–15.00 Sat. Coffees, speciality teas, baking, snacks & light meals. Historic premises & courtyard garden. See page 210.

Community Waffle House 1 West St ⟨⟩ 07535 761440 ⟨⟩ waffle.org.uk ⊙ 14.00–22.00 Tue–Sat. Belgian waffles, puddings, hot and cold snacks and drinks in a friendly, relaxed atmosphere. See opposite.

Far from the Madding Crowd Bistro & Bakery 3 Trinity Sq. Very newly opened at the time of writing but its freshly baked organic bread is already popular. Coffee and tea room, with a bistro open some evenings; times and contact details not yet fixed so search 'Axminster bistro and bakery' online for current situation. New owner Nathan is fully committed to organic, ethical food and is full of plans (including for bread-making courses), so do let us know how it turns out.

George Hotel George St ⟨⟩ 01297 33385 ⟨⟩ georgeaxminster.southcoastinns.co.uk ⊙ 11.00–23.00 Mon–Sat, 12.00–22.30 Sun. A competent, pleasant town-centre hotel with helpful staff, convenient for a full meal or just a drink or afternoon tea (good cake!) in comfortable surroundings. The menu is likely to change seasonally so check the website. See opposite.

River Cottage Canteen Trinity Sq ⟨⟩ 01297 631715 ⟨⟩ rivercottage.net ⊙ 09.00–21.00 Mon–Sat, 09.00–16.00 Sun. This is the essence of Slow, with fresh local produce and minimal food miles. The deli counter's goodies include local wines, cheeses, pies, poultry, meat, vegetables, preserves, home baking – and much more, but always on a small and non-mass-produced scale. The café and canteen attached to the shop follow the philosophy through and offer good, fresh, well-presented local food: breakfast, lunch, dinner, snacks, coffee etc. For details of other River Cottage activities, see page 223.

8 HAWKCHURCH

🏠 **Fairwater Head Hotel** (page 259), ⛺ **Crafty Camping**, Holditch (Dorset; page 260)

Devon reclaimed Hawkchurch from Dorset in 1893; thank goodness, or it wouldn't have belonged in this chapter. This charming, isolated village is worth the detour. Approached via narrow lanes enclosed by earth banks topped by high beech trees (their function as a hedge long gone) the village displays itself as quintessentially Devon, with a church opposite a pub (the Old Inn) and a community-run shop.

It is the **church** of St John the Baptist that brings the lover of village art here. The excellent church guide proudly declares that 'its early English sculpture is surely the finest to be seen in any of East Devon's churches'. I agree. Whereas other churches in the region have terrific carved bench ends, Hawkchurch's carved capitals are at least three centuries older and just as bizarre. Walk around the church, guide in hand, and marvel at the skill and ingenuity of these carvings. No-one knows what most of them mean – or indeed what many of them represent. Is that a man feeding a squirrel? And if so, why? It's certainly a red squirrel (which, of course, would have been the only sort in those days), you can see its ear tufts. Elsewhere it's a swan or goose that's being fed, and also, easily recognised, a seated man is feeding a dog. Then there is a confusion of serpents or dragons with a man biting on the tail of one, although another interpretation is that the creature is emerging from his mouth. My favourite, and the one in the best condition, is a ram and a goat, facing each other and playing musical instruments. The ram is playing a viol and the goat a set of panpipes or a recorder (tricky with hoofs). The church guide describes this as probably representing lust, although the two animals seem too immersed in their music to have any such ideas.

THE COMMUNITY SHOP

Chris Andrews

'Can I help you at all?' Hawkchurch Community Shop, like other such shops throughout the county, is a local shop for local people, staffed and managed entirely by volunteers and serving village residents and the occasional visitor seven days a week since May 2014. It sells the essentials like newspapers, wine (from Lyme Bay to Argentina) and milk, as well as local produce such as bread from Charmouth, biscuits from Morcombelake, curries from Kilmington, sausages from Axminster, free-range eggs from Fowler's near Sidbury, honey from local bees and other precious things. Its continued development as a local resource and social hub has meant that it has now outgrown its current Portakabin premises, which has led to a successful application to the National Lottery Community Business Fund for a £60,000 grant for a new larger shop on the same site, selling an increased range of merchandise and also incorporating a dedicated social space serving teas and coffees, which will complement the village hall and the pub. Work will be finished by the time you read this. You'll never leave!

There are also treasures on the outside walls, just underneath the roof on the south side. This feature is known as a corbel table and would originally have helped support the roof; they were reset in the Victorian restoration. Binoculars are a help here to fully appreciate the Norman carvings on both the north and southern aspects. Most delightful are a couple who ought to be husband and wife, one smiling, one gloomy (there's an excellent photo of these in the church guide). The tower, west window and clock were renovated in 2019, with the clock – installed in 1897 to celebrate Queen Victoria's jubilee – being sent away to be regilded.

9 TRILL FARM

🏠 **The Stables Guest House** (page 260)

Trill Farm, Musbury EX13 8TU 🕿 01297 631113 🖉 trillfarm.co.uk

For years I drove past the little sign to Trill when en route to Axminster from Seaton and thought only of budgies. I should have investigated sooner since Trill Farm is an exceptional place – embracing the Slow ethos more emphatically than anywhere else in this book. It was the long-term project of the founder of Neal's Yard Remedies, Romy Fraser, who wanted to combine her interest in sustainable living with education. This she has achieved at Trill Farm, a community of small businesses, all committed to the same goal: sustainability and respect for the environment. Their 300 organic acres support an orchard growing 20 variety of apples, sheep for wool, ponds that are now home to water voles, and much more. Their courses vary from one to four days and cover subjects such as creative writing, herbal medicine, foraging and Scandinavian woodwork – and some more surprising things such as game butchery and bark-tanning rabbit skins. This is truly using nature's bounty and wasting nothing.

"Trill Farm is an exceptional place – embracing the Slow ethos more emphatically than anywhere else."

Ash and Kate manage the vegetable garden with the help of local growers, trainees and volunteers – although garden is the wrong word for the two acres of productive land that produces over a hundred varieties of fruit and vegetables, and provides 3½ tons of salad every year to local restaurants – keep an eye out for 'Trill salad' on menus in the area, or visit their market stall outside Town Mill Bakery in Lyme Regis on Saturday mornings in the summer. Hand in hand with the kitchen garden is the **Old Dairy Kitchen**. Chris Onions, who runs this dynamic place, works with people who need a little more individual help and understanding, such as those in recovery from addiction and bereaved men who are taught simple cooking skills. His own skill can be appreciated at the farm lunches and dinners (see below). Finally, there's the main core of Trill Farm, their soaps and beauty products, sold in the shop and online, made using herbs grown on the farm. I watched, fascinated, as soap was prepared, sliced and packaged in a room that smelled deliciously of lavender.

All these products come together in the Trill Farm Seasons Box, which can be ordered online. 'Each item is a celebration of the organic and wild offerings of our land', they say. It will be unlike any similar hamper you have ever received.

¶¶ FOOD & DRINK

Crafty Tea Room Cooks Ln, Axminster EX13 5SQ ✐ 01297 639800 ♂ furzeleighdowndairy. co.uk ☉ 10.30–17.00 daily (closed Mon during school term & sometimes in Dec/Jan). A peaceful little café on Furzeleigh Down Farm's land, a short drive from Axminster; tables inside and out, with views of widespread rolling countryside. Ample parking, toilet, disabled-accessible and dog friendly, with a 'Chatter & Natter' table for single customers who may like company. Hot and cold drinks and snacks, cream teas and home baking. There's also ice cream available in containers to take home – it's made with milk from Furzeleigh Down's own Friesian Holstein cows, so its 'food miles' are just yards! Also on sale are jams and chutneys, as well as various handicrafts (hence 'Crafty Tea Room'). Cooks Lane is on Cycle Route 2, and there are walks nearby.

Trill Farm ✐ 07999 923089 ♂ olddairykitchen.co.uk. Farm lunches prepared by Chris Onions on Wednesdays, Saturdays and Sundays. Mainly vegetarian. Chris chooses the servings from what's available on the farm and guests sit at long tables, outside in good weather, and serve themselves from a large selection of yummy dishes and get immersed in conversation. It's reasonably priced, utterly delicious, and an opportunity to meet both locals and visitors. There are also multi-course monthly dinners, sometimes with guest speakers. Popular so book well in advance but there's always the possibility of being fitted in at the last moment.

10 MUSBURY

☗ **Castlewood Vineyard** (page 260)

There are all sorts of notable things about this well-kept village. For instance, Sir Winston Churchill lived here; not a lot of people know that. Because it was another Sir Winston. The Musbury man lived in the 17th century, and was the father of the first Duke of Marlborough who built Blenheim Palace. One of 11 children, John Churchill was a lesson in how to achieve greatness through political flexibility. He managed to maintain loyalty with both King James II and his successor William of Orange, and married Queen Anne's favourite, Sarah Jennings (yes, the Sarah Churchill of the film *The Favourite*). He was also, indisputably, a military genius and a great diplomat.

It is, however, the name Drake, not Churchill, which is commemorated in Musbury, with a row of three generations providing a strikingly unusual memorial in the church. They are kneeling one behind the other, brightened by flaking polychrome, and resplendent in their Elizabethan ruffs.

The Drakes lived at Ashe House (of which no trace is left) and were a separate branch of the family that produced the famous Sir Francis. The first Drake in the memorial to be knighted was Sir Bernard, an admiral for Queen Elizabeth I. Death, in those days, stalked the rich and poor alike. Sir Bernard died 'of a fever caught at the trial of prisoners from a Portuguese ship he had captured, the judge, 11 jurymen, and two other knights dying also'. So writes Arthur Mee in *The King's England*. Probably typhus, also known as 'jail fever' because of the filthy conditions in which prisoners were kept.

The Churchill connection is through Sir John Drake, whose memorial slab is set in the floor beneath his effigies of his relatives. His daughter, Elizabeth, married the 17th-century Sir Winston Churchill and brought him to Musbury after he had lost all his money supporting the wrong side just prior to the Civil War. It was their son, John, who managed his life more effectively to become Duke of Marlborough.

Present-day Musbury has a feeling of community which is reflected in how well the residents look after their church. It is also the starting point for a walk up to the best view in East Devon, from the top of Musbury Castle (see box, page 218). Don't look for dramatic ruins or crenellations; this is an Iron Age hillfort, built before the Roman Conquest, probably for protection against invaders or wild animals. It has never been excavated and little is known about it. What is known is that it's now a great place for rare flowers and butterflies. Musbury Castle is now under the care of the National Trust.

"Present-day Musbury has a feeling of community which is reflected in how well the residents look after their church."

Musbury Castle & beyond: orchids & sequoias

❋ OS Explorer 116 or (better) the Croydecycle maps *Musbury & Axminster* and *Lyme Regis*; start: Musbury Village Hall car park; approx 2 or 5 miles; moderate, with some steep hills

This is a tough but rewarding walk with several options: a circular stroll up and around this hillfort for the best high views in East Devon or an extension to the Pinetum at Uplyme (page 222). For the latter you will need to take a couple of buses to bring you back to your car at Musbury.

Park at the village hall car park in Musbury (if there is no event taking place in the hall; it's a private car park), and follow the East Devon Way (EDW) up past the church and down the drive marked Musbury Barton. The footpath takes you past farm buildings and up a steep track. Just after this track makes a right-angled turn to the left look for the stile on the right. Follow the EDW arrows across the field and over another stile. This field has probably never been ploughed so there are unusually large numbers of flowers here – in June you may see your first common spotted orchids. For more orchids – early purples in May – turn right along the EDW and explore the upper woodland where these orchids are mixed with bluebells. To continue your walk, however, instead of turning right into the woods, head uphill towards the highest point. It's a tough slog, but the views and flowers will help you forget your aching legs. At the highest point you will see the sea, the white cliffs of Beer Head and Seaton in the distance, and Musbury and the nearer villages and small towns in the area below you. In the summer you should also see plenty of butterflies, including perhaps the rare silver-washed fritillary.

After gazing at the view from the high point, follow the path around to the left and continue to walk on high ground, following the footpath into a field. The way is blessedly level here, with far-reaching views on the left. Keep going until you come to a weathered but beautiful seat carved from one piece of timber, set in an enclosed area facing the view. It was put there

Sunning itself above the village is Castlewood Vineyard (⌀ castlewoodvineyard.co.uk). Their sparkling wine can be bought online, at Lyme Winery or by appointment from the farm. Two self-catering cottages are also available (page 260).

11 LOWER BRUCKLAND NATURE RESERVE

🏠 **Higher Bruckland Farm B&B** (page 260)

✐ 07721 429077 ⌀ lowerbrucklandfarm.co.uk ⊙ Apr–Oct 11.30–17.00 Sat & Sun (check website for current opening times)

in memory of Adam James Hoare who died of cancer aged 20.

Continue to Mounthill Lane where you have a choice. Turn left and walk steeply downhill for a mile back to Musbury, or right and meet up with the EDW to Uplyme. Mounthill Lane is beguilingly peaceful, with

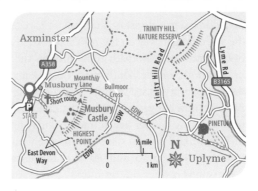

very little traffic, and it's a gentle downhill stroll to Bullmoor Cross, where the EDW meets the road, and then on to a junction where a little stone bridge takes you over the old railway line. The road section is a little over a mile. After the bridge, look for a stile on your left and go through a couple of fields. Cross Trinity Hill Road (with the option to turn left up to the nature reserve, page 224) and follow the bridleway to Woodhouse Hill where you turn right. Keep an eye out for a gated bridle path which climbs up adjacent to the Pinetum (page 222), giving you access to the highest part of the woods so you can walk downhill enjoying the trees and shrubs to the little gate at the bottom.

From here the easiest thing is to continue walking downhill into Uplyme, take some refreshment at the Talbot Arms and catch the next (hourly) bus to Axminster station where there's a connection with the bus to Musbury and Seaton. The alternative, if you're still full of boundless energy, is to continue on the EDW, following the River Lim downhill into Lyme Regis.

This privately owned and award-winning reserve encompassing five small lakes is particularly interesting for dragonflies, butterflies and waterfowl. Visitors strolling the paths (for which there is a charge) should also keep an eye out for the sculptures made by David Satterley who is a skilled woodworker as well as a farmer. He also created the waving figures by one of the lakes, animated by a water wheel.

His partner, Jo, runs Ratty's Tea Room where you can sit and enjoy a peaceful cuppa or light snack overlooking the first lake.

Dogs are not allowed in the reserve or tea room.

12 ROUSDON

🏠 **The Dower House** (page 259), 🏨 **Peek House** (page 260), **Rousdon Cottages** (page 260)

Rousdon is a private estate, and thus you are only supposed to drive past the splendid gateway on the A3052 before stopping at the bakery (page 149). However, a footpath runs through the estate from Stepps Road in Axmouth, or the South West Coast Path from Seaton, giving you the opportunity to see the very grand mansion, the ornate church of St Pancras (now converted to a holiday cottage) and the beautiful grounds with towering copper beech trees. Holiday lets make up almost half of the accommodation in the estate, so a self-catering holiday here allows you to enjoy the peace and beauty of the place to the full.

Rousdon's history centres round Sir Henry Peek. He made his money in tea, and shrewdly married Margaret Edgar, heiress of the Swan & Edgar London store, thus accumulating a great deal of money. They honeymooned in Lyme Regis, fell in love with the area, and in 1871 he bought the entire community of Rousdon. It's what rich people did in those days, although admittedly the population was only 16. Now he had the land he could indulge himself in building an opulent 18-bedroom mansion. The style is described as Franco-Flemish Tudoresque and it was – and still is – undoubtedly grand (Peek House now accommodates holidaymakers; page 260). Marble from a shipwreck was hauled up from the beach on donkeys and used to create a great fireplace and the main stairway in the house.

"The sheep and cattle that graze there now would not have pleased him: his animals were more exotic."

At the same time he rebuilt the Benedictine chapel. This had stood since the 13th century and was once thatched, but now little more than a ruin. No service had been held there for 50 years and it was being used by the farm to store timber. Although no longer used for worship, St Pancras' Church is still interesting, both for its architecture and for the rare revolving lych gate, which is beautifully carved and has a 'coffin slab' for resting the coffin on while opening the gate.

Sir Henry was a true Victorian benefactor, and having taken care of his workers' spiritual health, he set about ensuring that their children were both well educated and well fed. He built a village school and added a kitchen, believing that children could learn more easily with a full stomach. He was thus the pioneer of school dinners. For a penny the children could enjoy rabbit stew, bacon roly-poly and other treats cooked by the headmaster's wife and daughters. An inspector's report of 1883 stated 'What strikes one at once coming into the school is the healthy and vigorous look of the children' which he said was in marked contrast with those in neighbouring schools. The school is now Peek Hall, next to the bakery.

Once the building work was completed Sir Henry turned his attention to the grounds. The sheep and cattle that graze there now would not have pleased him: his animals were more exotic. One guest was surprised to encounter a giraffe while on a morning stroll, and a newly employed steward of the estate was prevented at the last moment from shooting an emu, thinking it was an overgrown hen pheasant. Omelettes made from the eggs of these birds were sometimes served to guests at Sir Henry's London home. He was a member of parliament and steered through the Open Spaces Act of 1878, which did much to preserve common land such as Wimbledon Common.

After Sir Henry's death in 1898 two more generations of Peeks lived at Rousdon but in 1937 it was sold to Allhallows School, which moved there from Honiton in 1938. The school closed in 1998 and the estate was bought by developers with the restrictions of a Conservation Area. These are strictly adhered to.

To Buy a Whole Parish: Rousdon & the Peek Family, by Nicky Campbell, describes this fascinating man and his estate.

13 COMBPYNE

This well-tended village (pronounced Coom-pine) has an appealing little 13th-century church with a distinctive saddle-back tower. A surly writer in 1840, quoted in the church guide, claims that 'its church, dedicated to St Mary, has little to recommend it'. The writer seems particularly disapproving of the size of the church. Too small, apparently. And of course that's what makes it so attractive to the modern visitor. Little churches hold a place of their own in our affections, but this one is exceptional because of the murals, which were only discovered in 1950, during renovations. The biblical texts probably date from the 17th century whilst their decoration may have been done two centuries earlier. But it is the rough sketch of a ship, scratched on the lime-washed wall, that is famous. It is thought to date from the 14th century and be a votive drawing of St Nicholas made by a seafaring parishioner. When it was discovered, the National Maritime Museum confirmed that the construction of the ship itself, with its pole masts and steeply stepped bowsprit, was consistent with vessels of the 13th–14th century. The mystery makes it all the more appealing, and it is accurately reproduced in one of the colourful kneelers.

Almost as old as the ship mural is the stained glass in the west window; this is probably from the 14th or 15th century.

It is thought that St Mary's may overlie a Saxon religious site, and nearby Rousdon's St Pancras' Church (page 220) was originally a Saxon chapel. After St Pancras had been closed for worship, its pews were transferred to St Mary's.

To complete your visit don't miss the charming model of the church in the graveyard where there is also a tombstone to Tristam Hine, a doctor who, when he retired, 'used to sally forth clad in carpet slippers and a blanket over his shoulders to give medical attention to Combpyne parishioners until their own doctor should arrive'.

Between Combpyne and the next place of interest, the Prescott Pinetum, the lanes are so narrow that motorists may suffer a loss of nerve but cyclists will enjoy one of the most interesting and traffic-free bits of East Devon countryside, as well as pass under the impressive Cannington Viaduct which once supported the branch line from Axminster to Lyme Regis, with a station at Combpyne. Constructed in 1903 this was a considerable engineering achievement,

"It is the rough sketch of a ship, scratched on the lime-washed wall, that is famous."

being one of the few such structures to be built of concrete. Subsidence during construction necessitated the unusual supporting pair of arches propping up one of the main arches. The railway closed in 1965.

14 UPLYME & THE PRESCOTT PINETUM

🏠 **Montana** (page 260), **Valley View HQ** (page 260), ⚑ **Hook Farm** (page 260)

Uplyme, as its name suggests, sits above Lyme Regis and is in Devon, while Lyme is across the border in Dorset. A petrol station-cum-shop provides most needs, and there's a bus link to Axminster (useful for walkers; page 218) and a friendly pub, the Talbot Arms. Uplyme is also the starting point for a delightful mile-and-a-half walk down to Lyme Regis following the little River Lim (part of the East Devon Way). It's described in a leaflet available in the Uplyme shop.

The **Pinetum** (rhyme it with arboretum) is managed by the Woodland Trust (⊘ woodlandtrust.org.uk) and hides away on the left side of Woodhouse Lane as it drops down into Uplyme. It's clearly marked on the OS map, and more clearly on the Croydecycle map, but is still very easily missed. Look for the pink East Devon Way arrows at the start of a bridle path (parking is best a little higher up the hill, opposite another bridle path that forms part of the circular walk). The Pinetum was donated to the Woodland Trust in 1977 by Captain John Prescott in memory of his father. The New World conifers from North and South America were planted between 1840 and 1853. There are some seriously impressive sequoias and a wellingtonia which is estimated at 150ft tall. Look out also for Prince Albert's

"This is also an excellent place for bluebells so early May is the perfect time for a visit."

yew (*Saxegothaea conspicua*) from South America which is probably the largest such tree in Britain. There are some equally stately native trees, too – massive oaks and towering beech trees, much higher than you would normally see. This is also an excellent place for bluebells so early May is the perfect time for a visit, when it is pungent with wild garlic and the hybrid rhododendrons are in bloom. Walk quietly up the steeply climbing path, listening for the drumming of greater spotted woodpeckers and the songs of other birds. The trees are not labelled but the information board helps to identify them.

To make this a circular walk continue uphill through the Pinetum until it emerges on to the bridle path where you turn left to walk back to your car or bike.

15 RIVER COTTAGE HEADQUARTERS

✆ 01297 630300 ⊘ rivercottage.net

Hugh Fearnley-Whittingstall and his River Cottage enterprise are a huge asset to the area and the essence of Slow in every way. This is the nerve centre. Tucked away in the countryside between Axminster and Lyme Regis, it isn't a place you can drive straight up to or visit as you pass by. Instead it's the venue for a variety of day and evening events (and some mouthwatering meals), but they are held on specific dates and at specific times; you may need to park a little way off, and walk or use their tractor transport for the final stretch. For details of the current programme see the very comprehensive website (you can book for events online), or phone. Apart from the understandably popular **dining events** (on most Friday and Saturday evenings, and Sunday lunchtime; they need pre-booking) in the 17th-century barn, and the well-attended one-day **cookery courses**, the programme includes four-day wellness retreats, arts and crafts courses, gardening courses and more. There's also some B&B accommodation available. Their **Food Fair** in May and **Festival** in August are lively events with music, food, masterclasses, demonstrations and a generally happy atmosphere, involving a large number of food- or craft-based local businesses; but they're having a break in 2020 and will resume in 2021.

"The ideal time to find reptiles is soon after rain when they come out to warm themselves."

For details of the River Cottage canteen and deli in Axminster, see page 213.

16 TRINITY HILL

This Local Nature Reserve is most easily accessed from the A35, a couple of miles east of Axminster, and is notable for the way the heathland is being managed to encourage heather (there are three types here) and discourage the rampant growth of bracken. Red ruby cattle are helping these conservation efforts by keeping down unwanted vegetation. This is one of the heathlands that hold Nightjar Night Walks (check ⌁ wildeastdevon.co.uk), when you have a good chance of hearing the 'churring' noise that these birds make. Nightjars are migratory, visiting us in the summer from southern Africa. Through careful habitat management their number has increased. You will be lucky to see one, however, since they are extraordinary well camouflaged as they rest on the ground. Diurnal birds include yellowhammer, linnet and reed bunting. Ravens are often seen and heard.

This is also a particularly good place for moths with appealing names such as the drinker and true lover's knot as well as the common emerald.

Trinity Hill is one of the best places in East Devon to see reptiles. Sharp-eyed walkers will notice the sheets of corrugated iron or roofing felt scattered around the reserve. These are to provide a quickly warmed shelter for the cold-blooded reptiles to raise their body temperature. The ideal time to find reptiles is soon after rain when they come out to warm themselves. Use binoculars to spot adders sunning themselves in the clearings close to gorse bushes (they are very shy animals and will retreat if alarmed). For this reason it's best to get to the reserve as early in the morning as possible, providing the sun is up, because walkers and their dogs frighten the reptiles into hiding.

Information on all East Devon's reserves can be found on ⌀ wildeastdevon.co.uk.

STEDCOMBE HOUSE

From the tram between Seaton and Colyford you may spot a striking, somewhat pepper-pot-shaped country house on a hillside across the estuary, about a mile upstream of Axmouth. This is Stedcombe House, built around 1697 by Richard Hallett of Lyme Regis. The Hallett family, ship owners, plied a lucrative trade in rum and sugar between Lyme and Barbados with – most probably – some slave-trading on the side. Several Lyme Regis merchants at the time were buying slaves in Africa, taking them to Barbados to work on the sugar plantations and bringing 'servants' back when they returned home. Hallett was one such, and in 1702 the Lyme Regis town court recorded that 'a Black Negro servant of Mr. Richard Hallett named Ando' was accused of rioting. Earlier, in 1662, Lyme Borough records mention 'a barbadoes boy' being paid to carry out a whipping. For more (surprising!) details search Lyme Regis museum's website, ⌀ lymeregismuseum.co.uk.

The Stedcombe estate – and house – remained in the Hallett family until 1890 when it was bought by Samuel Sanders Stephens, High Sherriff of Devon and notable philanthropist. It was he who, to great local acclaim and popularity, in 1907 paid for the removal in perpetuity of the toll charge on Axmouth bridge (page 191). When his family sold the estate in 1960 it was broken up; the house was abandoned and fell into a sorry state, riddled with dry rot, until new owners in the 1980s undertook massive and sympathetic renovation – so successfully that its Listed Building status was upgraded from II to I.

The house – built of red brick that was most probably baked on site, and with Dorset's Portland stone and Devon's Beer stone used for dressing – has enormous charm, with the spacious rooms and high ceilings of its period and superb open views. The style is simple and symmetrical, with clear, straight lines, making it a tidy rectangle topped by a neat square belvedere. Seen from a distance, across the estuary, it looks almost like a toy house dropped into a modelled countryside. It's a private home at present and there's no public access; but, if it appeals to you, you could always do an internet search to see whether that has changed. It's a beautiful and intriguing place.

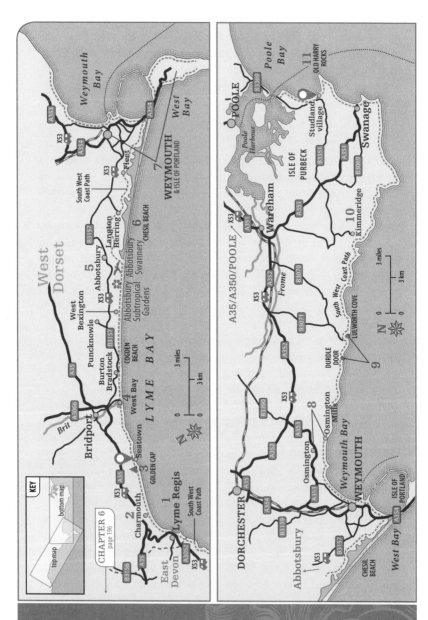

DORSET'S JURASSIC COAST

7

DORSET'S JURASSIC COAST

Alexandra Richards

> The view from Golden Cap is superb. Westward I could see the shining windows of Lyme, the white cliffs of Beer and the red cliffs of Seaton; eastward, the orange cliffs of Burton Bradstock, and the grand sweep of Chesil Beach fading into the grey nose of Portland Bill.

S P B Mais, *This Unknown Island*, 1932

Despite Dorset's many and great delights, in this guide we cover only the highlights of Dorset's section of the Jurassic Coast, which stretches from Lyme Regis on the Devon border to Old Harry Rocks at Studland. Bradt's *Slow Travel Dorset* by Alexandra Richards provides much more detail and is the book you should buy if you plan to spend a reasonable amount of time in Dorset.

 WET-WEATHER ACTIVITIES

Aquarium Lyme Regis (page 234)
Dinosaurland Fossil Museum Lyme Regis (page 235)
Town Mill Complex Lyme Regis (page 234)

GETTING THERE & AROUND

There are only two ways of seeing Dorset's Jurassic Coast properly: on foot along the South West Coast Path, or from the sea on one of the several cruises, listed in each relevant section, which explain the geology from the most advantageous viewpoint.

THE JURASSIC COAST BUS

The X53 Jurassic Coast Bus, the *Jurassic Coaster*, runs all the way from Lyme Regis to Poole. With a bit of planning you can stop off at various points, walk the South West Coast Path for four or five miles, and catch the next bus towards your destination.

THE SOUTH WEST COAST PATH

The South West Coast Path is the standout piece in Dorset's impressive repertoire of walks, combining heritage, flora, fauna, geology and spectacular coastal scenery. The UK's longest national trail, it runs for 630 miles from Minehead in Somerset to Poole in Dorset's east, tracing the coastlines of Cornwall, Devon and Dorset. The Dorset section is 86 miles. The path is easy to find and is waymarked by an acorn symbol. Easy to find is not the same as easy, however. The SWCP is a roller coaster of ups and downs with very few level stretches, so factor this in when planning a walk.

The South West Coast Path website (southwestcoastpath.org.uk) is extremely helpful for planning and its walk-finder tool can help you choose the right route for you. You can download a range of themed walks of varying lengths and levels of difficulty, including information about where to eat and drink en route. Another invaluable source of information is *Dorset & South Devon Coast Path* by Henry Stedman and Joel Newton published by Trailblazer (trailblazer-guides. com). Its combination of hand-drawn maps showing every necessary detail of the trail, and accommodation close to the path, makes it the perfect companion for anyone planning long or short walks along the Jurassic Coast.

The Dorset section of the SWCP offers some of the most spectacular seaside scenery and the path provides access to almost the entire length of the Jurassic Coast World Heritage Site. It passes through Lyme Regis and Charmouth, popular for fossil hunting and between Charmouth and Seatown is Golden Cap, the highest point on England's south coast (see box, page 242).

One warning, however. Cliff falls and landslips in the area sometimes lead to temporary inland diversions of the path, which can be quite lengthy. Always check the SWCP website before planning a cliff walk; you can also follow their route changes page on Facebook (southwestcoastpath)

One of the most rewarding walks is the section of the path between Lulworth Cove and Durdle Door, two of the most spectacular features within the Jurassic Coast World Heritage Site. Durdle Door, a near-perfect coastal arch of limestone rock, lies half a mile to the west of Lulworth Cove. The walk involves some moderately steep climbs along a remarkably well-preserved and photogenic section of coast.

Another highlight is the gentle four-mile walk from Studland along the cliffs to the dramatic chalk stacks of Old Harry Rocks (page 253), from where you can see across to another chalk formation: The Needles, off the Isle of Wight. Early mornings are the best time for this walk, when the sun casts its first gentle rays on the crisp, white rock.

The path provides plenty of opportunity for wildlife watching; on a clear day you may be lucky enough to spot basking sharks, seals or dolphins, particularly around Durlston Country Park near Swanage. Portland and Poole Harbour are good for watching resident and migrating seabirds, and you may catch a glimpse of rare butterflies on the Isle of Purbeck's chalk downland.

"On a clear day you may be lucky enough to spot basking sharks, seals or dolphins."

Walking maps

In addition to the relevant Ordnance Survey maps, ✤ Explorer 116 and ✤ OL15, there are eight Croydecycle maps at 5 inches to the mile which make planning walks so much easier, starting with *Lyme Regis* (Undercliff to Golden Cap) and ending with *Swanage & Studland*.

THE JURASSIC COAST BY BOAT

Travelling by boat along the Jurassic Coast can give you a real appreciation of the area's geology and the multi-layered cliffs that run along the coastline. West Dorset's two harbours, Lyme Regis and West Bay, both have a slipway for public use; visiting craft are welcome but there is a long waiting list for the moorings that are let on an annual basis. Lyme Regis Sailing Club (⌀ lymeregissailingclub.co.uk) offers temporary membership for visitors. Further information about using the harbours is available at ⌀ dorsetcouncil.gov.uk, while general information about exploring the Jurassic Coast by boat is available at ⌀ jurassiccoast.org.

You can take fishing, sightseeing and diving trips from both Lyme Regis and West Bay. Between Easter and October, Lyme Bay Rib charter (⌀ 07971 258515 ⌀ lymebayribcharter.co.uk) operates a **water taxi** between Lyme Regis and West Bay, and Jurassic Coast cruises departing from Lyme Regis. Lyme Rib Rides (The Cobb, Lyme Regis DT7 3JJ ✎ 07709 400300 ⚓ lymeribrides.com) provides similar services. For a bit of variation you can take the CoastLine X53 bus from Lyme Regis to West Bay and then the water taxi on your return trip. The Lyme Regis Pleasure Boat Company (✎ 07765 501539) offers self-drive hire boats from the harbour in Lyme Regis, if you prefer to explore the coast at your own pace.

Weymouth is known for its superb sailing and various Jurassic Coast cruises depart from there (page 249). Cruises also depart from Poole and Swanage (page 252).

LYME REGIS & CHARMOUTH

West Dorset is endowed with one of the most enticing sections of the Jurassic Coast. At its heart, just inside the Dorset border, lies the supremely characterful resort of Lyme Regis. Lyme, as it is often known, is a popular holiday destination for its quaint buildings, sheltered beach and fossil hunting. From here you'll find a choice of excellent walks, notably a particularly beautiful stretch of the South West Coast Path which incorporates Golden Cap, the highest point on the south coast. Nearby Charmouth is as rewarding for fossils as Lyme, and rather quieter.

1 LYME REGIS & SURROUNDS

🏠 **Alexandra Hotel** (page 260) **Dorset House** (page 261), **Hix Townhouse** (page 261)
Tourist information: Church St, Lyme Regis DT7 3BS ✎ 01297 442138 ⚓ lymeregis.org & (for local events) ⚓ whatsoninlyme.co.uk ⏰ 10.00–17.00 Mon–Sat.

Somehow Lyme Regis doesn't look real: with its rows of houses of every shape and size huddled together along the seafront beneath open fields and woodland, it looks more like a painting in a children's book, or perhaps a model town. You might half expect to see an oversized adult bending down peering through the windows of the cottages.

Lyme Regis snuggles up against the Dorset/Devon border, on the River Lym (or Lim). The Jurassic blue-grey cliffs on either side of the town are filled with layers of fossils, making the beaches excellent for fossil hunting. The narrow, twisting (and in parts steep) streets lead down through the town to the attractive seafront and the manmade harbour protected by the ancient breakwater known as The Cobb. The

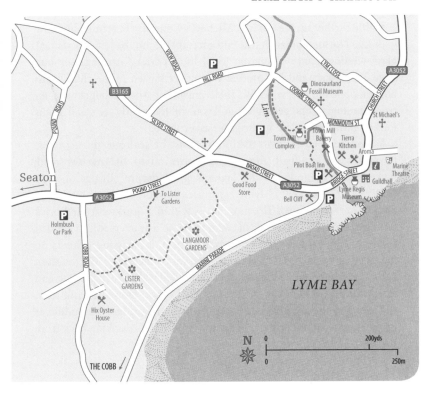

combination of picturesque town, fossils and jungly Undercliff has captured the imagination of artists and writers, from Jane Austen to John Fowles.

The town centre

The town is best explored on foot as the centre is compact, packed with small shops, eateries and art galleries, and there is little room for cars. At the northern end of the seafront you will find the tourist information centre, which, as well as the usual brochures on accommodation, eateries and activities, can provide tide times – essential if you plan to go fossil hunting. Nearby is the **Marine Theatre** (Church St, DT7 3QA ✆ 01297 442138 ⏱ marinetheatre.com), an active, traditional seaside theatre with regular performances. In 2019 it celebrated its 125th birthday, and hosted a performance of Sir Ian McKellen's one-man show celebrating his 80th.

231

A little further up the hill is **St Michael's Church**, a charming building with two Norman pillars in the entrance. Inside, on the left, is a stained-glass window commemorating fossil hunter Mary Anning (see box, page 236). Mary and her brother Joseph are buried in the churchyard almost opposite the window. Their grave is a site of pilgrimage for palaeontologists and geologists, and you will frequently see small fossils found on the beach left on the grave as a tribute.

As you head back down the hill towards the seafront, the eccentric tower of the guildhall almost encroaches on to the narrow road; tucked away behind it is the **Lyme Regis Museum** (Bridge St, DT7 3QA ✆ 01297 443370 ⌂ lymeregismuseum.co.uk ⊙ Easter–Oct daily, Oct–Easter Wed–Sun). The museum is within a quirky turreted brick building built in 1901 and, like the town, is a warren full of hidden corners to be explored. As you would expect, it has good exhibits on local geology and fossils, and Lyme's literary connections. The museum runs a programme of activities, such as guided walks, rock pooling and fossil hunting, which can be booked in advance. Down the hill from the museum the road crosses the River Lym; the bridge, the Buddle, is largely medieval underneath but you will need to be looking back from the seafront to see evidence of its age.

The eastern end of the seafront

A promenade leads northeastwards along the seafront from the town centre, past the Marine Theatre in the direction of Charmouth. The cliffs here have long been particularly unstable and in 2014 a new sea defence wall was built along this stretch as part of a broader project to stabilise the coastline, prevent erosion and save the houses in the East Cliff area from being washed into the sea. The sea wall provides a wide, elevated and flat platform along which to walk and enjoy the views around the bay to Charmouth and beyond. A large ammonite found during the construction by local consultant geologist Paddy Howe is set into the end of the wall. The new structure should also prevent the recurrence of an earlier problem: skeletons poking out of the cliff from the graveyard at St Michael's Church. The walk along the wall leads to Back Beach, known for its rock pooling and fossil hunting.

"The sea wall provides a wide, elevated and flat platform along which to walk and enjoy the views."

Around The Cobb

Lyme Regis is perhaps at its most enchanting viewed from The Cobb at sunset, when the sun illuminates the hills above the harbour and you can see the geological layers within the cliffs, stacked like a deck of cards. Sheltering behind the breakwater is a colourful array of fishing and pleasure boats. The Cobb has been protecting the harbour and the town from erosion since the 13th century. It was originally made from huge boulders inside oak walls and detached

"Sheltering behind the breakwater is a colourful array of fishing and pleasure boats."

from the land at high tide. It was joined to the land in 1756 and rebuilt in Portland stone in the 1820s, as the gently tilting serpentine wall that you see today.

It may look like a tiddler of a harbour but in its heyday Lyme Regis was a major port – the second largest in Dorset in the 14th century. Ships from Lyme Regis traded all over the world until the 20th century. Attached to the front of The Cobb's buildings, near the aquarium (page 234), is a venerable toll board dated 1879 and entitled 'Rates of Merchandise'. It lists the amount of tax levied on imports and exports to and from the harbour with incredible detail, such as 'for every barrel of salted beef, cod, herring … 4d', 'for every Hogshead of Ale, Beer or Porter … 6d', 'for each horse, mule, cow or ox … 6d'.

The Cobb has seen its fair share of drama, real and fictional. It was at The Cobb that James Scott, Duke of Monmouth, landed with his followers in 1685, intent on taking the throne from his uncle, James II. Monmouth, the son of King Charles II, chose Lyme Regis because the West Country was strongly Protestant. A month after they landed, Monmouth and his followers were defeated at the Battle of Sedgemoor in Somerset. Following the trial known as the 'Bloody Assizes', presided over by the notorious Judge Jeffreys, 292 Monmouth supporters were executed. A dozen of them were hanged, drawn and quartered on the spot where they had disembarked in Lyme Regis.

You won't be in Lyme Regis for long before finding mention of its connection with John Fowles's *The French Lieutenant's Woman*, the story of a romance between Sarah Woodruff and Charles Smithson, a fossil hunter. Fowles was living in a farmhouse in Lyme Regis when he wrote the book. The Cobb is the setting of the dramatic opening scene of the film, when Sarah, played by Meryl Streep, is standing alone looking out to sea. Lyme Regis's other literary claim to fame involves Jane Austen, who stayed in the town in 1803–04. The Cobb features in her novel *Persuasion*, which describes Louisa Musgrove falling from the steps. It's said that when Alfred Lord Tennyson visited Lyme, his hosts were keen to show him where the Duke of Monmouth had landed, but the poet exclaimed 'Don't talk to me of Monmouth, show me the exact spot where Louisa Musgrove fell!'

On The Cobb, within a building dating from 1723, is the small, unpretentious **Lyme Regis Aquarium** (✐ 01297 444230 ✐ lymeregismarineaquarium.co.uk ☉ Mar–Nov 10.00–17.00 daily), run by the Gallop family since 1958. It contains a modest collection of species found in the local waters. Alongside the sea creatures is a display of photographs showing films being shot in Lyme Regis, including *The French Lieutenant's Woman* and *Persuasion*. Mr Gallop proudly told me that the aquarium was used as a make-up room during the making of the latter. Tickets can be bought at a reduced rate on the aquarium's website.

Along the seafront (Marine Parade) is a string of pastel-coloured wooden beach huts, well equipped and well used. The slightest bit of sun has holidaymakers throwing open their doors. Like magicians pulling rabbits from hats, they reach into their hut and produce with a flourish a never-ending supply of deckchairs, beach games, umbrellas and, of course, the all-important tea-making paraphernalia. If this prospect tempts you, beach huts are available for daily, weekly or seasonal hire from the council (✐ 01297 445175 ✐ lymeregistowncouncil.gov.uk/book-a-beach-hut).

As well as the pebble beach, there is a manmade sandy one, complete with sand imported from Normandy, known as Front Beach. Lyme Regis is busy in summer and the area around Front Beach is where it shows. The sand is barely visible beneath the sun worshippers, the restaurants are buzzing and the shops are crowded with souvenir hunters.

The Langmoor and Lister Gardens provide a chance to step back from the crowds and admire the views of The Cobb and the coastline.

The Town Mill Complex

Mill Ln, DT7 3PU ✐ 01297 444042 ✐ townmill.org.uk ☉ mill tours Easter–Oct 11.00–16.00 Tue–Sun, Nov–Easter 11.00–16.00 Sat & Sun, plus w/days during school holidays

Around a cobbled courtyard, restored mill buildings house small shops showcasing local art, crafts and produce (including a potter and a brewer). The tour of the working watermill is worthwhile (in exchange for a donation), with its volunteer millers overflowing with enthusiasm and knowledge about its workings and its history dating back to the 11th century. Powered by the River Lym, the mill continues to produce stoneground flour, which is available in the mill shop. It also generates electricity, which powers the site.

Dinosaurland Fossil Museum

Coombe St, DT7 3PY 01297 443541 dinosaurland.co.uk mid-Feb–Oct 10.00–17.00, Nov–Feb opening hours vary so it is best to check beforehand

This museum in a former 18th-century chapel showcases fossils from the local area and beyond. There are dinosaur models and skeletons (good

TIPS FOR FOSSIL HUNTING

Brandon Lennon and the Lyme Regis tourist information centre gave me the following tips for fruitful and safe fossil hunting.

- Fossil hunting is usually most productive after stormy weather or rough seas, as cliff falls are frequent and the shingle is rapidly turned over, exposing new fossils.
- Landslides are common, so stay away from the cliffs when searching the beaches.
- Sturdy footwear is essential to negotiate the rocks, which are slippery when covered in seaweed.
- Keep an eye on tide times – you don't want to get stranded. The best time to collect is 1½ hours either side of low tide.
- Only search the loose beach material; do not dig into the cliffs.
- You will see some fossil hunters carrying hammers. These are not essential equipment but if you do decide to hammer at a rock, wear eye protection and heavy-duty gloves, and watch out for flying splinters.
- You can take home small fossils but the large ones should be left alone.
- If you find something of possible scientific interest (a local expert can tell you), you will need to register it with the Charmouth Heritage Coast Centre (page 240). While it will remain yours, scientists have the right to ask to study it during the six months after registration.

Guided fossil tours are available from **Lyme Regis Museum** (01297 443370 lymeregismuseum.co.uk), from **Brandon Lennon** (07854 377519 lymeregisfossilwalks.com) and from **Charmouth Heritage Coast Centre** (01297 560772 charmouth.org/chcc).

for children) and a natural history room containing assorted taxidermy of British animals. If you choose to search for fossils without an expert guide, a visit to the museum will help you understand their formation.

Fossil hunting around Lyme Regis

Made from soft clay layered with a few hard bands of limestone that formed on the bottom of the sea during the early Jurassic period, some 190 million

MARY ANNING – GROUNDBREAKING FOSSIL HUNTER

A female fossil hunter, dealer and palaeontologist who unearthed some of the most significant geological finds ever made, Mary Anning (1799–1847) was ahead of her time. Her discoveries were key to a fundamental shift in scientific thinking about the history of the Earth, and challenged religious views.

Mary was born into a humble family of religious dissenters in Lyme Regis. She and her brother, Joseph, were the only survivors of ten children born to Richard Anning, a carpenter and cabinetmaker, and his wife Mary. At the age of 15 months, Mary survived a lightning strike which killed three others; local legend had it the lightning turned her into a bright and observant child. Mary attended a Congregationalist Sunday School where she learnt to read and write. Congregationalist doctrine emphasised the importance of education for the poor, unlike the Church of England at the time. However, the family's position as dissenters against the Church of England caused them further discrimination than did poverty alone.

Richard Anning taught his children how to look for and clean fossils that had been hidden within the cliffs at Lyme Regis. They sold the 'curiosities' they collected on the seafront to the wealthy tourists who flocked to Lyme Regis in the summer.

Richard died in 1810, when Mary was 11 years old, and she supplemented the family's meagre income by continuing the fossil trade. Waves and landslides exposed new fossils, especially during winter, which needed to be collected quickly before they were washed out to sea. It was a dangerous living – landslides, treacherous tides and ferocious seas. In 1833, Mary narrowly avoided being killed by a landslide that buried her constant companion, a terrier named Tray. It has been suggested that Mary was the inspiration for the well-known tongue-twister 'she sells seashells on the seashore', written by Terry Sullivan in 1908.

Mary taught herself geology and anatomy and she, and her family, made some important discoveries. In 1811, Mary's brother Joseph found a skull protruding from a cliff. Over a period of months Mary painstakingly uncovered an almost complete 17ft-long skeleton of a 'crocodile'. The specimen was bought by the local lord of the manor, who sold it to William Bullock for his Museum of Natural Curiosities in London. The find caused years ago, the grey cliffs of the Lyme Regis area regularly offer up some valuable clues about life on earth in geological ages past. The Jurassic fossils within the cliffs are derived from sea creatures that lived when dinosaurs roamed the land. Landslides and waves cause fossils to fall from the cliffs on to the beaches below, making them prime fossil-hunting territory.

Heading out with an expert will help you to get the most from your fossil-hunting expedition and give you a greater understanding of how

quite a stir and brought Mary to the attention of scientific circles. The specimen was later named *Ichthyosaurus*, the 'fish-lizard'.

In 1828, Mary made another important discovery – the first complete skeleton of a flying reptile recorded in England. It was named *Dimorphodon* after its two kinds of teeth and appears to have been a fish eater.

The Anning family had established themselves as fossil hunters but remained very poor. In 1820 one of their patrons, Lieutenant-Colonel Thomas James Birch, organised an auction of specimens he had purchased from them. The sale raised £400, which he donated to the Annings, and the publicity cemented Mary's fame.

Mary's gender and social class meant she could not fully participate in the scientific community of the day. As a woman, she was not eligible to join the Geological Society of London and rarely received due credit for her work. However, she was visited by, and corresponded with, eminent scientists of the time and her opinions were valued. In 1838, Mary was given an annuity raised by members of the British Association for the Advancement of Science and the Geological Society of London.

Mary Anning died from breast cancer aged 47 and is buried in the churchyard of St Michael's in Lyme Regis, with her brother. A stained-glass window within the church, commissioned by the Geological Society of London, commemorates her life. On the wall of the Lyme Regis Museum is a blue plaque dedicated to her; the museum is believed to be on the site of Anning's home and her first fossil shop.

From humble beginnings Mary Anning eventually gained the respect of the scientific community and captured the imagination of the public. She may not have been eligible to join during her lifetime but her death was recorded by the Geological Society. In 2010, the Royal Society included Anning in a list of the ten British women who have most influenced the history of science.

Ammonite, a film depicting Mary Anning's life and starring Kate Winslet and Saoirse Ronan, was filmed in Lyme Regis in 2019. The filming was a big event for Lyme, with parts of the town becoming film sets and local people being costumed up as extras. It's due for release in 2020, so it seems Anning is finally receiving some of the recognition she deserves.

they are formed. Contact details for guided fossil tours are provided on page 235.

I was lucky enough to go fossil hunting with enthusiastic expert Brandon Lennon. As the son of an international geologist, who also lives locally and fossil hunts, Brandon has a fine fossil-hunting pedigree.

Brandon started by explaining the origins and significance of the Jurassic Coast; a large map erected by the local council on the seafront provided a handy prop and showed the relative ages of the coastline, with Lyme Regis and Charmouth being the oldest parts of the Dorset section at around 190 million years. As you head eastwards the cliffs are younger, and are a mere 65 million years old at Old Harry Rocks, the most easterly point of the Jurassic Coast. The Devon end is even older, approximately 250 million years old around Exmouth.

Brandon led me along Monmouth Beach, west of The Cobb, where we clambered across rocks and trudged through seaweed, keeping an eye out for spiral-shaped ammonites and other fossilised creatures. We were heading towards one of the area's *"We were heading* best-known fossilised phenomena, the *towards one of the* ammonite graveyard. About halfway to *area's best-known* the headland there was no doubting that *fossilised phenomena, the* we had found what we were looking for: a *ammonite graveyard."* ledge of limestone packed with the internal moulds of football-sized ammonites. Brandon explained that a catastrophic event or chemical reaction must have occurred to kill all these creatures at the same time. There were so many, and they were so clearly defined and uniform, that it looked as if an overly enthusiastic wallpaper designer had got carried away with an ammonite-shaped ink stamp. The ammonites of the graveyard are intriguing to admire but you should not attempt to extract them; to do so would be dangerous and would damage this amazing site.

Brandon handed me a sieve and we began sieving sand in rock pools to search for tiny fossils. He hit the jackpot with several dainty little ammonites. My find was less appealing – an ancient, fossilised gastropod. It didn't look like anything special, just a rather old and solid snail, and I would have discarded it if it hadn't been for Brandon's enthusiastic reaction.

We seized upon a particularly interesting-looking rock, which Brandon skilfully tapped with a hammer to reveal the edge of an ammonite. He advised me to have it cut from the rock by local expert, Paddy Howe, and so I did. Sadly, the rock around the fossil was not of a type that could be removed easily, so once the fossil was partly revealed (for the first time in hundreds of millions of years) Paddy was forced to stop to avoid damaging it. Nevertheless, it will go on display in my house as a reminder of my fossil-hunting day, and is all the more special because we found it.

Brandon explained that there is no reason why people should not take small fossils home, as it prevents them from being washed out to sea. The large ones, however, should be left alone.

Cruises, sailing & fishing

At the shore end of The Cobb you can arrange fishing trips, self-drive hire boats, Jurassic Coast cruises or a water taxi to West Bay (page 243). Harry May's deep-sea and mackerel-fishing trips (07974 753287 mackerelfishinglymeregis.com) come highly recommended by locals and visitors alike. If you fancy getting in some sea time, a mackerel-fishing trip is a pleasant way to spend an hour pottering around the bay. On a deep-sea fishing trip your catch is likely to be cod, conger and skate.

Sailing lessons are available from Lyme Regis Sea School (lrss.org. uk), and the Lyme Regis Sailing Club (lymeregissailingclub.co.uk) offers temporary membership for visitors.

¶¶ FOOD & DRINK

As you would expect of a bustling tourist town, Lyme Regis is packed with cafés and restaurants. They are concentrated along the main street and the seafront. Below is a selection, although take-away fish and chips eaten on the beach is always a good option.

Aroma 6 Bridge St (opposite the museum) 01297 445914 aromacafe.co.uk 10.00–16.00 daily, from 11.00 Sun. Owners Jon and Jodie have a background in horticulture and organic farming, and it shows in the care with which they run this award-winning café. Great coffee and very good food.
Bell Cliff 6 Broad St, DT7 3QD 01297 442459 09.00–17.00 daily. Centrally located restaurant and tea room with a small outdoor eating area with views over the bay. Does a good Dorset cream tea.
Good Food Store 21 Broad St, DT7 3QE 01297 442076 09.00–17.00 daily in summer & closed Sun in winter. A deli, bakery and organic produce shop, which also has a café. Good, wholesome, local food and plenty of gluten-free options.

Hix Oyster & Fish House Cobb Rd, DT7 3JP ✆ 01297 446910 ⌁ hixoysterandfishhouse. co.uk ⊙ 12.00–22.00 daily, Nov–Mar closed Mon. Reservation recommended. Lyme's best-known and most exclusive restaurant, owned by celebrity chef Mark Hix. Great if you want to treat yourself or someone else, especially if you like fish. At the end of the gardens above the seafront, it has sweeping views over the bay and the service is excellent. There is no parking but you can drop people off and park nearby.

The Lyme Bay 8–10 Bridge St, DT7 3QA ✆ 01297 444700 ⊙ 09.00–16.00 Sun & Mon, 09.00–22.00 Tue–Sat. In a prime spot overlooking the bay. Local food and tasty artisan bread and cakes.

Millside Restaurant 1 Mill Ln, DT7 3PU ✆ 01297 445999 ⊙ 10.30–14.30 & 18.30–21.00 Tue–Sat, 10.30–14.30 Sun. In a peaceful location near the old mill, serving a creative menu consistently prepared to a high standard. Plenty of vegan and gluten-free options.

Penny Black 37 Broad St, DT7 3QF ✆ 07951 865760 ⊙ 09.00–16.30 Mon–Sat. Vintage-style café inside an antique shop. Excellent cream teas and homemade cakes.

Pilot Boat Inn 1 Bridge St, DT7 3QA ✆ 01297 443157 ⊙ 08.00–23.00 daily. Right in the centre of Lyme Regis, this previously unassuming, traditional pub was given a makeover in 2018 and is now rather trendy, with a very pleasant courtyard. Plenty of vegetarian and vegan options.

Tierra Kitchen 1a Coombe St, DT7 3PY ✆ 01297 445189 ⊙ 09.00–16.00 Tue–Sun. The food philosophy at this vegetarian restaurant centres on local, seasonal, organic and wild. Even carnivores will enjoy the exciting dishes created here.

Town Mill Bakery 2 Riverside Studios, Coombe St, DT7 3PY ✆ 01297 444754 ⊙ 08.00–16.00 Thu–Tue. Bread, pastries and pizzas, made on site. Long, wooden tables reminiscent of school mealtimes and the open bakery provide a casual atmosphere.

2 CHARMOUTH

Smaller than Lyme Regis, Charmouth is billed as the quieter of the two, although the beach can feel pretty crowded in the summer. The bulk of Charmouth is about half a mile back from the sea, spread along either side of the main street, which runs between the coast and the A35. You can drive down to the seafront, where there is ample paid parking close to the beach.

The seafront is decidedly low-key – there is no fancy esplanade lined with shops, amusement arcades and hotels; instead there is a pebble beach, fossil-rich cliffs, a fossil shop, a café and the **Charmouth Heritage Coast Centre** (Lower Sea Ln, DT6 6LL ✆ 01297 560772 ⌁ charmouth.org/chcc; free admission). If you plan on collecting fossils or simply want to know more about the Jurassic Coast, the centre is

MRTOM-UK/I

RIVER, ESTUARIES & WETLANDS

The rivers Axe, Otter and Exe are home to a variety of wildlife, but it is the estuaries which attract flocks of waders and other waterfowl, making them a birding hotspot.

1 The Seaton Wetlands have a variety of carefully managed habitats, from ponds to marsh, with hides and even special birdwatching trams. 2 Avocets visit the Exe Estuary during winter months. 3 A rare visitor to Seaton Wetlands, osprey may be seen in the late autumn during their migration to Africa. 4 Beavers are once again making their home in the River Otter, closely monitored by the Devon Wildlife Trust.

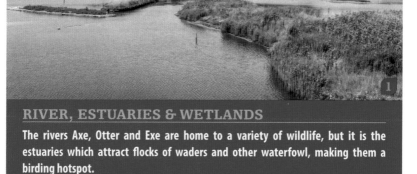

ANDREW M. ALLPORT/S

MATTHEWO2000/D

JOHN DIXON

FOTOVOYAGER/I

BESIDE THE SEA

Most of East Devon's beaches are pebble rather than sand, but this doesn't diminish their popularity – it just widens the attractions.

1 Axmouth Harbour, across the Axe from Seaton. 2 Colourful houses front the harbour at Weymouth. 3 Seaton's combination of the Axe Estuary and Lyme Bay makes it popular for watersports, including stand-up paddleboarding and kayaking. 4 Fishermen's cottages in Beer, built around 1873. 5 Budleigh Salterton's beautiful beach pebbles are known as Budleigh Buns.

SEATON BAY WATERSPORTS

PATIO/S

HELEN HOTSON/D

FAVOURITE PLACES

Museums, mansions, cottages and gardens: everyone has their favourite East Devon place. Nationwide the Donkey Sanctuary wins hands down, however!

1 À la Ronde, an intriguingly shaped National Trust house near Exmouth, includes a unique shell collection.

2 The dining room at Killerton House, part of the vast Killerton Estate which includes a village and a forest, as well as the manor house, all owned by the National Trust. **3** The little train at Beer's Pecorama delights children and adults as it tootles its way around the gardens. **4** Sidmouth's Donkey Sanctuary is the most popular free attraction in East Devon. **5** The largest public garden in the area is Bicton, where this glass house is even older than Kew's. Built in the 1820s it comprises 18,000 flat pieces of glass. **6** The clifftop labyrinth at Seaton is a symbol of life's journey; walk it for relaxation or meditation.

THE RURAL SCENE

East Devon isn't only about the coast. Inland lie peaceful villages with their pubs and churches, amid agricultural land and rolling hills cut by many rivers.

1 The River Axe. 2 Harvesting wheat near Sidbury. 3 Branscombe's 'blossomy cottage' is a riot of colour at almost any time of the year. 4 Bike rides organised by Velo Vintage have a foot – or pedal – firmly in the past. 5 The Lamb Grand National at the World of Country Life, Exmouth. 6 Cannington Viaduct supported a train line until 1965.

CURIOSITIES

East Devon has its share of festivals and oddities, some permanent, some annual and some transitory.

1 Local morris dancers preparing to strut their stuff. 2 The 15th-century 'House that Moved' in Exeter was hauled uphill to a new position. 3 This charming model of the church in Combpyne's churchyard is correct in every detail. 4 Ottery St Mary's annual Tar Barrel Ceremony is held on Guy Fawkes night.

worth a visit. The interactive displays and fossil touch table will appeal to most children, and there is a video microscope for you to examine your fossil finds. Displays on the coastal wildlife of the area, including two marine rock-pool aquariums, add another dimension. The centre provides a large and varied programme of events, including fossil hunting, ammonite-slice polishing and rock pooling.

Every Monday during the summer a large **flea market** is held in a field on the edge of Charmouth at Manor Farm Park.

At the eastern end of the village is a turning marked Stonebarrow Lane, which leads to Stonebarrow Hill. This National Trust land along the coast is a relatively uncrowded and peaceful vantage point from which to take in the sea views. Bridleways and the South West Coast Path pass through here and the small National Trust shop does a good trade selling teas, coffees and ice creams to walkers.

¶¶ FOOD & DRINK

Bank House Café DT6 6PU ☏ 01297 561600 ◷ 10.00–16.00 Mon, Tue, Thu & Fri, 09.30–16.00 Sat, 12.00–15.00 Sun, summer 09.00–1700 daily. Informal family-run café on the main street that is known for its Sunday roasts.

Fernhill Hotel DT6 6BX ☏ 01297 560492 ⬨ fernhill-hotel.co.uk ◷ dinner daily, lunch Sun. A smart restaurant, good service and delicious food combine to make a meal here very pleasant. A bar and grill offer more casual dining.

3 GOLDEN CAP TO WEST BAY

🏠 **Washingpool Farm** North Allington (page 261), **Symondsbury Estate** nr Bridport (page 261), **⚑ Downhouse Farm** (page 261), **Golden Cap Holiday Park** (page 261)

Beyond Charmouth the hump on the Jurassic Coast composed of greensand and known as Golden Cap lives up to its name: the top of the cliff has a warm golden glow, which can be seen for miles around, and at 626ft it is the highest point on the south coast. It can be reached on foot from Seatown or, less strenuously, from Langdon Hill Wood.

As you head eastwards on the A35 from Charmouth, you pass through **Morcombelake**, home of Dorset's well-known Moores Biscuits, and then **Chideock**, a village of attractive golden stone and whitewashed cottages, many of them thatched, and with a couple of decent pubs. A turning in the centre of Chideock takes you to **Seatown**, a modest seaside hamlet nestled between cliffs. It consists of a few houses, a pub

A walk to Golden Cap

❀ OS Explorer 116 or Landranger 193; start: Seatown or Langdon Hill ♀ SY420917; 4 miles; difficult (steep climb along the cliff top). For an easier walk, avoiding the steep climb, start the walk at Langdon Hill car park ♀ SY412930.

This walk takes you to the highest point on England's south coast and entails an appropriately steep section and far-reaching views. From the car park near the **Anchor Inn** in Seatown, walk up the hill into the village, climb the stile on the left and join the footpath, signed 'Coast Path Diversion'. Walk across the field, over a stile and through a small woodland. Cross another stile and bear right up the hill, signposted 'Golden Cap'.

Where the track forks, keep left. You will walk through open fields with **Golden Cap** directly ahead of you. It gets pretty steep in parts but the views give a great excuse for a pause. At the summit you will see a stone memorial to the Earl of Antrim KBE, chair of the National Trust 1966–77. The views of the coastline are spectacular, towards Lyme Regis in the west and West Bay in the east. Once you have had your fill of the view, follow the path down the steep hill to a gate and bear right over the fields towards the ruins of the 13th-century **St Gabriel's Chapel**. Keeping the chapel on your right, you will pass through two gates. Continue in the direction of Morcombelake. You will pass through **Filcombe Farm** and around the base of **Langdon Hill Wood**, which in spring is awash with bluebells and wild garlic. Head down the hill back to Seatown, where the Anchor Inn awaits.

To reach the National Trust car park at Langdon Hill, drive westwards through Chideock on the A35 and turn left at the top of the hill half a mile past the village centre, just before the dual carriageway ends. The turning you are looking for is a tiny, unmarked lane (known as Langdon Lane) just after the turning signposted 'Seatown'. A mostly level walk takes you around Langdon Hill Wood and on to Golden Cap. The route avoids the long, steep climb.

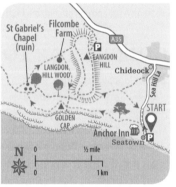

and a good campsite, all huddled close to a golden shingle beach. The Anchor Inn has cliff-top seating and terrific food.

The land along the coast around Seatown is owned by the National Trust and offers excellent walks. The hillside to the east of Seatown is steep and usually dotted with cows of assorted colours and sizes, who casually swagger to the cliff edge and gaze out to sea. From Seatown you can walk up and over the hill, and then another hill, to Eype Mouth and on to West Bay. It is a hilly two miles to Eype and the Downhouse Farm Café provides an excellent stop for refreshments. Eype, near Bridport, has a shingle beach, which is reached down a steep path from a cliff top car park (payable), and a couple of sizeable campsites.

¶¶ FOOD & DRINK

Anchor Inn Seatown DT6 6JU ✆ 01297 489215 ⊙ daily for lunch & dinner. A Palmers Brewery pub in a super seaside location, with a beer garden on the cliff top, serving exceptional food. This, and its location, keeps it very busy at weekends. Parking is paid but is refunded if you spend over £20 in the pub.

Felicity's Farm Shop Morcombelake DT6 6DJ ✆ 01297 480930 ⌂ felicitysfarmshop. co.uk ⊙ 09.00–17.00 Mon–Sat, 10.00–16.00 Sun. This large, family-run farm shop is conveniently located on the A35 and has plenty of parking. The shop is well stocked with local produce, deli items and gifts. Felicity's son, Tom, raises pigs nearby and his pork, bacon and sausages are deservedly popular. This is the perfect place to stock up for a picnic or a self-catering stay, and if you can't wait to try the food there is a small café onsite selling take-away food. The outdoor picnic tables are convenient, or, if you park on the southern edge of the parking space, you've a superb view across green countryside to the distant sea.

Garden Café Downhouse Farm, Downhouse Ln, Higher Eype DT6 6AH ✆ 01308 421232 ⌂ downhousefarm.org ⊙ Mar–Oct 10.00–18.00 Tue–Sun. This outdoor café serves delicious homemade food using the farm's own organic meats, vegetables and herbs. It is found down a very narrow lane or by diverting inland from the coastal path. Dog friendly.

4 WEST BAY

A mile from Bridport is its harbour West Bay, where the tidal River Brit flows into the sea through the sluice gates and harbour basin. A harbour was first recorded at West Bay in the 13th century and was known as Bridport Harbour until 1884. It was a centre of the boat-building industry until the late 19th century and many ships were built here during the Napoleonic Wars (1799–1815). Until 2013 West Bay was a working fishing harbour with a 'what you see is what you get' attitude and relatively little tourist infrastructure. Then came *Broadchurch*, with its recognisable West Bay landscape, and thousands of fans wanted to see it for themselves. You may recognise the rounded apartment block behind the harbour as the programme's police station, and the cliffs at

Harbour Cliff Beach are where Danny Latimer's body was found in the opening scenes of the first episode. A *Broadchurch* trail map leads you to these locations and more; enquire at the Bridport tourist information centre (✆ 01308 424901).

If you're not a *Broadchurch* fan you can enjoy the town for what it is. Above the pebble beach tower Triassic sandstone cliffs, and the pier looks out along the coastline from the Isle of Portland to Brixham in Devon. Lyme Bay Rib Charter operates a water taxi between Lyme Regis and West Bay (✆ 07971 258515 ⬧ lymebayribcharter.co.uk).

¶¶ FOOD & DRINK

Watch House Café West Bay DT6 4EN ✆ 01308 459330 ⬧ watchhousecafe.co.uk ⊙ hours vary, check the website. In an unrivalled location on East Beach is this sister to the well-known Hive Beach Café at Burton Bradstock (see below). It has a casual atmosphere and specialises in seafood and wood-fired pizza.

WEST BAY TO ABBOTSBURY

🏠 **The Seaside Boarding House** (page 260) 🏡 **Donkey Lane Cottage** (page 261)

West Bay to West Bexington on the coast path is 5½ miles, which a fit walker can do in two hours – although be warned, it's hilly – making this a good stop-off from the Jurassic Coast bus (X53) which runs close by. Slower walkers can go as far as Cogden Beach, then up to the road which is about half the distance. Or just to Burton Bradstock and have a leisurely lunch.

Burton Bradstock nestles at the base of the Bride Valley, at the point where the River Bride flows into the sea. Although there has been some modern development on the outskirts, photogenic thatched 17th- and 18th-century cottages remain around the church of St Mary the Virgin.

A pleasant shingle beach lies on the edge of the village, shielded by golden cliffs that regularly yield up their fossils. Apart from a National Trust car park and the popular Hive Beach Café (✆ 01308 897228) there are no other facilities of note at the beach.

West Bexington is a small settlement tucked away off the B3157 between Burton Bradstock and Abbotsbury. A lane leads down to a car park that extends over the pebble beach, making it one of the most accessible beaches for those with limited mobility. There aren't any shops at the beach and the only café is the new Club House restaurant (see below), which means the beach is usually far quieter than others in the area. However, it is popular with fishermen, who can be seen casting their lines into the sea whatever the weather.

Puncknowle lies slightly inland at the entrance to the beautiful Bride Valley, a landscape of hilly farmland dotted with pretty hamlets. Despite its spelling, Puncknowle is pronounced 'Punnel'. There is no agreed explanation for the 'Punck' part of the name but the second part is believed to refer to the knoll to the south of the village. On top of the knoll is a small, mysterious stone house. No-one is certain of its origins but its positioning high above the coast means it has long been used as a land and sea mark. In 1794 the knoll was the site of a signal station, one of a chain along the coast, and it has been suggested the house may have been associated with it.

The village has a simple charm – narrow roads lined with thatched, stone cottages and farm buildings, plus a decent pub (see below).

¶¶ FOOD & DRINK

The Club House Beach Rd, West Bexington DT2 9DG ✆ 01308 898302
✎ theclubhousewestbexington.co.uk ☉ 12.00–16.00 & 18.00–21.00 Tue–Sat, 12.00–16.00 Sun. The latest offering from the owners of Hive Beach Café (see opposite) and Watch House Café (see opposite). A bungalow opposite the beach has been transformed into a restaurant with a retro feel. The menu is, unsurprisingly given the location, fish-centric. Gets very busy at times. Reservation recommended.
Crown Inn Church St, Puncknowle DT2 9BN ✆ 01308 897711 ☉ lunch & dinner Tue–Sun. A handsome, thatched 16th-century inn serving tasty, traditional pub food. Popular with locals and visitors, the pub also houses a small village shop selling local produce and household essentials.

5 ABBOTSBURY

Approaching Abbotsbury by road from the west is an absolute delight, as you gaze down towards Chesil Beach and The Fleet lagoon, which are watched over by the sturdy St Catherine's Chapel. There are a few lay-bys where you can pull over and admire the view but it can get a bit frantic if there are streams of traffic in both directions. A more relaxing option is to head up to Abbotsbury hillfort to take in the views at your leisure. Before you begin the descent to Abbotsbury, take the small turning on your left signed 'Ashley Close only'. You can park and walk along the hillfort for practically aerial views of the coastline.

Abbotsbury is an estate village, owned by Ilchester Estates, so it is beautifully preserved with many adorable thatched cottages of golden stone. Its idyllic looks and a choice of traditional tea rooms make it worthwhile pottering territory. From the village it is an easy walk to the 14th-century **St Catherine's Chapel**, a lonely building dominating the landscape from its position high on a hill. From the chapel there are far-reaching views of Chesil Beach and The Fleet, and you can walk half a mile down the hill to the swannery and the beach from here.

Abbotsbury Swannery
New Barn Rd, DT3 4JG ✆ 01305 871858 ☝ abbotsbury-tourism.co.uk ⊙ mid-Mar–end Oct 10.00–17.00 daily

The Swannery on The Fleet Lagoon is home to around 600 swans (and various other canny birds who have taken up residence and exploit the very pleasant living conditions). It was established by Benedictine monks during the 1040s, when they farmed swans for food. Sir Giles Strangways bought the Swannery from Henry VIII in 1543 and it is still owned by his descendants, Ilchester Estates, making these among only swans in England not owned by the Queen.

The visit begins with a film and an exhibition. You can then wander along the paths among the nesting mute swans, and hides allow you to watch the birds out on the water. Children have the opportunity to help with feeding at 12.00 and 16.00, and mid-May to late June is a particularly exciting time to visit as this is when the cygnets hatch. Also on site are a well-stocked gift shop and a café.

Abbotsbury Subtropical Gardens
Bullers Way, DT3 4LA ✆ 01305 871387 ☝ abbotsbury-tourism.co.uk ⊙ 10.00–17.00 daily

Established in 1765 by the first Countess of Ilchester as a kitchen garden, this has developed into a colourful 30-acre garden filled with rare and exotic plants from all over the world. Many of the plants were first introductions to Britain, discovered by the descendants of the countess.

6 CHESIL BEACH
🏠 **Moonfleet Manor** (page 260)

Stand on Portland Heights or outside St Catherine's Chapel above Abbotsbury and look out to sea and you will be treated to the most extraordinary sight – a wide, golden, shingle bank rising out of the water and running along the coastline, with a lagoon sheltering sheepishly behind it. If you saw such a thing in Dubai you might assume it was the zany creation of a capricious sheikh, but this is Dorset and Chesil Beach is all natural.

Stretching for 18 miles between West Bay and Portland, Chesil Beach is the largest of three major shingle structures in Britain. The shingle bank, which reaches around 40 feet at its highest point, was formed by rising seas *"Home to an abundance* at the end of the last Ice Age. Its rounded *of birdlife, wading birds* pebbles have been graded in size by strong *can be seen all year."* tidal currents; they are as small as peas at the western end and the size of oranges at the Portland end. For centuries the size of the pebbles has been helping locals, mostly smugglers and fishermen, pinpoint where they are landing on the beach.

The lagoon, known as The Fleet, extends from Abbotsbury to Portland and contains a mixture of salt and fresh water. Home to an abundance of birdlife, wading birds can be seen all year, while Brent geese from Siberia and red-breasted merganser (fish-eating duck) visit in winter.

At the southern end of The Fleet, just before you head over the causeway from Weymouth to Portland, is the Fine Foundation Chesil Beach Centre (Portland Beach Rd, DT4 9XE ✐ 01305 206191 ◌ dorsetwildlifetrust.org.uk/chesil-beach-centre) and a pay-and-display car park with direct access to Chesil Beach. The centre is run by Dorset Wildlife Trust and provides information on Chesil Beach, the Fleet and Portland. Binoculars allow you to watch seabirds feeding on the sand flats and there is live video from cameras filming on the bed of the lagoon. It is worth checking whether any sections of the beach are closed, as during nesting season (usually April to August) parts are off-limits. The centre also runs events (see website for details), and there is a good café. From the centre a boardwalk leads to Chesil Beach.

Glass-bottom boat trips run by DWT provide the opportunity to explore The Fleet and get a closer look at its bird and sealife (The Fleet Explorer, Ferryman's Way, Wyke Regis, Weymouth DT4 9YU ✐ 01305 206191 ◌ dorsetwildlifetrust.org.uk/things-do/your-community/fleet-explorer ◔ Easter–Oct daily). The trips last one hour and can be booked at the Fine Foundation Chesil Beach Centre.

Since Chesil Beach is almost impossible to walk along, the South West Coast Path follows the inland side of The Fleet, midway along which

Langton Herring makes a handy access point for the water's edge, while Fleet village is the smugglers' haunt fictionalised by J Meade Falkner in his 1898 adventure novel *Moonfleet* (page 260), filmed in 1955 with Stewart Granger.

WEYMOUTH TO OLD HARRY ROCKS

At the southeastern end of Chesil Beach is the town of Weymouth and the peninsula known as the Isle of Portland. Further east lies the Isle of Purbeck, which offers unspoilt beaches and wild heathland.

7 WEYMOUTH & PORTLAND

Tourist information: ⌀ visit-dorset.com/explore/towns/Weymouth. Also (for brochures, maps, tickets, etc) Pavilion Theatre, The Esplanade, Weymouth DT4 8AD & Heights Hotel, Portland DT5 2EN ⌀ heightshotel.com.

Depending on how you look at it, Weymouth is either confused about what it wants to be or multi-talented, having to juggle being a working town, a port and a seaside resort. In 2012 it added another achievement to its CV – Olympic venue. It was quite a coup for Weymouth, and for Dorset, when the Weymouth and Portland National Sailing Academy (WPNSA) was chosen to host the sailing events for the London 2012 Olympic and Paralympic Games. Thanks to the WPNSA, the area now has world-class facilities to complement its superb sailing waters.

"A bustling seaside town, Weymouth attracts thousands of holidaymakers in summer."

A bustling seaside town of around 52,000 people, Weymouth attracts thousands of holidaymakers in summer, earning it the rather dubious nickname of 'England's Bay of Naples', or more recently 'Weybiza'.

During the 18th century Weymouth was touted as a health retreat. King George III came to Weymouth in 1789 to try out one of the first bathing machines, a hut on wheels drawn into the water by horses where one could bathe supervised by an attendant. It is said that while he bathed 'God save the King' was dutifully sung from another hut. The king visited regularly until 1810, a fact that is commemorated by a chalk carving on a hillside at Osmington depicting the monarch on horseback (see opposite). The promise of healing and royal patronage made Weymouth highly fashionable and rows of elegant houses sprung up along the esplanade to cater for well-to-do visitors.

Linked to Weymouth by a causeway is the Isle of Portland, famed for its stone quarries and its lighthouse at Portland Bill, which warns shipping to steer clear of Dorset's southernmost point. A highlight is **Portland Castle** (Liberty Rd, Castletown DT5 1AZ ✆ 01305 820539 ☉ most of the year daily but parts are closed at times for private events; English Heritage), an extraordinarily well-preserved fort built by Henry VIII in the 1540s to protect against French and Spanish invasion after his break from the Catholic Church.

⚓ CRUISES & EXCURSIONS

Coastline Cruises Brewery Quay, DT4 8TJ ✆ 01305 785000 ⌂ coastlinecruises.com. Cruises along the coast from Weymouth Bay. Also a Portland ferry service and private charter.

Jurassic Safari – 4x4 tours ✆ 01305 772324 ⌂ jurassicsafari.co.uk. See coastal Dorset from a different perspective.

MV Freedom 11 Redcliff View, DT4 8RW ✆ 07974 266867 ⌂ mvfreedom.co.uk. Trips along the Jurassic Coast or around Portland Harbour in a boat equipped for the disabled.

Weymouth Bay Rib Charters ✆ 07872 140753 ⌂ weymouthbayribcharters.co.uk. High-speed 20-minute rigid inflatable boat rides around the bay.

8 OSMINGTON & OSMINGTON MILLS

Although just four miles from Weymouth, Osmington seems a world away from the bustling town. Its narrow street is lined with thatched cottages and the backdrop of verdant hills leaves you in no doubt that you have re-entered rural Dorset. To the north of the village of Osmington is the White Horse, a depiction of George III on horseback, carved into the chalk hillside in 1808 in honour of

"The backdrop of verdant hills leaves you in no doubt that you have re-entered rural Dorset."

the king, to commemorate the summers he had spent in the Weymouth area. At 279ft long and 327ft high, the carving is clearly visible from the A353 to the east of Weymouth.

On the coast is Osmington Mills, with a rugged coastline and views towards Portland. The South West Coast Path runs along the cliffs, dipping down to the Smugglers Inn, a popular pub with an inviting garden. It is easy to see why this building, parts of which date from the 13th century, has a long association with smugglers as its location is perfect for bringing contraband ashore – right on the coast at the bottom of a gulley.

Osmington Mills is another excellent stopping-off place from the *Jurassic Coaster* bus with some very good cliff and beach walking. This is also the last possible bus-assisted walking as the bus route swings inland on its final journey to Poole.

¶¶ FOOD & DRINK

Craig's Farm Dairy East Farm, Osmington DT3 6EX ✆ 01305 834591 ⌂ craigsfarmdairy. co.uk ☉ summer & autumn daily. Tea rooms and farm shop on a working dairy farm, where the dairy's own ice cream is sold.

The Smugglers Inn Osmington Mills DT3 6HF ✆ 01305 833125 ☉ daily. A perfect stop-off for walkers on the South West Coast Path (with Burning Cliff above Ringstead Bay to the east and Black Head to the west) this large pub has lots of eating areas and a huge beer garden on either side of the stream, and its menu offers plenty of variety. There is a fee for the car park but you can redeem it at the bar for orders over £15. Gets very busy in summer.

THE ISLE OF PURBECK & THE END OF THE JURASSIC COAST

Tourist information: White House, Shore Rd, Swanage BH19 1LB ✆ 01929 766018 ☉ 10.00–17.00 Sun–Fri, 09.00–17.00 Sat

One glance at the map tells you that the Isle of Purbeck is not actually an island, but a peninsula of some 60 square miles bordered to the south and east by the English Channel and to the north by Poole Harbour and the River Frome.

The peninsula is dissected by the Purbeck Hills, a chalk ridge which runs westward from the sea near Old Harry Rocks across the Isle of Purbeck to Lulworth Cove, and whose shape hints at the origin of the name 'Purbeck' – supposedly from the Saxon 'pur', meaning bittern or snipe, and beck meaning 'beak'.

9 LULWORTH COVE & DURDLE DOOR

🏠 **Lulworth Estate** (page 261)

The Lulworth Estate covers some 20 square miles and includes Lulworth Cove and Durdle Door, two of the most spectacular and best-known features of the Jurassic Coast. Lulworth Cove is a scallop-shell shape (almost a full circle) sculpted by the sea, which broke through a fault in the limestone beds at the mouth of the cove and ate away at the soft clay inland. Durdle Door, an impressive limestone arch eroded by waves, lies half a mile to the west.

The hilly coastline and looping bays backed by pale-coloured cliffs are topped with grassland and flowers; if you walk only one small section of the South West Coast Path, let it be this one. The stretch west from Lulworth Cove over Hambury Tout to Man o' War Bay and Durdle Door is only 1¼ miles. It is steep in parts but at the top of those climbs you are rewarded with almost aerial views of the coastline. You can park either in the car park above Durdle Door or at Lulworth Cove but bear in mind that the refreshments are at the Lulworth Cove end.

The approach to West Lulworth and Lulworth Cove is via a narrow lane; there is a car park at Lulworth Cove but like all car parks on the estate it is payable. The **Lulworth Heritage Centre** (BH20 5RH ✎ 01929 400587) near the car park makes a handy starting point. The free exhibition contains information on

"At the top of those climbs you are rewarded with almost aerial views of the coastline."

the geology, geography and social history of the area, including its long farming tradition. You won't be surprised to learn, given the shape of the cove, that it was a popular haunt for smugglers, who exploited its seclusion. The heritage centre stocks local maps, walking guides and wildlife identification guides.

From there it is a short stroll to **Lulworth Cove** along a narrow street lined with the usual trappings of a seaside touristy spot – guesthouses, tea rooms, and shops selling brightly coloured buckets, spades and rock-pooling nets. Thankfully, however, it lacks that slick, smarmy, touristy feel and instead retains the scruffy charm of a fishing village enhanced by the presence of rickety rowing boats lying at odd angles beside the street. Running down one side of the street is a stone wall and on the other side a stream, one of the many springs which feed the cove and make its waters some of the coldest in Dorset.

As you walk down the hill you will see a mint-coloured cottage, the Dolls House (✎ 01929 400587), which is said to have been brought from Canada and rebuilt here in 1860. Within is a delightfully old-fashioned fudge shop and tea garden. At the cove, boats lie scattered around the slipway and moored in the calm water, reinforcing that fishing village feel. The cove is ringed by a well-sheltered shingle beach and the waters are popular with snorkellers.

The car park above Durdle Door is reached by driving through the large Durdle Door Holiday Park. On a clear day the views along the coast stretch as far as Portland. It is a steep walk down (and back up!) to Durdle Door, where there is a pebbly beach. The sea washes back and forth through the arch, making a washboard of the rocks below. On the way down to the beach is a lookout point with views of **Durdle Door** in one direction and Man o' War Bay in the other. The beach at Man o' War Bay is accessible only at low tide.

If you've made it this far you will want to take as close a look as possible at the youngest part of the Jurassic Coast, ideally from the sea or the coast path. There is a good selection of walks that bring you near to the iconic cliffs and sea stacks, but perhaps the best option of all is to take a boat trip close to the coast. If you are feeling particularly adventurous, you may like to try coasteering, available at Lulworth (✆ 01929 400155 ⬚ lulworthoutdoors.com).

⚓ CRUISES

Dorset Cruises Parkstone Bay Marina, Turks Ln, Poole BH14 8EW ✆ 01202 724910 ⬚ dorsetcruises.co.uk. Offers a range of cruises from Poole Quay, including themed cruises showcasing local produce.

Greenslade Pleasure Boats Poole Quay BH15 1HJ ✆ 01202 669955 ⬚ greensladepleasureboats.co.uk. Offers cruises of Poole Harbour, Wareham River and Swanage.

Marsh's Boats The Stone Quay, Swanage BH19 2LN ✆ 01929 427309 ⬚ marshsboats.co.uk. From April to October offers cruises along the Jurassic Coast from Swanage, and fishing trips.

10 KIMMERIDGE

🏰 **Clavell Tower** (page 261)

The small village of Kimmeridge lies about a mile from the bay of the same name and consists of a clutch of stone and thatched cottages in the midst of some fine farmland. The bay is part of the privately owned Smedmore Estate and you pay a toll to drive from the village to the bay, where there is plenty of parking. Kimmeridge Bay lies within the **Purbeck Marine Wildlife Reserve** (⬚ dorsetwildlifetrust.org.uk), one of the first underwater reserves in the country. It is wide and sheltered, backed by dark shale cliffs and with calm waters for swimming: the shallow waters mean this is fine rock-pooling country at low tide. The Fine Foundation Wild Seas Centre (Kimmeridge Bay, BH20 5PF

⌁ 01929 481004 ⌁ dorsetwildlifetrust.org.uk/wild-seas-centre ⊙ Apr–
Oct 10.30–17.00, Nov–Mar closed) has displays on local marine life and
organises events for children.

On top of the cliff to the east of Kimmeridge is **Clavell Tower**, its soft
pink-and-cream colouring and its Tuscan colonnade combining to give
it a certain wedding-cake quality. It was built as a folly in 1830–31 by
Reverend John Richards, who took the name Clavell when he inherited
the Smedmore Estate. The three-storey tower fell into disrepair and
due to coastal erosion ended up perilously close to falling into the sea.
Between 2006 and 2008 the Landmark Trust dismantled the tower,
repositioned it 82ft further from the cliff and restored it. It is now
available to rent as luxury holiday accommodation (page 261).

The Etches Collection Museum
of Jurassic Marine Life

BH20 5PE ⌁ 01929 270000 ⌁ theetchescollection.org ⊙ 10.00–17.00 daily

This small, modern museum in the centre of the village contains fossils
collected from Kimmeridge Bay over 30 years by local Steve Etches,
who is now often found preparing fossils in the on-site workshop. The
collection is unusual for having been gathered from just one site by
just one person. The high-tech and interactive features are fun for both
adults and children. Families should try out the iPads, which when you
answer a series of questions correctly generate a 3D animated image of
the fossilised creature above their remains in the museum. The entrance
fee gives you entry for 12 months.

¶¶ FOOD & DRINK

Clavell's Village Café and Farm Shop BH20 5PE ⌁ 01929 480701 ⊙ Apr–Oct 10.00–
17.00 daily, Nov–Mar closed Mon. In a charming cottage opposite The Etches Collection.
Much of the produce is grown on the farm and the food served in the café is excellent. Watch
out for evening events during summer.

11 OLD HARRY ROCKS

🏠 **Pig on the Beach** (page 260)

Studland, which has a beautiful sandy beach, is the starting point for
walks to Old Harry Rocks, the stark white chalk stacks which stand in
the water just off the cliffs at Handfast Point. Carved by millions of years
of erosion by the sea, Old Harry Rocks mark the most easterly point of

A walk from Studland village to Old Harry Rocks

✤ OS Explorer OL15; start: Bankes Arms ⚲ SZ038824; 3 miles; easy

Although the beaches at Studland provide a view of Old Harry Rocks, the chalk stacks are much more impressive viewed up close. This can be done either by boat from the sea or by walking out along the chalk ridge towards the cliffs along a section of the South West Coast Path. There is a National Trust car park next to the Bankes Arms.

Early in the morning, in time to see the first rays of sunshine hitting the cliff faces, is a beautiful time of day for this walk. The waters are at their calmest then and the views towards the Isle of Wight are at their clearest. After a short descent and climb at the start, it is a mostly level walk along the chalk ridge. There are opportunities for bird- and butterfly watching on the way, as well as views of Studland Bay and Poole.

You can return the same way or extend the walk by heading up the hill following the coastline to the summit of Ballard Down. As you approach Ballard Point, the South West Coast Path continues on towards Swanage. To walk back to Studland you need to head through the gate on the right. After the descent past the Glebeland Estate, you arrive at the edge of Studland. The **Manor Farm Tea Rooms** (✆ 01929 450511), within converted farm buildings, is a good spot to reward yourself with a Dorset cream tea.

the Jurassic Coast, which is also the youngest. They are said to take their name from a 15th-century pirate, Harry Paye, who regularly attacked ships leaving Poole Harbour. Standing at Handfast Point on a clear day you can see a similar chalk formation off the coast of the Isle of Wight, called The Needles. They serve as a physical reminder that the Isle of Wight was once joined to the mainland at this point by a chalk seam, of which both Old Harry Rocks and The Needles were part.

FOLLOW BRADT

For the latest news, special offers and competitions, subscribe to the Bradt newsletter via the website ⚲ bradtguides.com and follow Bradt on:

🄵 BradtGuides 🆈 @BradtGuides
🄾 @bradtguides 🄿 bradtguides You Tube bradtguides

ACCOMMODATION

This small sample of the accommodation available in East Devon has been chosen with an eye to geography and because it is unusual, or in some ways embodies the Slow philosophy. Not surprisingly, prices in all types of accommodation are at their highest during school holidays and especially in August. As well as avoiding the crowds there is much to be said for visiting out of season when real bargains can be found.

For this edition we have separated the increasingly popular 'glamping' from camping since they have very little in common. All accommodation suggestions are listed under the heading for the area in which they are located.

In Devon by far the most popular accommodation is self-catering, offered by a large number of agencies, listed below, and indicated in the text by 🏠. Hotels and B&Bs are shown by 🏡, glamping by ⛺ and campsites by ⛺. Go to ⌔ bradtguides.com/edevonsleeps for further reviews and additional listings.

1 EXETER & THE EXE ESTUARY

Hotels

The Globe 34 Fore St, Topsham ⌔ theglobetopsham.co.uk. A former 16th-century coaching inn with 21 en-suite rooms and one self-catering apartment.

Lympstone Manor Courtlands Ln, Lympstone EX8 3NZ ⌔ lympstonemanor.co.uk. A luxury country-house hotel owned by celebrity chef Michael Caines. See page 63.

Salutation Inn 68 Fore St, Topsham ⌔ salutationtopsham.co.uk. Historic inn with four en-suite bedrooms and two suites, plus an upmarket restaurant.

Self-catering

Peters Tower Lympstone ⌔ landmarktrust.org. uk. Stay in a 130-year-old clock tower! One of Landmark Trust's most eccentric properties, bang in the middle of Lympstone with estuary views. Sleeps two, in bunk beds. Strong legs needed for the spiral staircase.

Route 2 apartments Topsham ⌔ route2topsham.co.uk/accommodation. Four small, practical, modern apartments, three with one bedroom and one with two. Above the Route 2 Café-Bar and cycle sales/hire/repair shop, with estuary views.

SELF-CATERING AGENCIES

Blue Chip holidays ☞ bluechipholidays.co.uk. Southwest specialists.

Canopy & Stars ☞ canopyandstars.co.uk. Sawday's glamping selection.

Classic Cottages ☞ classic.co.uk. West Country specialists.

Classic Glamping ☞ classicglamping.co.uk. Safari tents, shepherd's huts and more.

Devon Farms ☞ devonfarms.co.uk. Stay on a working farm.

Devon Holiday Cottages ☞ devonholidaycottages.com. A wide selection of East Devon places.

Helpful Holidays ☞ helpfulholidays.co.uk. A wide variety in East Devon.

Landmark Trust ☞ landmarktrust.org.uk. This charitable organisation rescues historic buildings in danger of dereliction, restores them, and then rents them out for holidays. Furnishings respect the history and character of the place, and there are no televisions or telephones. A genuine Slow retreat, in fact. Because their properties fit the Slow ethos so exactly, both its places in this region are listed.

Lyme Bay Holidays ☞ lymebayholidays.co.uk. A large selection of cottages in and around Lyme Regis.

Milkbere Holiday Cottages ☞ milkberehols.com. Cottages along the Jurassic Coast.

Quality Unearthed ☞ qualityunearthed.co.uk. Luxury glamping in yurts, safari tents, cabins, tree houses and more.

Toad Hall Cottages ☞ toadhallcottages.co.uk. West Country specialists.

Camping

Exmouth Country Lodge & Prattshayes Farm Maer Ln, Exmouth EX8 5DB ☞ exmouthcountrylodge.com. Two separate camping areas, one for tourers and the other a free-pitching tent-only field. Also a small 'bell tent village' if you've no kit. Good facilities. Same owners as Exmouth Watersports (page 70).

2 FROM THE M5 TO HONITON

Hotel

The Pig at Combe Gittisham ☞ thepighotel. com. Part of the Pig chain of hotels; a gracious Elizabethan manor house set in acres of parkland. A wide range of rooms at varying prices. See page 93.

Self-catering

Killerton Estate Holiday Cottages ☞ nationaltrustholidays.org.uk. Five National Trust cottages dotted around the Killerton Estate (page 76).

Glamping

Deer Park Tree House Weston, Nr Honiton EX14 3PG ☞ deerpark.co.uk. An amazing adults-only luxury treehouse. This is definitely *not* camping!

3 THE CULM VALLEY & THE BLACKDOWN HILLS

Self-catering

The Old Kennels ☞ theoldkennels.co.uk. The Loft is popular for those doing an arts course here but can be booked separately without doing a course. Sleeps Four.

Twistgates Farm Cottages Upottery EX14 9PE ⌂ twistgatesfarm.co.uk. Three updated traditional beamed cottages (sleeping two, four and five) plus a two-person apartment and a self-contained double bedroom.

Glamping & camping

Grey Willow Yurts Smeatharpe ⌂ greywillowyurts.co.uk. Three 'Yabins' – a combination of yurt and cabin. Shared showers and toilets.

Kingsmead Centre Clayhidon, nr Cullompton ⌂ kingsmeadcentre.com. A campsite in the northern Blackdown Hills that caters for everyone: glamping (bell tents and yurts) tent camping and caravans.

The Nest, Tree House Combe Raleigh ⌂ treeholidays.co.uk. Back-to-nature but in total comfort in the Blackdown Hills.

4 THE RIVER OTTER & THE HEART OF DEVON'S AONB

Hotels

Tumbling Weir Hotel Canaan Way, Ottery St Mary ⌂ tumblingweirhotel.com. A friendly, family-run hotel with ten en-suite bedrooms, near Ottery St Mary's historic weir. See page 123.

B&Bs

The Salty Monk Sidford ⌂ saltymonk.com. A boutique B&B, with seven stylish rooms and an excellent secluded restaurant. See page 148.

Southern Cross Guest House Newton Poppleford ⌂ southerncrossdevon.co.uk. Inexpensive, friendly accommodation on the 9/9A bus route with easy access to Exeter and Sidmouth. See page 141.

Self-catering

Cadhay Manor ⌂ cadhay.org.uk. Exceptional self-catering holiday accommodation for up to

22 people in the manor, old stables and coach house (page 127). See ad, 2nd colour section.

The China Tower Bicton ⌂ landmarktrust. org.uk. This octagonal castellated tower was given by Lady Rolle to her husband as a surprise birthday present! Sleeps 4. Strong legs needed for all those stairs.

Mazzard Farm Holiday Cottages Ottery St Mary ⌂ mazzardfarm.com. Seven cottages sleeping from two to ten with space for additional cots. Child-friendly. Eight acres of woodland with a variety of wildlife. See ad, 2nd colour section.

Glamping & camping

Cuckoo Down Farm Yurts West Hill ⌂ luxurydevonyurts.co.uk. Four safari lodges and two yurts, beautifully furnished, with wood-burning stoves.

Hunger Hill Yurts Nr Newton Poppleford ⌂ yurt-holidays.co.uk. Five yurts with shared bathrooms and toilets.

Knightstone Farm Glamping Safari Tent Nr Ottery St Mary ⌂ knightstonesafaritent.co.uk. A roomy safari tent sleeping four, plus a shepherd's hut, in a family-run dairy farm.

Oakdown Holiday Park Weston ⌂ oakdown. co.uk. An award-winning 'green' caravan and camping park adjoining the Donkey Sanctuary.

5 THE SEASIDE TOWNS

Hotels

Elizabeth Hotel Sidmouth ⌂ hotels-sidmouth. co.uk/hotels-booking/the-elizabeth. One of the fine Regency buildings in Sidmouth's sea-front parade. Family-run. Light, modern bedrooms overlooking Lyme Bay, and a good restaurant.

B&Bs

Baldash Cottage B&B Branscombe ⌂ baldashcottage.co.uk. Luxury accommodation (two bedrooms and one suite) in a newly restored, thatched, stone-built cottage in its own ten-acre wooded valley. Set just 100m from Baldash Lodge self-catering (see opposite).

Fring House B&B Seaton ⏚ fringhouse.co.uk. Two luxury B&B rooms and a self-catering apartment, in a quiet residential road within walking distance of the town centre and beach.

Gatcombe Farm Seaton ⏚ gatcombe-farm-devon.co.uk. Farmhouse B&B (two rooms, twin/double/family) on a 230-acre family-run working farm, near the Jurassic Coast. Watch calves being fed, or the 360 dairy cows being milked by five Lely Robots.

Long Range Hotel Vales Rd, Budleigh Salterton ⏚ thelongrangehotel.co.uk. Family-run, in a pleasant garden. Seven comfortable en-suite rooms, most with lovely views over the Axe Valley.

Mariners B&B & Apartments Seaton ⏚ marinershotelseaton.co.uk. Eight en-suite bedrooms, most with panoramic views of Lyme Bay. Promenade and beach just across the road. Also two self-catering apartments.

The Old Farmhouse Sidmouth ⏚ theoldfarmhousesidmouth.co.uk. Within walking distance from the town and sea, a 16th-century farmhouse and adjoining cottage with five en-suite bedrooms. Evening meals by arrangement.

Pebbles B&B 16 Fore St, Budleigh Salterton ✆ 01395 442417. Delightful B&B with three en-suite rooms only yards away from Budleigh's famous pebbles and the South West Coast Path. Super sea views. Despite the name, has no connection with Pebbles the Apartment (see right).

Self-catering

Baldash Lodge (see **Baldash Cottage B&B**, see opposite) Luxury self-contained self-catering accommodation for two people (double bedroom with four-poster), in peaceful surroundings. Located 100m from Baldash Cottage.

Forge Cottage Branscombe ⏚ nationaltrustholidays.co.uk. In the heart of picturesque Branscombe village, this traditional thatched cottage sleeps four in two bedrooms.

Fring House Seaton. A peaceful two-person apartment (double bed): see details under Fring House B&B, see left.

Margells Branscombe ⏚ landmarktrust.org.uk. A beautiful thatched cottage with exposed oak beams and a well-preserved 16th-century interior. Sleeps five.

Mariners B&B & Apartments Seaton (see under *B&B*, see left). Two seafront apartments with balconies overlooking Lyme Bay, sleeping two and four.

Pebbles the Apartment 32B Fore St, Budleigh Salterton ✆ 01395 471766 ⏚ pebblesapartment.com. A luxury, sea-facing, first-floor flat for two adults (one king-size bed), close to the beach.

Camping

Coombe View Farm Branscombe ⏚ branscombe-camping.co.uk. Peaceful camping in a sloped green field with views to the Jurassic Coast (only a mile away).

Salcombe Regis Camping & Caravan Park & Campsite EX10 0JW ⏚ salcombe-regis.co.uk. A green, family-run, 16-acre site for touring caravans, motorhomes or tents (also static caravans for hire). The nearest park to Sidmouth. Served by the *Sidmouth Hopper* (see box, page 153) running between Sidmouth town and the Donkey Sanctuary.

6 DEVON'S FAR EAST

Hotels

The Dower House Rousdon ⏚ dhhotel.com. An elegant country house with a heated outdoor pool and ten rooms. See ad, 2nd colour section.

Fairwater Head Hotel Hawkchurch ⏚ fairwaterheadhotel.co.uk. A lovely leafy hotel with 16 characterful rooms and an acclaimed restaurant.

The George Hotel Axminster ⏚ georgeaxminster.southcoastinns.co.uk. A historic hotel in the centre of town, newly reopened after high-class refurbishment. See page 212.

B&Bs

Higher Bruckland Farm B&B Combpyne ⌂ higherbruckland.co.uk. Three en-suite rooms on a working dairy farm, including a family suite and a ground-floor disabled-adapted room.

The Old Bakehouse Colyton ⌂ theoldbakehousebandb.co.uk. Comfortable twin and double rooms in a period cottage. In the centre of Colyton, within sound of the church bells.

The Stables Guest House Trill Farm, Musbury ⌂ trillfarm.co.uk. In line with the ethos of Trill Farm (page 215), there is underfloor heating and solar thermal panels so all energy is sustainable. Terrific farm-produced breakfasts and courses to attend.

Self-catering

Castlewood Vineyard cottages Musbury ⌂ castlewoodvineyard.co.uk. Two stone-built Grade II-listed cottages on a dairy farm overlooking the vineyard. No guesses where you'll get your wine!

Montana Nr Lyme Regis ⌂ uniquehomestays.com. Just two miles from Lyme on the Devon side of the county border. An architect-designed retreat with far-reaching woodland views. Sleeps ten. Dog-friendly.

Peek House Rousdon ⌂ peekhouse.co.uk. The west wing of the Rousdon Mansion with seven bedrooms; also available is Billiard House with five bedrooms.

Rousdon Cottages ⌂ lymebayholidays.co.uk (among others). Several self-catering cottages in Rousdon Estate, including the converted St Pancras' Church.

Shute Barton Gatehouse ⌂ landmarktrust.org.uk. Described as looking like a toy castle, complete with castellations. Huge fireplace and decorative plaster ceiling. Sleeps three.

Shute Barton House ⌂ nationaltrustholidays.org.uk. Part of a stately medieval manor house; sleeps ten; the accommodation includes the medieval great hall on the top floor.

Valley View HQ Uplyme ⌂ valleyviewhq.co.uk. Leys (Grade II-listed) luxury self-catering in rural Uplyme, close to Lyme Regis. Spacious converted high-spec barn sleeps eight in four en-suite rooms; annex sleeps two.

Glamping

Crafty Camping Holditch, Dorset ⌂ canopyandstars.co.uk. Only just over the Dorset border. A superb two-storey treehouse designed by IBA-award-winning Guy Mallinson. Also a shepherd's hut, tipi, yurts and bell tent, all tucked away in woodland.

Lower Keats Glamping Tytherleigh ⌂ lowerkeatsglamping.co.uk. Six secluded six-person safari tents with en-suite bathrooms.

Camping

Hook Farm Uplyme ⌂ hookfarmcamping.co.uk. A secluded, spacious and leafy campsite.

7 DORSET'S JURASSIC COAST

Hotels

Alexandra Hotel Lyme Regis ⌂ hotelalexandra.co.uk. Upmarket hotel in an 18th-century house on the hill above Lyme Regis Harbour, with views of the coast.

Moonfleet Manor Fleet ⌂ moonfleetmanorhotel.co.uk. Family-friendly, comfortable, flexible accommodation in the historic 17th-century house and adjacent coach houses, overlooking the Fleet and Chesil Beach. Features as the home of the Mohune family in J Meade Falkner's classic adventure novel *Moonfleet* (page 248).

Pig on the Beach Studland Bay ⌂ thepighotel.com. Popular, smart hotel in an 18th-century house close to the bay. Shepherd's huts and converted dovecotes also available.

The Seaside Boarding House Burton Bradstock ⌂ theseasideboardinghouse.com. Luxurious accommodation: all nine rooms have sea views. Very good restaurant.

B&Bs

Dorset House Lyme Regis ⬦ dorsethouselyme. com. An outstanding B&B with luxurious rooms and locally sourced breakfasts, plus a sustainability ethos.

Hix Townhouse Lyme Regis ⬦ hixrestaurants. co.uk. Luxury guesthouse owned by chef Mark Hix and close to Hix Oyster & Fish House, where you'll receive a discount. Beautifully decorated rooms. Breakfast is via a hamper delivered to your room.

Self-catering

Clavell Tower Kimmeridge ⬦ landmarktrust. org.uk. Unique accommodation for a couple in a clifftop tower. Book well ahead. See page 253.

Donkey Lane Cottage Burton Bradstock ⬦ burtonbradstockcottages.co.uk. A pretty thatched cottage in the village centre, sleeping three in two bedrooms.

Lulworth Estate ⬦ lulworth.com/stay. The Lulworth Estate has a range of self-catering properties, from cosy cottages to expansive manor houses for large groups. Camping, self-catering and pods are available at the estate's Durdle Door Holiday Park.

Symondsbury Estate Symondsbury, nr Bridport DT6 5HG ⬦ symondsburyestate.co.uk. Ten self-catering cottages and houses of varying sizes, all finished to a high standard. There are also three double en-suite rooms if you don't need self-catering.

Washingpool Farm North Allington Bridport DT6 5HG ⬦ washingpool.co.uk. Two cottages on a working farm with superb farm shop and café. Coarse fishing available.

Camping

Downhouse Farm Higher Eype ⬦ downhousefarm.org. Two shepherd's huts on a working organic farm with sea views. On the South West Coast Path. No electricity.

Golden Cap Holiday Park Seatown ⬦ goldencapholidaypark.co.uk. Campsite right on the coast. Spacious, modern cabins, safari tents and bell tents.

NOTES

NOTES

INDEX

Entries in **bold** refer to major entries; those in *italic* refer to maps.

INDEX OF ADVERTISERS